The
WILD FOOD
COOKBOOK

ROGER PHILLIPS

The Countryman Press
Woodstock, Vermont

Book design and composition by S. E. Livingston

Published by The Countryman Press,
P.O. Box 748, Woodstock, VT 05091

Distributed by W. W. Norton & Company, Inc.,
500 Fifth Avenue, New York, NY 10110

The Library of Congress has cataloged the hardcover edition as follows:

Phillips, Roger, 1932–
Wild food.

Bibliography: p.
Includes index.
1. Wild plants, Edible–United States–Identification.
2. Cookery (Wild foods) I. Foy, Nicky. II. Hurst,
Jacqui. III. Title.
QK98.5.U6P54   1986   581.6'32'0973'   86-128
The Wild Food Cookbook
ISBN 978-1-58157-218-6

Printed in the United States of America

10 9 8 7 6 5 4 3 2 1

Contents

INTRODUCTION

When I was seven, an eccentric, bohemian teacher at my school used to send me and my classmates into the local wilderness of suburban London to find sufficient nettles for our lunchtime soup. Thus began my lifetime love affair with wild food.

When I was 47, I decided to combine my love of nature with my love of food, so I produced a book that would help like-minded people to find, cook, and enjoy some of the numerous wild plants that have been known for centuries to be edible. Once *Wild Food* was published in Europe, my mind kept wandering to North America. What kinds of edible plants grew in abundance, waiting to be collected and consumed? Finally, curiosity overcame common sense, and I decided to tackle the huge task of exploring the edible wild plants of North America and publishing an American *Wild Food*. As the venture would take several years to complete and would necessitate traveling thousands of miles to find, collect, cook, and photograph the plants I needed, my wife, Nicky, and I decided it had to be a family affair—and we would take our baby daughter, Phoebe, with us.

So twice a year, we packed our bags, displayed ABSENT ON LOCATION signs on our London studio, and went on the road. Everyone thought we were crazy traveling with such a tiny tot (she was three months old when we began), but although there were a couple of occasions when she did succumb to germs and jet lag, basically she loved the excitement of new places and faces; and she soon became an avid berry and mushroom hunter—and taster too! How many little English girls of three have visited the Great Lakes and the Grand Canyon, the Cascades and the Appalachians, the Sonoran Desert and Skyline Drive? America has now become her second home, and within minutes of landing on US soil she is saying, "Hi, guys," as though she had been born and bred to it.

THE AIMS OF THIS BOOK

In producing *Wild Food*, I have tried to do two things that I felt had not been covered before in one volume.

First, I wanted to make sure that the book could be used as a basic reference for all the best-known recipes traditionally associated with wild food—cranberry sauce, blueberry muffins, dandelion coffee, lime tea, elderflower wine, cattail shoots, wapato roots—and so I have included all the standard recipes. But second, I wanted to go farther than this. By exploring and developing some of the other fascinating sources of wild food, such as seaweeds and mushrooms, I could show that there were several groups of wild plants that had been left largely unexploited, and yet they provide a great many of the most nutritious and tasty dishes for the adventurous food hunter's table.

Two principles have guided my choices throughout. I have included only those plants that can be found in sufficiently large quantities to make eating them worthwhile—and, much more important, those plants whose survival will not be endangered by gathering them for the pot. Furthermore, I have tried to select one or two really successful recipes for each plant rather than include all possible recipes. The rationale for this is illustrated by the mushrooms. In the recipes in the mushroom chapter almost any of the 50 or so species that appear in the book can be used successfully. But the actual recipes selected for each species are those that, after numerous testing-and-tasting sessions, I think best suit the flavor and texture of that particular mushroom.

The recipes have been gleaned from a variety of sources. Historical research into old cookbooks, explorers' diaries, traders' accounts, and anthropological studies of Indian tribes and customs revealed an enormous number of ideas about how to cook wild plants, many of them far too elaborate and impracticable for modern cooks, but nevertheless fascinating reading. I am also indebted to numerous contemporary authors and magazines for recipes I have either quoted verbatim or adapted slightly to suit my ingredients; and last, and by no means least, I have regularly invaded the kitchen of friends and acquaintances to steal their cherished secrets.

As a result of this research, I collected a wide variety of recipes—far more than could possibly be used. So, in order to find out which ones I personally liked the best, I made every single recipe and included in the book only those that seemed really worthwhile, even though it meant rejecting about two-thirds of the material.

HOW TO USE THIS BOOK

The book is arranged by sections, and the sections, as far as possible, follow the seasons of the year. This means that if you are going wild food hunting in the spring, you will find details about the plants and accompanying recipes appropriate to this time of year in the front sections of the book. Conversely, if you collect some interesting berries or mushrooms in the fall, you can look in the book's later sections for ideas of what to do with them. However, should you want to look up a particular recipe or plant, the index, which lists recipes and both common and botanical plant names, will guide you to the entries.

Seaweeds

Seaweeds must be, without doubt, one of the most wasted natural resources in North America as well as in Europe. Fortunately, our ever-growing interest in Japanese cooking is making us more aware of the benefits that the numerous seaweeds on our coasts can provide.

Among the most nutritious plants in the world, seaweeds contain high proportions of proteins, minerals, and vitamins, notably vitamins A, B_1, B_{12}, C, and D. Sea lettuce, for instance, has more vitamin A—the "growth vitamin"—than butter does, and many of the green seaweeds contain a higher concentration of vitamin B_{12} than can be found in liver. Seaweeds contain about 2.5 percent protein by weight, so that laver, for one, contains a higher proportion of protein than do soybeans. Another virtue: all species are rich in minerals and trace elements because seawater has almost exactly the same proportion of minerals as human blood.

Seaweed hunting

Botanical Information

To avoid misunderstanding, I must make clear at the outset that this book cannot and should not be used as a field guide for the identification of the edible wild plants included in the text. That job must, of necessity, be left to specialized works on trees and shrubs, on wildflowers, on seaweeds, on mushrooms. The force of this will become apparent when it is realized that in North America there are more than 3,000 species of mushrooms alone, both edible and poisonous. The mushroom hunter must be able to make minute comparisons of one species with another, and to do this he needs a comprehensive field guide on the mushrooms of his particular region. A number of the standard field guides and other specialized works are listed in the bibliography. In describing each edible plant in the text, I have accordingly confined myself to giving information on times of growth, flowering, and fruiting, and on habitat and distribution. Since I found that a common name was often shared by two or more plants, I have included the Latin name in each entry to resolve any ambiguities.

Poisonous Mushrooms and Other Poisonous Plants

Since these are a fact of life in North America as well as elsewhere in the world, it is essential that you be certain of your identification before eating any plant. If you are in any doubt, no matter how small, consult an expert or an authoritative, specialized book. If either of these resources is unavailable, leave the plant alone. In some localities it is possible to take a field course in mushroom identification under the tutelage of an expert. In any event, learning to identify mushrooms takes time and effort, but if you persevere and conquer the difficulties, you will find that cooking and eating wild mushrooms is a not-to-be-missed culinary treat.

Protection of Wild Plants

It is my firm belief that increased knowledge of and interest in the flora of our countryside will lead to greater personal thought about how plants may be best protected and encouraged. This statement might seem to be at odds with a book about the collection and consumption of wild plants, fruits, and roots, but man cannot live without eating, and as I have already pointed out, I have included recipes only for plants that are in no danger of extinction. It is a fact that the greatest threat to our wild flora is loss of habitat caused by building, road making, draining, and farming. Careful gathering of wild plants is not itself an ecological menace.

I would like to emphasize again to the prospective wild food hunter that only plants growing in profusion should be harvested and then only in such quantities that the viability of each colony is not endangered.

Herbs, flowers, seaweeds, and mushrooms
are all easy to preserve by drying.

Drying

Drying is a very useful method of preserving, especially for herbs, seaweeds, and mushrooms. I have found that the most practical and effective method is to rig up a wire rack about 3 inches above a radiator; this allows a good current of hot air to flow around the plants and enables them to dry very quickly. Alternatively, you can buy a drying cabinet, which is excellent for drying mushrooms, herbs, seaweeds, or berries.

Winemaking and Beer Brewing

There are two approaches that can be taken to making wines from wild fruits and flowers. The first aims to preserve the taste and flavor of that particular flower or fruit that has been collected, while the second is to produce a wine that is as near as possible to a commercial wine made from grapes. I prefer the first approach, and in every instance I have accordingly balanced the ingredients to bring out the essential taste of the fruit or flower that is the main constituent. The result, I hope, is a series of wines that have really authentic country flavors. Each recipe in this book has been designed to produce a dry, rather than a sweet, wine. If you have never made wine or beer at home but would like to try it, consult a good book on the subject. One such is Charles Foster's *Home Wine Making, Brewing and Other Drinks.*

Yeast: For both wine and beer, I have used brewer's yeast, which is available in packet form in supermarkets and in specialty food shops. It can be "started" very rapidly by putting the contents of the packet into a mug, with a little sugar and warm water, and then leaving the solution in a warm place for about an hour.

Sterilization: This is essential because winemaking vessels that have not been properly sterilized are the most common cause of failure in winemaking. A strong solution of Campden tablets can be used for this purpose, or proprietary brands of cleaning and sterilizing powder are available in winemaking shops. Sterilize corks by boiling them for 15 minutes.

The Photographs

All the photographs, except those on the title pages, have been taken in natural light using a Nikon FM camera with a 50mm lens on a tripod. The film used was Kodak Ektachrome 64 ASA, which was pushed one stop in development. This enabled me to stop the lens down to f16 and yet not have to use too slow a shutter speed, thus reducing wind movement.

I have endeavored, wherever possible, to take the recipe photographs in conjunction with the plants from which the dishes were made and in the natural habitat of the plants. Obviously, this required a lot of traveling and hard work, but it gave me the opportunity of doing food photographs against a great variety of lovely natural backgrounds, which made working on this book continuously exciting, interesting, and stimulating.

chapter one
LEAVES, SHOOTS, FLOWERS & HERBS

WATERCRESS

Watercress, *Nasturtium officinale*, a perennial herb, grows in shallow, moving water in brooks and springs and flowers from April to October.

Found throughout North America.

Although originally cultivated, watercress has subsequently naturalized so extensively that it can be found almost anywhere, at any time. Its generic name, *Nasturtium*, is derived from the Latin *torus nasus* (writhing nose) and refers to the pungency of the plant; its species name, *officinale*, means that it was originally on the official list of medicinal plants and is referred to in Dioscorides's *Materia Medica* of AD 77. Rich in vitamin C and minerals, watercress is an excellent addition to the diet. Traditionally it was used to garnish parsnips or, in Ireland, boiled with bacon. Nowadays it is used in soups, salads, sandwiches, and stir-fries.

CAUTION: When collecting wild watercress, the fear is of liver-fluke pollution. Stan Williams, who owns a watercress farm, told me that the danger spreads from cattle and particularly from sheep. If the cress is growing by a stream where there are no sheep or cattle in any stretch above where you are, it will be fine to eat fresh, but if there are cattle present, it should be very thoroughly washed before eating raw. However, if the watercress is cooked, any danger will be removed, so I tend to think of wild watercress soup as the ideal way of eating it.

When collecting watercress, pick the more mature shoots before they flower; on some plants the leaves have a bronze tint, on others they are dark green. Do not pull the plant up by the roots; instead, cut the tops off the shoots. Wash the cress thoroughly and use it promptly; refrigerating destroys the texture. If you want to keep it, it stays fresher more or less submerged in water.

Watercress Soup

SERVES 4

- 2 BUNCHES WATERCRESS
- 2 LARGE POTATOES
- 1 TABLESPOON BUTTER
- 1 TEASPOON VEGETABLE OIL
- 2 CUPS CHICKEN STOCK
- ½ CUP HALF-AND-HALF
- SALT AND PEPPER TO TASTE

Wash the cress thoroughly and chop it coarsely. Peel and slice the potatoes, or cube them if you like. Put the butter and oil in a large saucepan and heat over a low flame until the butter is melted. Add the potatoes and cook them very gently, covered, until they are soft, then add the stock and simmer, uncovered, for 15 minutes. Next, add the watercress and simmer, again uncovered, for another 7 minutes. Transfer the mixture to a blender and liquefy at high speed. Then stir in the half-and-half, check for seasoning, and chill the soup in the refrigerator. It makes a delightful summer soup, but it is equally good served hot for a winter starter and it freezes well.

WINTERCRESS

Common Wintercress or **Yellow Rocket**, *Barbarea vulgaris*, is a biennial or perennial herb that grows in moist meadows, on brooksides, and in ditches and damp woods. It flowers from April to August.

Found in CT, DE, n.e. GA, IA, IL, IN, KY, MA, MD, s. ME, MI, MN, n.e. MO, NC, NH, NJ, NY, OH, PA, RI, SC, TN, VA, WI, WV. In Canada: NS.

The generic name, *Barbarea*, is derived from the fact that this used to be the only green plant that could be gathered and eaten on Saint Barbara's Day, which falls on December 4. Introduced from Europe, where it was commonly cultivated, common wintercress was eaten by early settlers as a salad or potherb.

I find it makes a delicious vegetable when lightly boiled. In salads it provides a nice, rather peppery addition, similar to watercress. To increase the plant's productivity, remove the flowering stems as they appear and pick the outer leaves as the plant regrows.

Chickweed Soup and Salad. Eating your garden weeds is a great solution to weeding.

Wintercress

CHICKWEED

Common Chickweed, *Stellaria media*, an annual herb, grows in waste places, cultivated ground, dooryards, moist woods, and thickets, and flowers almost all year round.

Found throughout North America.

Abundant in the East and Midwest, chickweed is a marvelous plant because it is available virtually throughout the year, though it tends get a bit straggly and dusty in high summer. The whole plant can be eaten, and it is best gathered when it begins to flower. Snip off the tender leaves and stems with scissors and lay them neatly in a basket to save preparation time later on. You can pull the plant up by the roots, but as well as diminishing your supply this method requires more cleaning time in the kitchen.

Chickweed Salad

SERVES 4

2 LARGE BUNCHES CHICKWEED
4 CRISP APPLES, CORED AND CHOPPED INTO CUBES
2 TABLESPOONS CHOPPED FRESH CHERVIL
    OR PARSLEY
6 TABLESPOONS OIL-AND-VINEGAR DRESSING

Wash the chickweed, dry it in a salad spinner or with paper towels, and mix it with the apples. Add the chervil to the dressing and blend. Pour the dressing over the salad and toss lightly.

Chickweed Soup

SERVES 4

2 BUNCHES CHICKWEED
3 PINTS CHICKEN STOCK
6 SCALLIONS, WHITE AND GREEN PARTS,
    THINLY SLICED
1 LARGE POTATO, PEELED AND DICED
SALT AND PEPPER TO TASTE
1 CUP HALF-AND-HALF

Trim the chickweed of any damaged leaves and tough stems; wash in cold water and dry in a salad spinner or with power towels. Reserve a few sprigs for garnishing. Put the stock into a large, heavy saucepan and bring to the boiling point. Immediately lower the heat and add the scallions, potato, and chickweed. Simmer, covered, for 10 to 15 minutes. Do not cook longer or the soup will lose its flavor. Add the salt and pepper, then puree the soup in a blender. Return it to the saucepan and stir in the half-and-half. Heat the soup through but do not let it boil. Garnish with the reserved sprigs of chickweed and serve hot.

This is a delicious soup, and as the chickweed can be so readily found in abundance, it is well worth trying. I like it with the addition of a few sorrel leaves mixed with the chickweed, if they are available. This soup is just as good served cold and freezes well too.

Spring beauty

SPRING BEAUTY & MINER'S LETTUCE

Spring Beauty, *Claytonia virginica*, a perennial herb, grows in rich woods, thickets, wet fields, and clearings, and flowers between March and May.

Found mainly in AL, AR, CT, DE, GA, IA, IL, IN, e. KS, KY, n. LA, MA, MD, MI, MN, MO, MS, NC, n. NE, s. NH, NJ, NY, OH, e. OK, PA, RI, SC, TN, VA, s. VT, WI, WV.

Miner's Lettuce, *Montia perfoliata*, an annual herb, grows along shaded roadsides, in moist valleys, near springs, and on lower mountain slopes. It flowers from January to July.

Found mainly in CA, ID, MT, w. ND, w. NV, OR, w. SD, n. UT, WA, WY. In Canada: s. BC.

The name *miner's lettuce* goes back to gold rush days. Early California gold miners ate the plant to avoid scurvy when fresh fruit and vegetables were in short supply. As late as 1891, the members of the Health Expedition to California did likewise. Frederick Vernon Colville (1895) wrote that they "used large quantities of this plant when they came out of the desert and ascended the mountains to the west, having lived for several months without green vegetables of any kind." The Indians were very fond of miner's lettuce. V. K. Chesnut (1902) says that the Yuki called it *go-shin*, and among the Indians of Mendocino County "the whole plant was either eaten raw or cooked with salt and pepper for greens."

The young white-and-pink-striped blossoms are rather hot-flavored, and the leaves and stems have a mild, cress-like flavor. All make an attractive addition to salads, and although the small corms take time to dig up in sufficient quantity, they are worth the effort. Euell Gibbons (1962) says the small tubers (fairy spuds) of the spring beauty are very tasty boiled for 15 minutes in salted water, then peeled and popped in the mouth. "They have the sweetness and flavor of boiled chestnuts, although they are softer and smoother in texture," is his verdict.

Miner's lettuce

STINGING NETTLE

Stinging Nettle, *Urtica dioica*, a tall perennial with very bristly, stinging hairs, grows on roadsides, in waste areas, on trails and streambanks, and at the margins of woods. It flowers from the end of June to September.

> Found mainly in CT, IL, IN, KY, MA, MD, ME, MI, MN, NH, NJ, NY, OH, PA, RI, w. VA, WI, WV. In Canada: NB, NFLD, NS, s. ONT, s. QUE.

The stinging characteristics of the nettle gave rise in Europe to a number of epigrams, for example:

> *Tender-handed stroke a nettle*
> *And it stings you for your pains*
> *Grasp it like a man of mettle*
> *And it soft as silk remains*

During World War II, I attended a village school run by a wonderful bohemian woman called Miss Raymond. There were only about six children over the age of six (the rest of the school consisted of babies) so, as there was very little to eat at that time, we six were sent out every morning to pick nettle tops. These were boiled by the cook into a most unsavory pulp, and when it was time for the babies' lunch, we, the long-suffering, had to push it down their unwilling gullets. The babies, quite rightly, rejected it, usually into the faces of the feeders.

Believe it or not, I love nettles now.

High in protein, minerals, and vitamins (A and C in particular), nettles have long been recognized in Europe as excellent edible wild plants. We were therefore amazed when we came to the United States to discover that nobody we met had ever heard of, let alone tasted, the delights of nettle soup. Thinking it was just the company we kept, we scoured our American wild food guides and found but one mention of nettles, stinging or otherwise. We have now decided to take it upon ourselves to convert the American palate. Admittedly, although nettles grow in numerous states, they are not usually found in abundance, so once you have discovered a supply, cherish the secret.

Nettle Beer and Nettles as a vegetable

The best time to collect nettles is when the young shoots are not more than an inch high. Pick the whole of the shoots, or, if you're gathering later in the year, just the tops and the young, pale green leaves. Wear gloves and cut the nettles with scissors, laying them tidily in a basket to facilitate sorting later on. Cooking will eliminate the stinging quality of the nettles.

Nettles as a Vegetable

Wash fresh, young nettle tops (about 30 per serving) and put them into a saucepan without any additional water. Add a teaspoon of butter (per serving) and pepper and salt to taste. Simmer gently for about 10 minutes, turning the nettles constantly, until they have the consistency of cooked spinach. The flavor is rather bland, so serve with a sprinkle of nutmeg and butter.

Nettle Beer

MAKES ABOUT 3 GALLONS

100 NETTLE TOPS, 2 INCHES LONG
3 GALLONS WATER
6 CUPS SUGAR
½ CUP CREAM OF TARTAR
1 TABLESPOON BREWER'S YEAST

"Boil nettles in water for 15 minutes. Strain and add the sugar and the cream of tartar. Heat and stir until dissolved. Wait until tepid, then add the yeast and stir well. Cover with muslin and leave for 24 hours. Remove the scum and decant without disturbing the sediment. Bottle, cork and tie down."

This recipe was given to me by Lyndsay Shearer of Bucky, who found it in the "Common Place Book" of her grandmother May Buchan. It is quoted verbatim.

I have made nettle beer many times, and in practice it seems best to let it ferment in the bucket for 4 days, thus avoiding too much fizzing when you open the bottles. Your first sip will dispel any doubts about the excellence of this beer. It is light and refreshing, an ideal drink on warm, early-summer evenings. Before serving, add a sprig of mint and an ice cube.

Nettle Soup

SERVES 4

½ GALLON NETTLE TOPS, LIGHTLY PRESSED DOWN
1 LARGE ONION
1 CLOVE GARLIC
2 MEDIUM-SIZED POTATOES
2 TABLESPOONS OLIVE OIL
4 CUPS HOMEMADE CHICKEN STOCK
     OR CANNED CHICKEN BROTH (DILUTED)
SALT AND PEPPER TO TASTE
½ CUP HALF-AND-HALF
2 SLICES BREAD, CUBED
1–2 TABLESPOONS BUTTER

Using gloves and scissors, trim away the stems from the nettle tops, then wash the tops well. Peel and finely chop the onion, garlic, and potatoes, and fry them for 3 to 4 minutes in a large saucepan with the olive oil. At the same time, heat the chicken stock to the boiling point. When the vegetables have cooked the specified time, stir in the nettle tops and the hot chicken stock. Boil the mixture fairly rapidly for 15 minutes, or until the potatoes are cooked. Transfer the mixture to a blender and liquefy at high speed. Return the soup to the pan to keep hot, seasoning it with salt and pepper. Then pour it into a large bowl and stir in the half-and-half. Serve with croutons made by sautéing bread cubes in butter.

WILD ASPARAGUS

Wild Asparagus, *Asparagus officinalis*, a perennial herb, grows in sandy fields, on roadsides, and in disturbed sites, and flowers between May and June.

Found throughout North America.

Euell Gibbons's account of hunting wild asparagus when he was 12 has given this plant an almost symbolic significance for wild food aficionados; yet Peter Kalm, who traveled around the colonies in the 1740s, fails to comment on its delicious edible qualities when he speaks of it in his diary: "We frequently saw asparagus growing near the enclosures in a loose soil on uncultivated sandy fields. It is likewise plentiful between the maize, and was at present full of berries, but I cannot tell whether the seeds are carried by the wind to the places where I saw them; it is however certain, that I have likewise seen in growing wild in other parts of America."

C. S. Rafinesque (1828–30) points out that asparagus was highly acclaimed for its medicinal qualities: "The shoots a well-known vernal luxury, very healthy, diuretic, giving a strong smell to urine, purifying the blood but the excessive use is said to bring on gout. A peculiar substance, asparagines, found in them. Valuable diet in many diseases of the breast, heart, kidneys and bladder, it allays the inordinate action of the heart."

Gibbons is right. Wild asparagus is a marvelous vegetable and can be used in many ways: in cream of asparagus soup; with stir-fry vegetables; in quiches and flans, served hot or cold; or boiled and served either hot with butter or cold with vinaigrette dressing.

Wild Asparagus in Ambush– A Modern Version

SERVES 8

8 FRESH FRENCH BREAD ROLLS
3 POUNDS ASPARAGUS
BUTTER
HOLLANDAISE SAUCE

Wash the asparagus stalks carefully to remove any grit, cut them into lengths to fit the rolls, and steam or boil them until they are tender (10 to 12 minutes). Cut the tops from the rolls and remove the soft interior from the bottom halves. Three minutes or so before the asparagus is done, toast the tops and bottoms of the rolls under the broiler, and then butter them. Arrange the hot, cooked asparagus on the bottoms and dress with hollandaise sauce. Cover each roll with its toasted top and dribble a little more sauce over the roll crosswise.

Serve as a separate course or as an hors d'oeuvre. Knife and fork are called for.

This recipe is based on the one in James Beard's *American Cookery* (1972), but harks back to the traditional one favored by Mrs. Harland, Mrs. Rorer, and other great 19th-century cookery writers.

Japanese knotweed

JAPANESE KNOTWEED

Japanese Knotweed, *Polygonum cuspidatum*, a large, perennial herb, sometimes as tall as 9 feet, grows on roadsides, in waste places, and in neglected gardens, and flowers from July to September.

Found mainly in CT, DE, KY, IA, IL, IN, MA, MD, ME, MI, MN, ND, NH, NJ, OH, PA, RI, n. SC, VA, VT, WI, WV. In Canada: NB. NFLD, NS, s. ONT, s. QUE.

Japanese knotweed is a rampant weed that spreads very quickly, so once you have found some you should not have any difficulty in gathering enough for experimenting with different dishes. In early spring, when the plant is a foot high or less, cut the top 3 inches off each shoot and strip the leaves that have opened. The tender shoots can be boiled or steamed and eaten with butter or vinaigrette dressing, or they can be pureed with milk, salt, and pepper to make a soup.

Alternatively, if you find them a bit sour, you can cook the shoots as you would rhubarb, with a goodly amount of sugar or honey, and make sauces, pies, and jams.

Japanese Knotweed Crumble

SERVES 4

6 CUPS CHOPPED KNOTWEED SHOOTS
6 TABLESPOONS HONEY
½ CUP RAISINS
1 CUP FLOUR
¼ CUP BUTTER
¼ CUP SUGAR
½ TEASPOON CINNAMON

Simmer the knotweed, honey, and raisins until the knotweed is soft (about 4 minutes). Meanwhile, using a fork, rub the butter into the flour, then add the sugar and cinnamon, and continue to work the mixture until it resembles fine bread crumbs. Line a well-greased pie dish with the knotweed mixture (strain off any excess liquid) and top with the crumble mixture. Bake at 375°F for 15 minutes, or until nicely browned on top. Serve hot with custard or cream.

Field cress

FIELD CRESS
OR COW CRESS

Field Cress or **Cow Cress**, *Lepidium campestre*, a tall herb with a very hairy stem, grows along roadsides and in fields and waste places. It fruits from May to September.

Found throughout North America except in the hot southern states.

Collect the young leaves and shoots in spring or early summer and use a few raw in salads to add a slight tang to milder salad leaves. For a cooked vegetable, pick only the young tops—the stems are very woody. Blanch them in boiling water for 30 seconds, drain, and repeat. Then add fresh boiling water to cover and simmer them for 2 minutes. Drain well again and serve with butter, salt, and pepper to taste. Cooked this way, field cress has a good, spinach-like flavor.

CATTAIL

Cattail, *Typha latifolia*, a tall, perennial herb with large underground roots, grows in marshes, ponds, and shallow water. It flowers from the end of May to July.

Found throughout North America.

The Indians and early explorers found the cattail to be a fantastically useful plant. Not only could one or another part of it be eaten virtually all year round, but the fluff could be used in place of feathers to stuff beds and pillows, the leaves could be used for chair seats and for caulking barrels, the rushes for making mats and roofs.

In spring dig up the small sprouts, which are edible raw or boiled or baked. A few weeks later, "cossack asparagus"—the tender white shoots from the base of the plant below the water level—can be cooked or eaten raw in salads. Later in the year the green bloom spikes are also tasty boiled, and the pollen from the flowers can be shaken off and used in baking.

SWEETFLAG or CALAMUS

Sweetflag or **Calamus**, *Acorus calamus*, a perennial herb with a large underground rhizome, grows in boggy ground on the borders of streams, lakes, and ditches. It flowers from May to August.

Found mainly in AL, AR, CA, CO, CT, DE, FL, GA, IA, n. ID, IL, IN, KS, LA, MA, MD, ME, MI, MN, MO, MS, MT, NC, ND, NE, NH, NJ, NM, NY, OH, OK, OR, PA, RI, SC, SD, TN, n.e. TX, VA, VT, WA, WI, WV, WY. In Canada: s. ALTA, s. BC, s. MAN, s. ONT, s. QUE, s. SASK.

CAUTION: Sweetflag can be distinguished from the poisonous wild irises by its fragrant, yellow-green leaves. Irises have blue-green leaves with an unpleasant odor when cut.

Traditionally used for their medicinal properties, the blossoms, leaves, and roots of sweetflag have a strange, very strong, aromatic smell and flavor. A tablespoon of the dried, grated roots can be infused in boiling water to make a tea that many find soothing for indigestion or heartburn. However, the traditional method of eating them was candied. The colonists took the large rhizome and boiled it for three days to make it palatable! We decided to follow Euell Gibbons's suggestion and use the young, inch-high leaf shoots.

Cossack Asparagus

SERVES 4

32 TENDER 8-INCH SHOOTS
COLD WATER TO COVER
2–4 TABLESPOONS BUTTER
   OR 2–4 OUNCES MILD CHEESE

After discarding the coarse outer leaves, put the shoots in water and bring to a boil. Simmer them, covered, until tender (4 to 5 minutes). Drain and serve with generous knobs of butter. Or place the shoots on foil, cover them with slices of cheese, and pop them under the broiler until the cheese melts.

Candied Sweetflag Root

MAKES 25 PIECES

25 INCH-HIGH UNDERGROUND STEMS
SEVERAL CHANGES OF BOILING WATER
4 CUPS SUGAR
2 CUPS WATER
GRANULATED SUGAR

Wash and clean the stems, place them in a saucepan of boiling water, and cook them, uncovered, for 30 minutes. Change the cooking liquid at least three times with fresh boiling water. When the pieces are tender, drain them and set them aside. Heat the sugar and the 2 cups of water in another saucepan to make a syrup, add the sweetflag pieces, and boil them for another 30 minutes. Drain them again and place them on waxed paper. Allow them to dry for several hours, then roll them in granulated sugar.

Our friends reacted strongly to these unusually flavored candies. Gail found the smell so unpleasantly pungent while the stems were cooking that she could not bring herself to even taste the candies, but her husband, Bob, liked them so much that he had consumed the whole plateful by nightfall!

WILD LEEK, ONION & GARLIC

Wild Leek, *Allium tricoccum*, a strongly scented herb, grows in rich, moist woods and bottoms, frequently under maples, and flowers in June and July.

> Found mainly in CT, DE, IL, KY, MA, MD, ME, MI, NH, NJ, PA, RI, TN, VA, VT, WI, WV. In Canada: w. NB, s. QUE.

Nodding Wild Onion, *Allium cernuum*, a perennial herb, grows on ledges and rocky or wooded slopes to high altitudes, and flowers from July to August.

> Found mainly in AZ, w. CO, ID, IL, IN, KY, MD, MI, n. MN, MT, w. NM, NY, OH, OR, PA, TN, UT, w. VA, WA, WI, WV, w. WY. In Canada: s. ALTA, s. BC, MAN, s. ONT, s. SASK.

Wild Garlic, *Allium canadense*, a perennial herb, grows in low woods, thickets, and fields, and on the prairie. It flowers between April and July.

> Found mainly in AL, AR, CT, DE, FL, GA, IA, IL, IN e. KS, KY, LA, MA, MD, ME, MI, MS, MO, NC, e. ND, e. NE, NH, NJ, NY, OH, e. OK, PA, SC, e. SD, TN, e. TX, VA, VT, WI, WV. In Canada: s. NB, s. NS, s. ONT, s. QUE.

All the many species of wild onion *(Allium)* are more or less edible and nutritious despite their strong, penetrating odor. A number of Indian tribes ate the nodding wild onion, *A. cernuum*, either raw in salted water or roasted in ashes, although Thomas Heriot (1585) says that the natives did not eat the wild leeks found growing in profusion around Virginia: "There are also leeks, differing little from ours in England that grow in many places where they were, we gathered and eat many, but the natural inhabitants never."

Valery Havard (1895) says that many explorers ate wild onions to supplement their diet, but "it was their abundance all over the land which gave them their value rather than their quality!" One early explorer would seem to disagree. Captain Meriwether Lewis, on his way up the Missouri

Wild garlic

ble: "On this island I met with great quantities of a small onion . . . I gathered about half a bushel . . . and the men also gathered considerable quantities . . . I think it is as pleasantly flavored as any species of that root I ever tasted. I called this beautiful and fertile island after this plant–'Onion Island.' A year later Lewis discovered that wild onions had another useful function. "To dispel the wind which the roots called cows and quawmash are apt to create . . . we boil a small onion which we find in great abundance, with other roots and find them also an antidote."

Although Captain Lewis praised wild garlic as food, the settlers of Virginia found that it had a disastrous effect on the milk and meat of their cattle. Peter Kalm, writing in 1749, reports that "A species of leek *(Allium canadense)*, very like that which appears only in woods or hills in Sweden, grows at present on almost all corn fields mixed with sand. The English here call it Garlick. On some fields it grew in great abundance. When the cattle grazed on such fields, and ate the garlick, their milk, and the butter which was made of it, tasted so strangely of it that they were scarce eatable. Sometimes they sold butter in the Philadelphia markets, which tasted so strongly of garlick that it was entirely useless. On this account, they do not suffer milking cows to graze on fields where garlick abounds: this they reserve for other species of cattle. When the cattle eat much of this garlick in summer, their flesh has likewise such a strong flavour that it is unfit for eating. This kind of garlick appears early in spring, and the horses always passed by it without ever touching it."

The bulbs of *Allium* can all be roasted, boiled, or braised, and used to season soups or stews. The pickled bulbs are delicious either on their own or used in salads.

River, made the following entry in his journal on April 12, 1805: "found a great quantity of small onions in the plain where we encamped; had some of them collected and cooked, found them agreeable." Later on, July 22, Lewis records christening an island in the Missouri after its principal vegeta-

Wild Vichyssoise

SERVES 4

2 LARGE POTATOES
15 WILD LEEK BULBS, PEELED AND CUBED
2 PINTS CHICKEN STOCK
SALT AND PEPPER TO TASTE
4 TABLESPOONS HEAVY CREAM
CHOPPED CHIVES OR WILD ONION,
   FOR GARNISH

Bring the first four ingredients to a boil in a large saucepan, then cover and simmer for 15 minutes. Cool the soup, then puree it in a blender. Chill in the refrigerator and when cold check the seasoning. Serve with a tablespoon of cream swirled into each bowl and sprinkle with chopped chives or wild onion.

This delicious summer soup is also good served hot in the winter if you can find enough leeks to make extra for the freezer.

HOPS

Hop, *Humulus lupulus*, a perennial climber, grown in hedges, thickets, and waste places, and flowers in July and August.

Found throughout North America.

In the best-known American books about edible wild plants, I could discover no mention of eating hops, yet I found them growing all over the place as I traveled through the United States to do this book. In fact, American hops are now so plentiful they are used by English brewers.

Although hops for brewing beer were not introduced into England until the 16th century, they had been used on the Continent from the earliest times. There is a reference to the use of hops in beer-making in the Finnish epic *Kalevala*, thought to date back some 3,000 years. The planting of hops was forbidden in the reign of Henry VI, but in the 16th century Flemish settlers began cultivating hops in Kent, which is still the most important hop-growing county in Britain.

When hops were first imported to England in about 1520, the more bitter drink they produced was rejected by many people and was even banned by Henry VIII, who loved spiced ale, and "interfered in everything from religion to beer barrels." Before hops were introduced, the traditional drink in England, in both town and country, was ale, which was brewed from malt and yeast only, or from malt, yeast, and honey flavored with heath tops, ground ivy, marjoram, yarrow, broom, or any other bitter or aromatic herbs.

The hop is first mentioned by Pliny as a garden plant.

The Romans used only the young shoots, in spring, as a vegetable. Hops used to be sold in markets, tied in bundles, for table use. The young tops can be eaten raw in salads, and the early foliage may be used as a potherb.

Hop Top Omelet

SERVES 2

4 EGGS
SALT AND PEPPER TO TASTE
A HANDFUL OF HOP TOPS, 2 INCHES LONG,
   WASHED AND DRIED
1 TABLESPOON OLIVE OIL

Lightly beat the eggs, add the seasonings, and stir in the hop tops. Fry in the olive oil in a medium-hot pan until fairly firm, then cut in half and serve.

This unusual Italian-style omelet is neither folded nor turned and is ideal for a light lunch.

Hop Top Soup

"Take a large quantity of hop tops, in April or May, when they are in their greatest perfection; tie them in bunches twenty or thirty in a bunch; lay them in spring-water for an hour or two, drain them well from the water, and put them to some thin pease soup; boil them well, and add three spoonfuls of the juice of onions, some pepper, and salt; let them boil some time longer; when done, soak some crusts of bread in the soup."

From Mrs. Charlotte Mason's *The Lady's Assistant* (1755).

I made my version of this soup by sautéing a chopped onion in butter, then adding 4 cups of chicken stock, a can of peas, and a large handful of hop tops, then cooking the soup gently for 30 minutes. I flavored it with a touch of cayenne pepper and served it with large croutons to my hungry family of four.

Hop Beer

MAKES 1 GALLON

2 CUPS HOP FLOWERS
1¼ GALLONS WATER
⅔ CUP MALT
1 CUP SUGAR
2 TEASPOONS BREWER'S YEAST

Boil the hops in the water for 15 minutes in a 2-gallon pail, then strain off the liquid into a bucket through fine muslin or cheesecloth. Mix in the malt and the sugar. Activate the yeast, and add it after the liquor has cooled down. Cover the pail with muslin and let the liquor stand for 5 days, then decant it into screw-top bottles, leaving the sediment behind. Test the bottles weekly to see that they do not get too fizzy. If you find they are flat, add a teaspoon of sugar to each bottle and leave for a week. The beer can normally be drunk 10 days to 2 weeks after you start making it. Pour it carefully into a jug, leaving any sediment behind.

Orange-flowered jewelweed

JEWELWEED

Orange-Flowered Jewelweed or **Spotted Touch-Me-Not**, *Impatiens capensis*, is an annual herb with a juicy stem or orange, spotted flowers. It grows in wet areas near swamps, streams, and ponds, or in moist woodlands, and flowers from June to September.

Found mainly in n. AL, n. AR, AK, CT, DE, FL, GA, e. IA, IL, IN, KY, MA, MD, ME, MI, MN, MO, NC, NH, NJ, NY, OH, OK, PA, RI, SC, TN, VA, VT, WI, WV. In Canada: all provinces.

Yellow-Flowered Jewelweed or **Pale Touch-Me-Not**, *Impatiens pallida*, is an annual herb with a juicy stem and pale yellow, spotted flowers. It grows in moist, shady woodlands and wet meadows, often in chalky soils, then flowers from July to September.

Found mainly in CT, n. GA, IA, IL, IN, KS, KY, MA, MD, ME, MI, MN, MO, w. NC, e. ND, NH, NJ, NY, OH, PA, n.w. SC, n. TN, w. VA, VT, WI, WV. In Canada: s. MAN, NB, s.w. NFLD, NS, ONT, QUE, s. SASK.

CAUTION: Do not eat the shoots frequently, as they may contain a concentration of calcium oxalate crystals.

The tender young shoots of both species can be eaten, as long as they are gathered before they exceed 5 or 6 inches in height. They should be boiled and drained at least twice before eating with butter and seasoning. The seeds are delicious eaten raw or used as a topping on desserts. Medicinally, fresh jewelweed juice alleviates the pain of nettles and the itching of poison ivy. The stems can be boiled to make an extract, which, if frozen, keeps its medicinal qualities.

SORREL

Sorrel, *Rumex acetosa*, a coarse herb, grows in fields and meadows, and on roadsides. It flowers from June to September.

Found mainly in CT, MA, ME, NH, NY, n. PA, RI, VT. In Canada: all provinces.

Sheep's sorrel, *Rumex acetosella*, a tall annual or perennial herb, grows in sour, worn-out soil on disturbed sites, and in waste places and old fields. It flowers from June to October.

Except for the southernmost states from AZ east to GA and FL, found throughout North America.

CAUTION: Sorrel can cause digestive upset if eaten continually—it contains small amounts of oxalic acid—but a good sorrel soup once in a while is harmless. Some *Rumex* species have been known to cause dermatitis in susceptible individuals.

Introduced from Europe, these species of *Rumex* spread rapidly and are referred to several times by early writers. In a diary entry of 1749, Peter Kalm says that the Virginians boiled sheep's sorrel with cogweed, copperas, and cloth to produce a very durable black dye. Edward Palmer (1870) tells us that the Indians living along the Colorado River called sorrel *yerba colorada* (colored grass) and used the roots for tanning hides, the seeds for flour. The Rio Grande Indians made a poultice from the leaves of the sour dock and combined them with salt to cure headaches.

Sorrel was obviously popular with American settlers during the last century. There are several recipes for making soup and vegetable dishes in the cookbooks of the period.

Sorrel has been used as a salad from the most distant times. It was extensively cultivated in Britain until Henry VIII's reign, when it was ousted by the large-leaved French sorrel (*Rumex scutatus*). John Pechy (1694) tells us that "the Juice may be mix'd with Broths, or the Leaves boyl'd in them. In summer 'tis good sauce for most meats." Traditionally, sorrel was used in country districts as a green sauce with cold meat. The plans were ground down in a mortar and the resulting puree mixed with vinegar and sugar.

In France, sorrel is put into ragouts, fricassees, and soups, and forms the chief constituent of the favorite *soupe aux herbes*. The name *sorrel* comes from the Old French *surelle*, which derives from *sur* (sour) and refers to the characteristic acidity of the plant. The juice of the leaves will curdle milk and is used by the Laplanders as a substitute for rennet. In England, where children eat sorrel leaves on the way to school, they are known as sour dabs.

When preparing sorrel, do not use steel knives, and avoid cooking it in a nonstick saucepan: The plant's chemicals react with iron.

Sorrel Sauce

MAKES 2 CUPS

1–2 CUPS SORREL LEAVES
2 CHOPPED SHALLOTS OR 1 HEAPING
    TABLESPOON CHOPPED ONION
2 TABLESPOONS DRY WHITE VERMOUTH
¼ CUP DRY WHITE WINE
¼ CUP WATER
3 LARGE EGG YOLKS
1 CUP (2 STICKS) LIGHTLY SALTED BUTTER
SALT AND PEPPER TO TASTE

Strip the sorrel leaves off the stems, wash the leaves, and cut them into small strips. Boil the shallots in a saucepan with the wines and the water until the liquid has almost vanished. Put the shallots and egg yolks into a blender, whiz at top speed for 30 seconds, and return to the pan. In another saucepan, cut up and melt the butter, and stir in half the sorrel strips. When the butter is almost boiling, remove the pan from the heat and pour the mixture onto the egg yolk and scallion puree very slowly, stirring vigorously; then increase the stirring speed as the sauce thickens. Now add salt and pepper to taste and gradually add the rest of the sorrel strips. Reheat the sauce over gentle heat or in a bain-marie. Do not overheat or the eggs and butter may curdle. Serve with poached salmon, trout, or sea bass.

This recipe by Jane Grigson was first published in the *Observer* magazine.

Sorrel Salad

SERVES 4

1 SMALL HEAD LETTUCE
   (RED OR RUBY LETTUCE IS NICE)
1 BUNCH SORREL LEAVES
1 TEASPOON SALT
½ CLOVE GARLIC, CRUSHED
1 TABLESPOON FINELY CHOPPED MIXED FRESH HERBS
2 TABLESPOONS OLIVE OIL
BLACK PEPPER

In gauging how many sorrel leaves to gather, count on their making up half the salad, and the lettuce making up the other half. Wash the greens, shake them well, carefully pat them dry with paper towels, and tear them into bite-sized pieces. Put the salt in the bottom of a large wooden salad bowl; add the garlic, then the herbs, then the greens. Sprinkle the olive oil over them and toss gently until all the leaves are coated, then grind black pepper over them to taste.

This makes a lovely, sharp, tangy salad. The bitter taste of the sorrel is the reason for putting no vinegar or lemon in the dressing.

Buttered Sorrel

After washing sorrel and removing the stalks, put it into a pan with only the water clinging to it. Cover closely and simmer for 10 minutes. Strain in a colander, pressing the leaves well with a saucer to remove as much water as possible. Return them to the pan, add a good knob of butter, season well with salt and pepper, and toss the sorrel over low heat until every leaf is coated with butter. Serve very hot.

Allow about ¼ pound of raw sorrel per person, as it boils down considerably. This makes a most interesting vegetable with a tart flavor, like unsweetened rhubarb.

Sorrel Soup

SERVES 4

1½ CUPS SORREL LEAVES
10 LETTUCE LEAVES
1 LARGE ONION
1 LARGE POTATO
2 TEASPOONS BUTTER
3–4 CUPS CHICKEN STOCK
   OR CANNED CHICKEN BROTH (DILUTED)
1 CUP MILK
SALT AND PEPPER TO TASTE

Wash the sorrel and lettuce leaves and break them into pieces. Chop the onion and slice the potato. Melt the butter in a large saucepan, add the sorrel, lettuce, and onion, and cook over low heat, without browning, until the vegetables are soft. At the same time, heat the chicken stock to boiling point. Add the potato and stock to the sorrel mixture and simmer uncovered for 20 to 30 minutes, until the potato is cooked. Put the mixture through a sieve or puree it in a blender. Return the puree to the saucepan, add the milk and the seasonings, and heat through. Serve with fried croutons.

An egg yolk beaten and added at the last minute makes a richer soup. I have also used chickweed in place of lettuce and it is just as good. The soup freezes well.

Adapted from Liz Roman's *Fenland Village Cookery Book* (1977).

Sour dock

SOUR DOCK

Sour Dock or **Curled Dock**, *Rumex crispus*, a large herb with curled leaves, grows in old fields and waste places and on roadsides.

It flowers from June to September.

Found throughout North America.

CAUTION: Sour dock should not be eaten continuously. It contains small amounts of oxalic acid, which can cause digestive upset.

Like sorrel, sour dock was popular among early settlers as a potherb or salad ingredient. Pick the young leaves in spring (older ones get stringy) and blanch them in two changes of boiling wa-

ter. Simmer for 2 to 4 minutes in a third change of boiling water, then serve with butter, salt, and pepper. The taste is similar to that of sorrel though a little sharper.

Sour Dock Soup

SERVES 4

1 TABLESPOON BUTTER
½ CUP FINELY CHOPPED ONION OR SCALLIONS
1 TEASPOON MIXED DRIED HERBS
2 LARGE POTATOES, PEELED AND CUBED
12 OR MORE YOUNG SOUR DOCK LEAVES,
    BLANCHED TWICE
3–4 CUPS WATER
SALT AND PEPPER TO TASTE
HALF-AND-HALF (OPTIONAL)

Heat the butter in a large saucepan and sauté the onion and herbs until soft but not brown. Add the potatoes and stir for a minute or two, then add the sour dock leaves and water. Bring to a boil, then simmer gently for 20 to 30 minutes. Cool, puree in a blender, and add the seasonings to taste. Serve either hot or cold, with a little half-and-half added to thin the soup if necessary and give it a smooth, creamy texture.

BULL THISTLE

Bull Thistle, *Cirsium vulgare*, a biennial herb, grows in clearings and pastures, on roadsides, and in waste places. It flowers from June to October.

Found throughout North America.

Introduced from Europe, the many species of thistle have spread throughout the United States. As we learn from the journals of Lewis and Clark, they were used as a food source by both Indians and explorers.

On January 21, 1806, Lewis wrote: "The root of the thistle, called by the natives 'Shan-ne-tah-que' . . . is white and nearly as crisp as a carrot; when prepared for use by the same process before described of the white bulb of pashohequo quawmash (that is, baked in a pit) it becomes black, and is more sugary than any fruit or root that I have met with in use among the natives; the sweet is precisely that of the sugar in flavor; this root is sometimes eaten also when first taken from the ground without any preparation, but in this way is vastly inferior."

A few finely chopped young thistle leaves add a crunchy texture and a slightly sour flavor to mild salad greens. They can also be cooked as a pot-herb, but be sure to remove the spines carefully, using gloves to protect your fingers. Pour boiling water on the leaves to cover, and cook them over medium heat, with the lid on, for 3 minutes. Then drain and serve with butter, salt, and pepper for a mild but pleasant-tasting vegetable. The young stems can be peeled and eaten raw or cooked.

Lotus lilies

Bull thistle

LOTUS LILY OR YELLOW NELUMBO

Lotus Lily or **Yellow Nelumbo**, *Nelumbo lutea*, a perennial, aquatic herb, grows in ponds, quiet streams, estuaries, and tidal waters, flowering between July and September.

Found in AL, AR, CT, DE, FL, GA, e. IA, IL, IN, e. KS, KY, LA, MA, MD, s. MI, s.e. MN, MO, MS, NC, s. NY, OH, e. OK, PA, SC, TN, e. TX, VA, s. WI, WV.

Captain Meriwether Lewis, in the notebook in which he made botanical notes and recorded meteorological data during the winter of 1803–4, gives an extensive description of the yellow nelumbo and says the Indians ate the seeds either raw or roasted and prepared the roots in the following way: "They enter the ponds where it grows, barefooted in autumn, and feel for it among the mud which being soft and the root large and near the surface they readily find it, they easily draw it up it having no fibrous or colateral roots to attach it firmly to the mud, they wash and scrape a thin bleack rind off it and cut it crosswise into pieces of an inch in length, when it is prepared for the pot it is of a fine white colour boils to a pulp and makes an agreeable soupe."

All parts of the plant are edible at some time in the year. In spring the unopened leaves and young stalks can be cooked as a vegetable or used in salad; in early summer the immature seeds are tasty raw or boiled; in autumn, you can collect the roots to boil, bake, or puree like sweet potatoes. The mature seeds can be winnowed and ground into flour or roasted; in this state they resemble chestnuts.

PICKERELWEED

Pickerelweed, *Pontederia cordata*, a perennial herb, grows along muddy shores or in the shallow water of ponds, streams, and lakes.

It flowers from June to November.

Found mainly in AR, AL, CT, DE, n. FL, GA, IA, IL, IN, e. KS, KY, LA, MA, MD, ME, MI, e. MN, MO, MS, NC, NH, NJ, OH, e. OK, PA, RI, SC, TN, e. TX, VA, VT, WI, WV. In Canada: NB, NS, s. ONT, s. QUE.

Pickerelweed

The young leaves should be gathered before they have fully unfurled and then added to salads or cooked, with the leafstalks, for 5 to 6 minutes and served with butter and seasoning as a potherb. The fruits each contain a single seed, which is highly nutritious and can be dried and roasted, then incorporated into cereals of the muesli type, or ground into flour and used in baking.

DANDELION

Dandelion, *Taraxacum officinale,* a perennial herb with a large taproot, grows on lawns, in waste grassy areas, and on open ground. It flowers from March to September.

Found throughout North America.

O fficial remedy" is the approximate translation of the Latin name, and for hundreds of years the dandelion has been widely used for its health-giving properties. Rich in vitamins and minerals, it was especially advocated for eating in the spring, when the young leaves would help to revitalize winter-weary bodies. The common name is derived from the French *dent-de-lion* (lion's tooth), which refers to the toothed edges of the leaves, or possibly to the white pointed roots.

Therapeutic use of the dandelion was first recorded by the Arab physician and herbalist Avicenna in the 10th century, and in the 13th century it occurs in the Welsh herbal of the physicians of Mydrai. The dandelion has been used as a food plant in many regions of America and Europe. In Minorca the islanders subsisted on it when a swarm of locusts destroyed other vegetation.

The young leaves are often eaten as a salad, especially in France, but the full-grown leaves are too bitter to be used. The young leaves are also served as a vegetable, cooked like spinach, or as a vegetable soup, and the flowers are fermented to make wine. Dandelion roots may also be used in salads, grated or chopped (the two-year-old roots are best), but the roots are more frequently roasted and used as coffee (see page 172). Dandelion beer is a rustic, fermented drink, common at one time in many parts of Canada. In Britain, dandelion stout was a favorite of the many herb beers brewed in the industrial towns. Dandelions were also fermented in combination with nettles and yellow dock.

In the past, dandelions were cultivated in kitchen gardens, where they sometimes attained a large size. The leaves can be induced to last through the winter by removing the flower buds as they appear. In France, dandelions can still be bought in the markets under the name *pissenlit*.

Pick the young leaves in spring, and during the rest of the year choose only the youngest leaves from the heart of the plant. Strip the leaves from the plant by hand, trim off the excess stalk, and wash well. If you want to avoid staining your hands brown, wear gloves! If the leaves are left to stand in water overnight, this will greatly improve them, as it does all wild salad plants.

Dandelion Nitsuke

½ POUND TENDER DANDELION GREENS,
    PICKED BEFORE THE FLOWERS BLOOM
1 TABLESPOON SESAME OIL
3 TABLESPOONS SHOYU
    OR 1 TABLESPOON MISO
    THINNED WITH 2 TABLESPOONS WATER
1 TABLESPOON WHITE SESAME SEEDS, TOASTED

"Wash the greens well and chop them finely. Heat the oil in a heavy skillet, add the chopped greens, and sauté over medium heat for 2 to 3 minutes. Season with shoyu or thinned miso and simmer until dry. Serve sprinkled with toasted sesame seeds.

"VARIATION: To prepare dandelion roots, scrub them well, then mince. Sauté in a little sesame oil over medium heat for 3 to 4 minutes. Season with shoyu or thinned miso and simmer until dry. Use sparingly as a garnish with rice. A traditional remedy for arthritis."

From Lima Ohsawa's *The Art of Just Cooking* (1974).

Salade de Pissenlit au Lard

SERVES 4

TENDER YOUNG DANDELION LEAVES
1 TABLESPOON WINE VINEGAR
1 CLOVE GARLIC, CRUSHED
¼ TEASPOON SALT
¼ TEASPOON PEPPER
4 SLICES BACON, CUT INTO SMALL PIECES
2 SLICES BREAD, CUBED

Gather enough of the leaves to make four generous servings. Wash the leaves several times, dry them in a salad spinner or with paper towels, and chop them coarsely. Put them into a large salad bowl and toss with the vinegar, garlic, and seasonings. Fry the little pieces of bacon until crisp and dry, then remove them from the pan and fry the cubed bread in the bacon fat to make crispy croutons. Toss together the bacon and croutons and any bacon fat still in the pan and spoon them on the salad. Serve immediately.

This is a delicious little side salad to serve either as an hors d'oeuvre or with a rich meat dish—a favorite with the French and with French food lovers the world over.

Wilted Dandelions

"Cut the roots from a quarter-peck (2 quarts) of dandelions, wash the leaves through several cold waters, drain and shake until dry. Take a handful of the leaves and cut them with a sharp knife into small pieces, and so continue until you have them all cut. Beat one egg until light, add to it a half-cup of cream, and stir over the fire until it thickens; then add a piece of butter the size of a walnut, two tablespoons of vinegar, salt and pepper to taste. Now put the dandelions into this, and stir over the fire until they are all wilted and tender. Serve hot."

From *Mrs. Rorer's Philadelphia Cook Book* (1886).

Dandelion-Flower Wine

MAKES 1 GALLON

1 QUART DANDELION FLOWERS
½ GALLON BOILING WATER
5 CUPS SUGAR
2 TEASPOONS BREWER'S YEAST
2 ORANGES
EXTRA BOILING WATER (COOLED)

Pick the dandelions on a sunny day. Fill a quart jar with flowers, pressing them down lightly as you add them; cut off any green stalks that may remain. Put the flowers into a bucket and pour on the boiling water. Leave for 2 to 3 days, then strain through a wine bag into a gallon jar. Stir the sugar into 5 cups of water and cook over medium heat until the sugar has completely dissolved. Activate the yeast. Allow the sugar syrup to cool to lukewarm before adding the yeast to it, then add them to the gallon jar. Now grate the rind and squeeze the juice from the oranges into the jar and make up a full gallon of liquid with the cooled, boiled water. Seal the jar with an air lock and leave until fermentation has finished. Siphon the wine into a clean jar and leave for as long as possible—it improves with keeping.

This recipe makes a medium-dry wine with a slightly resinous flavor, a taste that grows on you. I also tried cutting the green ends (calyxes) off each flower with a pair of scissors before proceeding and found that this reduces the resinous taste.

Dandelion Beer

MAKES 1 GALLON

1 QUART YOUNG DANDELION PLANTS
1 LEMON
2 TEASPOONS FINELY CHOPPED GINGER
1 GALLON COLD WATER
3 CUPS LIGHT BROWN SUGAR
1 TABLESPOON CREAM OF TARTAR
1 TABLESPOON BREWER'S YEAST

Wash the plants and remove the hairy roots without breaking the main taproots. Squeeze the lemon and put the juice aside; peel the rind off the lemon in strips (no pith should be left). Put the plants into a pail with the ginger, the lemon rind, and the water. Boil for 10 minutes, then strain out the solids. Put the sugar and cream of tartar in the fermenting vessel and pour the liquid over them. Stir until the sugar is dissolved. When the liquid is lukewarm, add the yeast and the lemon juice, and leave the vessel, covered with a folded cloth, in a warm room for 5 days. Strain out all the sediment and bottle in screw-topped cider or beer bottles. This beer is ready to drink in about a week, when it hisses as the stopper is loosened. It does not keep very long.

Test the bottles daily to see that they don't get too fizzy. Even after only 2 days in the bottles, the beer is smashing.

Apart from being a very popular country tipple, dandelion beer was the drink most favored in the past by workers in the iron foundries and potteries of England. It is refreshing and particularly good for relieving stomach upsets or indigestion and for clearing the kidneys and bladder.

Dandelion Coffee

The roots should be dug from September to March. Drinking chocolate is sometimes mixed with the coffee to improve the flavor. A detailed recipe for dandelion coffee is given on page 172.

Coltsfoot

COLTSFOOT

Coltsfoot, *Tussilago farfara*, a perennial herb, grows in damp soils and on waste ground and brooksides. It flowers from March to May, before the leaves appear.

Found mainly in CT, MA, ME, MI, MN, NH, NJ, NY, OH, PA, RI, VT, WI. In Canada: NB, NFLD, NS, s. ONT, s. QUE.

Traditionally, coltsfoot has been used to make cough drops, tea, seasoning, and wine. To relieve asthma and coughs, the leaves were dried and crumbled, then smoked like tobacco; or they were steeped in boiling water to make tea. A rich and tasty cough syrup was concocted by boiling the fresh leaves in water, adding sugar, bringing the extract to the boiling point again, and bottling. To make cough drops, boiling was continued until the syrup formed a hard ball when dropped into cold water. Gather the leaves before they get too tough.

Coltsfoot Wine

MAKES 1 GALLON

5 PINTS COLTSFOOT FLOWERS
JUICE OF 2 LEMONS
4½ CUPS SUGAR
GENERAL-PURPOSE YEAST
2 TEASPOONS BREWER'S YEAST

Traditionally, this wine was made from the petals only, but I have found that to cut away the stem and some of the outer green calyx with a pair of scissors is quicker than picking off the petals one by one, and does not adversely affect the flavor of the wine.

Prepare the coltsfoot flowers and place them in a plastic 1½-gallon bucket. Pour 3 pints of boiling water on the flowers and let them soak for 24 hours, pressing them occasionally with a wooden spoon. Then strain off the flowers through muslin or cheesecloth, squeezing hard at the end to extract all the flavor. Add the lemon juice and activate the yeast. Boil the sugar in 3 pints of water until dissolved and add it to the flower extract. When the extract has cooled, add the yeast, cover with cloth, and let the must ferment for 3 days, then transfer it to a gallon-sized fermentation jar. Fill the jar with cold boiled water to within 2 inches of the top, and seal with an air lock. Leave in a warm place, 60° to 70°F, until fermentation has ceased (about 6 weeks), then siphon the wine into a clean jar, leaving the main sediment behind. Seal with a sterilized cork and leave for a month. You can filter the wine to get a sparkling result, but if you prefer not to, leave it in the jar until the sediment has all settled out, and then siphon it off. Bottle and cork with sterilized corks.

Coltsfoot Cream

SERVES 4

2 CUPS SMALL COLTSFOOT LEAVES
1 TABLESPOON BUTTER
WATER
2 TABLESPOONS SESAME SEEDS,
    TOASTED IN A SKILLET

Chop the leaves and sauté them in the butter for 2 to 3 minutes. Add enough water to cover and cook them until soft. Strain, add the sesame seeds, and beat to a smooth cream. This makes an excellent vegetable.

DAYLILY

Daylily, *Hemerocallis fulva*, a large perennial herb with fleshy, fibrous roots and tubers, grows along roadsides and in vacant lots, fields, and thickets, and flowers from May to July.

Found mainly in AL, AR, CT, DE, n. FL, GA, IA, IL, e. KS, KY, LA, MA, MD, ME, MI, MN, MS, MO, NC, e. NE, NH, NJ, NY, OH, e. OK, PA, RI, SC, TN, e. TX, VA, VT, WI, WV. In Canada: s. NB, s. NS, s. ONT, s. QUE.

CAUTION: This plant has laxative properties, so eat in moderation.

Although the daylily is found throughout the eastern United States, it is not ordinarily eaten; yet the Chinese and Japanese have long recognized the superior edible qualities of the flower buds. Opened, they can be dipped in batter and lightly fried; unopened, they can be boiled and eaten as a vegetable rather similar in taste to green beans. Alternatively, they can be added to soups and stews to give body and texture. The flower heads make an attractive decoration on fresh summer salads. The tiny young tubers are rather laborious to clean but make a crunchy addition to salads; if boiled, they are sweet and nutty in flavor, a bit like sweet corn. Daylily flowers and buds can be easily dried by placing them on sheets of paper in a warm, dry room for 10 days. Sealed in jars, they will then keep all year and can be easily revived by soaking in water.

Daylilies Japanese Style

SERVES 4

½ POUND SMOKED SALMON, THINLY SLICED
1 CUP PLAIN, BOILED RICE
2 CARROTS, CUT INTO FINE MATCHSTICKS
½ CUP ALFALFA SPROUTS
4 DAYLILY FLOWERS
4 TABLESPOONS SOY SAUCE

Cut the salmon into 12 rectangles, each 1½ x 3 inches in size, and carefully roll them into small sausages. Place three salmon rolls on each plate together with a small pile of rice. Decorate with carrot matchsticks, alfalfa sprouts, and, lastly, a daylily flower. Serve with a tiny bowl of soy sauce.

The fun of serving this deliciously light, tasty, and nutritionally well-balanced meal lies in using the ingredients to make an artistic effect on the plate. Watching Japanese chefs in sushi bars makes it look incredibly easy, but therein lies the skill. It is actually surprisingly difficult to achieve a simple, beautiful arrangement.

FIREWEED

Fireweed, *Epilobium angustifolium*, a tall, perennial herb, grows in burned woodlands, clearings, and damp ravines. It flowers from July to September.

Found in AK, AZ, CA, CO, CT, DE, IA, ID, IL, IN, MA, MD, ME, MI, MN, w. NC, ND, NH, NJ, NM, NV, NY, OH, OR, PA, RI, SD, e. TN, UT, VA, VT, WA, WV, WY. In Canada: all provinces.

Because the seeds must be subjected to high temperatures before they can germinate, this plant often springs up on recently burned ground or, as in World War II, on blitzed land–hence the names *fireweed* and *bomb-site plant*.

Fireweed

Most parts of the plant can be used for food. The roots, if dug up in spring, may be boiled as a vegetable or added to casseroles. The young shoots should be collected in late spring, peeled, and eaten like asparagus, either boiled or baked in butter. On the Gaspé Peninsula, the French Canadians call the herb wild asparagus. The leaves and shoots together may be used as a potherb; the leaves themselves can be used as a salad or vegetable, or as a substitute for and adulterant of tea.

The herb is still popular as a vegetable in certain countries in Europe, especially in Russia, where it is used to make kaporie tea. In British Columbia, the Indians peel the stalks and eat the gelatinous pith fresh or cook it as a soup. Other tribes use the core as a flour for bread-making. Finally, the shoots may be used to make a beer-like liquid that, in certain parts of Siberia, is mixed with hallucinogenic juice of the fly agaric fungus (*Amanita muscaria*). This brew has effects that are said to be comparable to the combined effects of gin and LSD!

Despite all these exotic tales of eating fireweed, I have been unable to make it palatable. It is far too bitter to enjoy as any kind of vegetable.

RED CLOVER

Red Clover, *Trifolium pratense*, a biennial or perennial herb, grows on roadsides and in fields, clearings, and grassy places. It flowers from May to September.

Found throughout North America.

The Indians ate clover in several ways. Sometimes the foliage was eaten fresh before the plant flowered or, as among the Digger tribe, it was cooked by placing moistened layers of plants one upon another in a stone oven. The Apache Indians boiled it with dandelions, grass, and pigweed; the Pomo tribe held special clover feasts and dances in the early spring to celebrate the plant's appearance.

In Europe it is among the most generally cultivated fodder plants, but it is unknown as a human food. Its value as food for cattle is reflected in the phrase *to live in clover*, and its ability to enrich the soil, and thus fertilize the next corn crop, gives rise to the saying "Clover is the mother of corn." To dream of clover foretells a happy marriage; to find a four-leaved clover brings good luck and gives the possessor the ability to see fairies.

Clover leaves can be cooked as a vegetable, like spinach, and both the leaves and the flowers can be used in sandwiches and as a flavoring or garnish.

Red Clover Wine

MAKES 1 GALLON

2 QUARTS CLOVER BLOSSOMS
1 GALLON WATER
5 CUPS SUGAR
JUICE OF 3 LEMONS
JUICE OF 2 ORANGES
1 PACKET BREWER'S YEAST

Pick the clover blossoms when they are well out but before they start to go brown, and put them in a plastic bucket. Bring the water and sugar to a boil, pour it over the flowers, and add the fruit juices. Put the yeast in a glass with a little sugar, and set it near a radiator. By the time the water has cooled to lukewarm, the yeast will have started and can be stirred into the bucket. Cover the bucket with cheesecloth and allow the must to ferment for 5 days. Strain it into a jar, seal with an air lock, and let it ferment until it has entirely stopped working. Rack it off into a clear jar, let it stand until it has completely settled out, and then bottle. Alternatively, as you rack the wine off its sediment, put it through a fine filter and bottle immediately. The wine will be white, not red or pink as you might have hoped, and if you ferment it in a rather warm room as I do, it may be a little too dry. If this is the case, a tiny amount of sugar syrup will sweeten it nicely.

This is a light, refreshing wine that can, and probably will, be drunk immediately.

Red Clover Salad–A Garden and Wild Leaf Mixture

SERVES 4

4 CHICORY LEAVES
4 LEAVES MUSTARD GREENS
4 SWISS CHARD LEAVES
4 RUBY LETTUCE LEAVES
4 NASTURTIUM LEAVES
2 SPRIGS FLAT-LEAVED OR ITALIAN PARSLEY
2 WILD ONIONS, FINELY CHOPPED
PETALS FROM 6 WILD ROSES
16 CLOVER FLOWERS

DRESSING:
2 TEASPOONS DIJON MUSTARD
¼ CUP VINEGAR
¾ CUP OLIVE OIL
½ TEASPOON SALT
¼ TEASPOON PEPPER

Collect the first six ingredients from the garden, wash and dry them, and keep them in a plastic bag in the refrigerator while you collect the wild ingredients. Wash and dry them too. Now make the dressing. Blend the mustard and vinegar with a wire whisk, then add the oil drop by drop, whisking continuously, so that the ingredients emulsify. Finally, add the salt and pepper and whisk again. Place all the salad ingredients in a large bowl and toss thoroughly with the dressing.

This selection of wild and garden salad leaves is only a suggestion. Any combination of leaves will be fine as long as they offer a variety of flavors–hot, bland, bitter–that offset and complement one another in interesting ways.

Quickweed

QUICKWEED

Quickweed, *Galinsoga ciliata*, an annual weed, grows in gardens, yards, and waste places, and flowers from June to November.

Found throughout North America.

This plant is well known as an edible pot-herb and has quite a distinctive, rooty flavor. Simmer the leaves in boiling water for 2 to 3 minutes and serve with butter, salt, and pepper.

FIDDLEHEAD OR OSTRICH FERN

Fiddlehead or **Ostrich Fern**, *Matteuccia struthiopteris*, a tall perennial, grows in rich, very wet swampy soil in woods and on streambanks and the edges of ponds. It flowers from July to October.

Found mainly in AK, DE, e. IA, IN, MD, ME, MI, MN, e. ND, NH, NJ, NY, OH, PA, VT, WI, WV. In Canada: all provinces.

LEAVES, SHOOTS, FLOWERS & HERBS

CAUTION: This plant may be carcinogenic. Extensive research has been carried out in Europe on the much-consumed bracken fern, *Pteridium aquilinum*, which is now thought to be, in fact, carcinogenic. The finding is not necessarily applicable to the other common ferns, including the ostrich fern, but to be on the safe side, do not eat fiddleheads in great quantities or continually.

Fiddlehead ferns. Note the old, dark flower stems in the center.

Ferns are hard to categorize because a number of different ones are called fiddlehead on account of their tightly coiled young leaves, which can be collected in April or May. To recognize the real fiddlehead ferns, look for the previous year's dead flowering stems. They are about a foot high, and growing right in the middle of them you will see the new fronds with their tight, upright form (see photo). Remember, this fern grows only in really damp, boggy ground.

Fiddleheads are delicious to eat. The scaly rootstocks used to be eaten boiled or roasted by the Abnaki Indians of northern England and Quebec. Nowadays the young fronds are more commonly relished, so much so that they are now obtainable in some food stores in late spring or early summer. They must be boiled for 15 minutes or steamed for 10 to 12 minutes and then served with butter and seasoning—my favorite way to eat them. I find them similar in flavor to asparagus, though with a somewhat milder taste, more like lettuce.

SWEET GALE

Sweet Gale, *Myrica gale*, a small, aromatic shrub, grows in swamps and shallow water. It flowers from April to June and fruits from July until January.

> Found mainly in AK, CT, MA, MD, ME, MI, n. MN, NC, NH, NY, PA, RI, TN, VT, w. WA, n. WI, WV. In Canada: ALTA, LAB, NB, NFLD, NS, ONT, QUE.

The leaves of sweet gale have long been dried and used for making a delicate tea. The berries, dried and crushed, can be used as a spice for flavoring soups, stews, and meat. In England, where the plant is also known as bog myrtle, the leaves were used for flavoring ale. The Swedes put a sprig of gale into neat spirits, which they then leave for a couple of minutes before serving it with bleak roe, a special delicacy.

Sweet Gale Mead

MAKES 1 GALLON

¾ CUP FRESH SWEET GALE LEAVES
1 GALLON WATER
1 POUND HONEY
JUICE OF 1 LEMON
¼ TO ½ TEASPOON BREWER'S YEAST

Put the leaves in a 1½-gallon metal or plastic bucket, bring the water to a boil in a second bucket, and pour it on the leaves. Add the honey and the lemon juice, and stir until all the honey is dissolved. Activate the yeast and add it to the bucket when the water has cooled to lukewarm. Cover the bucket with muslin or cheesecloth and let the must ferment for 4 to 5 days. Strain off and bottle in screw-topped bottles.

The mead will be ready to drink in a week. After bottling, keep testing the bottles to see that they don't get too fizzy; my first bottles ended up all over the ceiling! If they do not fizz at all, add a teaspoonful of sugar to each one and leave for a week. Mead has an exotic, medieval flavor that you may hate or love.

CHICORY

Chicory, *Cichorium intybus*, a perennial herb with a deep root, grows along roads and in fields, vacant lots, and waste places. It flowers from June to October.

Found throughout North America.

Chicory is one of the most striking plants because of the intense blue of its blossoms. Although the flowers last for only one day, they bloom successively for a month or more on the same plant.

The young leaves can be used in a salad or cooked as a vegetable. The roots can be boiled, but though they taste something like parsnips, they are unexciting and barely worth the effort. The roasted roots are ground and commonly used as an adulterant in coffee or as a coffee substitute. In many southern cities coffee flavored with chicory is greatly preferred to pure coffee.

Chicory Flower and Cottage Cheese Salad

SERVE 3–4

6 LARGE, CRISP LETTUCE LEAVES
1 CELERY STALK, THINLY SLICED
2 CUPS COTTAGE CHEESE
6–8 CHICORY FLOWERS

Line a large salad bowl with the lettuce leaves. Stir the celery into the cottage cheese and pile the mixture into the center of the bowl. Finally, decorate with the chicory blossoms.

The slightly bitter flavor of the flowers makes them an ideal accompaniment to cottage cheese. Serve this salad only at lunchtime as the flowers fade and die later.

CREEPING THYME

Creeping Thyme, *Thymus serpyllum*, a low, aromatic, perennial herb, grows on roadsides and in old fields, dry grasslands, and rocky soils. It flowers in July and August.

Found mainly in CT, DE, IN, MA, MD, ME, MI, NC, NH, NJ, NY, OH, PA, RI, VA, VT, WV. In Canada: NB, NS, s. ONT, PEI, s. QUE.

Thyme is my favorite herb. It makes an excellent addition to roasting meat—chicken, heart, and especially liver—and gives a nice strong flavor to an herb omelet. Most mushroom dishes benefit from it, as do salad dressings and vinegar. Wild thyme can sometimes be rather mild in flavor compared with the cultivated forms, so remember to be lavish with it. The leaves can be used to make a tea that is good for colds and throat complaints. Thyme can be dried and stored with very little loss of flavor.

Thyme and Sour Cream Dressing

¼ CUP FINELY MINCED THYME
2 TABLESPOONS OLIVE OIL
2 TEASPOONS LEMON JUICE
1 SMALL CLOVE GARLIC
1 CUP SOUR CREAM
½ TEASPOON SALT
¼ TEASPOON PEPPER

In a jar, combine the thyme with the olive oil, lemon juice, and a squeeze of garlic. Shake the jar well so that the oil breaks up and emulsifies with the lemon juice. Then stir the dressing into the sour cream and season with the salt and pepper.

This makes a gorgeous dressing, especially for beetroot, cucumber, carrot, or any kind of bean salad.

Thyme and Parsley Stuffing

MAKES 1½ CUPS

1 TABLESPOON OIL
1 SMALL ONION, FINELY CHOPPED
2 SLICES BACON, FINELY CHOPPED
2 CUPS FRESH BREAD CRUMBS
1 TABLESPOON SHREDDED SUET, LARD,
    OR VEGETABLE SHORTENING
1 TABLESPOON FINELY CHOPPED THYME
1 TABLESPOON CHOPPED PARSLEY
¼ TEASPOON SALT
⅛ TEASPOON PEPPER
1 TABLESPOON LEMON JUICE
1 TEASPOON GRATED LEMON ZEST (NO PITH)
1 EGG

Heat the oil in a frying pan, add the onion and bacon, and sauté them lightly until the onion is soft. Put the bread crumbs in a bowl and add to them the onion, bacon, and all the rest of the ingredients except the egg. Mix well. Beat the egg lightly and stir it into the stuffing as a binder.

This is an ideal stuffing for chicken or turkey. When my mother, Elsie, makes it, she stuffs the neck end of the bird and sews it in. The stuffing expands a bit and cooks solid, so that it can be carved into thin slices. The recipe makes enough to stuff the neck of a 4- or 5-pound chicken. For larger fowl, increase accordingly.

COMMON PURSLANE

Common Purslane or **Pusley**, *Portulaca oleracea*, an annual herb with yellow flowers that open only on sunny mornings, grows close to the ground in gardens, and flowers, then fruits, from June to November.

Found throughout North America.

Although one of our most common and nutritious wild plants, purslane is now thought of solely as a weed. This was not always so. In colonial times, according to the Reverend Manasseh Cutler (1785), purslane was eaten as a potherb and regarded as little inferior to asparagus. The Paiute Indians also ate purslane greens (Palmer, 1878) and the ground seeds as well. By the end of the 19th century, F. V. Colville (1895) could write that purslane's chief economic value was supposedly as food for hogs, but he highly recommends it as food for humans: "As a potherb . . . it is very palatable, still retaining when cooked a slight acid taste. It can be heartily recommended to those who have a liking for this kind of vegetable food."

The leaves, stems, and flower buds of purslane can all be eaten. To keep your patch flourishing, it is best first to snip off the young leaf tips. Use them raw in a variety of salads or cook them lightly and serve them with butter as a crunchy green vegetable. Alternatively, the slightly mucilanginous texture of the leaves helps to thicken soups and casseroles. Many people like to fry purslane leaves with chopped bacon.

Having read that Indians made flour from the tiny black seeds that ripen in capsules when the plant is mature, Euell Gibbons dried the whole mature plants on a plastic sheet for two weeks, then sieved and winnowed them to accumulate the seeds. These he ground and mixed half and half with wheat flour to make pancakes, which he pronounced "delicious."

A woman who sold Mexican purslane in bunches at a Tucson street market, told me that Mexicans eat purslane as a side dish. They boil the leaves for a few minutes, then fry them in oil with a little chopped onion, adding slices of cheese and serving it when the cheese is hot and melting.

Tzatziki with Purslane
SERVES 4–6

1½ CUPS PLAIN YOGURT
1 MEDIUM-SIZED CUCUMBER,
    PEELED AND CUBED
2 CLOVES GARLIC, CRUSHED
1 CUP COARSELY CHOPPED PURSLANE LEAVES
SALT AND PEPPER TO TASTE

Combine all the ingredients and mix thoroughly. Put the mixture into a serving bowl and decorate with purslane sprigs.

This wild food version of a traditional Greek hors d'oeuvre has a refreshingly crunchy texture and is a good accompaniment for charbroiled meat.

Plantain

PLANTAIN

Plantain, *Plantago major*, an annual or perennial herb with thick, often hairy leaves, grows along roadsides and in waste places, and flowers from June to October.

Found throughout North America.

This common weed was introduced into North America from Europe, and it spread with such rapidity that some early botanists were uncertain whether it was a native or introduced plant. As Peter Kalm wrote in his diary in 1748, "The broad plantain, or *Plantago major*, grows on the high-roads, foot-paths, meadows, and in gardens, in great plenty. Mr Bartram had found this plant in many places on his travels, but he did not know whether it was an original American plant, or whether the Europeans had brought it over. This doubt had its rise from the savages (who always had an extensive knowledge of the plants of the country) pretending that this plant never grew here before the arrival of the Europeans. They therefore gave it a name which signifies the Englishman's foot; for they say, that where a European had walked, there this plant grew in his footsteps."

According to Jonathan Carver, who traveled here in the 1760s, one species of plantain was known as rattlesnake plantain because the Indians believed that its leaves were charmed, and if applied immediately to a rattlesnake wound would prevent all dangerous symptoms from appearing.

Mrs. Child (1836) confirms that the species appears to have medicinal properties: "Plantain and house-leek boiled in cream, and strained before it is put away to cook, makes a very cooling, soothing ointment. Plantain leaves laid upon a wound are cooling and healing."

Plantain has long been recognized as a salad herb or vegetable, but unless you pick very young fresh leaves they are inclined to be rather stringy. Blanch the leaves by plunging them into boiling water for 30 seconds, drain, and repeat. Then simmer them in a little freshly boiling water for about 4 minutes. Drain and serve with butter, salt, and pepper. Although I have tried plantain several times, both raw and cooked, it is not a great favorite with me.

FENNEL

Fennel, *Foeniculum vulgare*, an aromatic, perennial herb, grows in dry fields and on roadsides. It flowers from June to September.

Found mainly in AZ, CA, CO, KS, MI, NE, NM, OH, OK, PA, TX, UT.

Another herb that never seems to be mentioned in historical accounts or wild food guides, fennel was introduced from Europe and now grows wild in many parts of the United States.

The Romans cultivated fennel for its aromatic seeds and edible shoots, which they ate as a vegetable. Roman bakers are said to have put the herb under their loaves to improve their flavor. The Anglo-Saxons also frequently used fennel in both cookery and medicine. Traditionally, fennel was grown to eat with fish, in particular with salt fish, during Lent. Matthew Robinson, in *The New*

Family Herbal and Botanic Physician (n.d.), suggests: "One good old custom is not yet left off, viz to boil Fennel with fish, for it consumes that phlegmatic humor, which fish copiously produces, though few know why they use it."

In medieval times fennel was used as a preventive against witchcraft and other evil influences, and was hung above doors at midsummer. It was believed to restore lost vision and to give courage, and was included in victory wreaths, as Longfellow writes in "The Goblet of Life":

> *It gave new strength, and fearless*
> *   mood,*
> *And gladiators, fierce and rude,*
> *Mingled it in their daily food;*
> *And he who battled and subdued,*
> *A wreath of fennel wore.*

Snakes were said to eat fennel before sloughing their skins to renew their youth, but for those who sought to cultivate it, "Sow fennel, sow trouble."

Charcoal-Broiled Fish on Fennel

Collect the stems and leaves of well-grown fennel and hang them upside down in the sun to dry. They can then be kept for months or used as soon as they are dry enough to burn.

Take any fish for broiling; trout, mackerel, or mullet—the more oily fish—are best. Clean out the fish, leaving on the head, and stuff it with fresh fennel leaves, butter, and lemon slices. Put a good bed of dried fennel sticks on your grill and place the fish on top. The sticks will soon catch fire, but do not lose faith—it is this burning of the fennel that gives the fish its special flavor. Let the fish cook on both sides until it begins to break up slightly when prodded.

Serve with a fennel sauce to emphasize the flavor. Melt 3 tablespoons of butter and sauté 1 heaping tablespoon fennel in it over low heat for 30 seconds. Blend in 2 tablespoons of flour and cook for 1 minute, stirring constantly. Work in milk by degrees and simmer until the sauce is creamy and smooth. Add salt and pepper, and stir in another tablespoon of butter. Serve with mackerel or other fish.

This is an exciting accompaniment, especially to dull white fish.

Fennel

Quickweed

DILL

Dill, *Anethum graveolens*, a strong-smelling, upright annual, grows along roadsides and in waste places, and flowers from July to August.

Found mainly in CA, CT, IA, IL, IN, MI, MN, NJ, NY, OH, PA, WI.

Dill has been used since Egyptian times as an aid to digestion, and in these days of rich and often oily foods it is still a useful way to relieve indigestion. Soak a couple of tablespoons of crushed dill seeds in 2 cups of water overnight, then strain and sweeten with a little honey. A tablespoon of this mixture after a heavy meal is an excellent way to calm the stomach. Smaller doses can also be given to young children.

The pretty, feathery leaves and the mauvy brown seeds of dill can be used in a wide variety of fish, egg, and meat dishes as well as with vegetables or in salads. The leaves lose their flavor when cooked for any length of time so they are best used raw or in sauces that require only a few minutes of cooking.

Gravad Lax (Scandinavian Pickled Salmon)

SERVES 4

1½ POUNDS SALMON—THE TAIL END
2 TABLESPOONS SEA SALT
1 TABLESPOON SUGAR
12 BLACK PEPPERCORNS, CRUSHED
1½ TABLESPOONS CHOPPED DILL

SAUCE:
3 TABLESPOONS DIJON MUSTARD
1 TABLESPOON SUGAR
1 EGG YOLK
6 TABLESPOONS OLIVE OIL
2 TABLESPOONS WINE VINEGAR
2 TEASPOONS FINELY CHOPPED DILL
SALT AND PEPPER TO TASTE

First, fillet the fish into two triangles, then thoroughly mix the salt, sugar, peppercorns, and dill. Spread a quarter of this mixture over the bottom of a flat dish, then place one of the triangles of salmon in the dish, skin-side down. Spread half the remaining mixture on the upturned side. Then place the second triangle of salmon, skin-side up, on top of it. Finally, spread the rest of the mixture on the skin, cover with a piece of foil, and weight the fish down with a board. Put in the refrigerator or a cool place and leave for up to 5 days, turning the salmon occasionally.

To make the sauce, beat the mustard, sugar, and egg yolk until creamy. Then very gradually add the oil, followed by the vinegar, dill, salt, and pepper.

When you are ready to eat the salmon, slice it very thin and decorate each serving with a sprig of dill. Serve it with buttered whole wheat or rye bread. The sauce should be served in a bowl so that people can help themselves to as much or as little as they want.

This is a very traditional Scandinavian recipe from Sheila Howarth's *Herbs with Everything* (1976).

Dill Sauce

MAKES ABOUT 2 CUPS

1½ TABLESPOONS BUTTER
1½ TABLESPOONS FLOUR
1½ CUPS BEEF STOCK, HEATED
2 TABLESPOONS CHOPPED FRESH DILL
1½ TEASPOONS LEMON JUICE
1½ TEASPOONS BROWN SUGAR
SALT AND PEPPER TO TASTE
1 EGG YOLK

Melt the butter, blend in the flour, and gradually add the hot stock. Cook over low heat, stirring continuously, to make a smooth sauce. Add the dill, lemon juice, sugar, and seasonings, and cook over medium heat for 1 minute. Then cool slightly before whisking in the egg yolk.

This is a traditional 17th-century recipe and is delicious served with boiled beef or mutton.

COMMON MILKWEED

Common Milkweed, *Asclepias syriaca*, a perennial herb, grows in thickets, on roadsides, in dry fields, and on the margins of woods. It flowers between June and August.

Found mainly in the following states: CT, DE, GA, IL, IN, IA, KS, KY, MA, MD, ME, MI, MO, NC, NE, NH, NJ, NY, OH, PA, RI, SC, TN, VA, VT, WI, WV.

CAUTION: All parts of this plant contain a bitter principle that is known to be toxic to some animals and may also be poisonous to humans.

Peter Kalm gives a very interesting account of milkweed's uses in a diary entry of 1749: "The Asclepias Syriaca, or as the French call it, le Cotonier, grows abundant in the country . . . When the stalk is cut or broken it emits a lactescent juice and for this reason the plant is reckoned in some degree poisonous. The French in Canada nevertheless use its tender shoots in spring, preparing them like asparagus; and use of them is not attended with any bad consequences, as the slender shoots have not yet had time to suck up

Milkweed flower buds

anything poisonous. Its flowers are very odoriferous, and when in season, they fill the woods with their fragrant exhalations, and make it agreeable to travel in there, especially in the evening. The French in Canada make a sugar of the flowers, which for that purpose are gathered in the morning, when they are covered all over with dew. This dew is expressed, and by broiling yields a very good brown, palatable sugar. The pods of this plant, when ripe, contain a kind of wool, which encloses the seed, and resembles cotton, from whence the plant has got its French name. The poor collect it and fill their beds, especially their childrens, with it instead of feathers."

Almost all parts of the milkweed can be eaten, as long as the bitter principle is removed by blanching. The young shoots can be cooked and eaten like asparagus, and the unopened flowers and young pods also make good cooked vegetables. The young pods should be picked before they become elastic when pressed. They are rather mucilaginous, like okra, and can be added to soups or stews as a thickener.

HOW TO BLANCH MILKWEED

Remember, this plant may be poisonous to humans unless the bitter principle is properly removed. To do this, plunge the milkweed (pods or stems or whatever you are using) in boiling water for 1 minute. Discard the water and repeat the process three more times (four in all). It is essential to use boiling water: If milkweed is put in cold water and brought to a boil, the bitterness will remain in the plant, whereas several blanchings seems to remove it effectively.

Milkweed Provençale

SERVES 4

2 TABLESPOONS OLIVE OIL
1 CUP THINLY SLICED ONION
2 CLOVES GARLIC, CHOPPED
SALT AND PEPPER TO TASTE
4 CUPS BLANCHED MILKWEED PODS
2½ CUPS SKINNED AND QUARTERED TOMATOES
1 TABLESPOON CHOPPED PARSLEY

Remember, this plant may be poisonous, so blanch the pods carefully according to the directions above. Heat the oil in a fairly deep frying pan and fry the onion, garlic, and seasonings over medium heat until browned. Stir in the milkweed pods and tomatoes, and bring the mixture to a boil over high heat. Bubble for 1 minute, then turn the heat down and simmer for about 15 minutes, until the pods are cooked and the juices have reduced and thickened. Finish with the parsley.

This is an excellent accompaniment to veal scallops or broiled liver.

Milkweed and Chicken Curry

SERVES 4

20 SMALLISH MILKWEED PODS, BLANCHED
6 TABLESPOONS OLIVE OIL
4 CLOVES GARLIC, FINELY CHOPPED
1 TEASPOON SALT
½ TEASPOON BLACK PEPPER
12 CARDAMOM SEEDS, SLIGHTLY CRUSHED
1 TEASPOON GROUND CORIANDER
1 TEASPOON CURRY POWDER
1 TEASPOON GROUND CUMIN
2 TABLESPOONS TURMERIC
2 LARGE ONIONS, CHOPPED
1 LARGE RED OR GREEN BELL PEPPER, CHOPPED
4 LARGE CHICKEN PIECES
2 CUPS YOGURT

Remember, this plant may be poisonous, so blanch the pods carefully according to the directions above. Heat the olive oil in a large pan and fry the garlic, salt, pepper, and spices for 2 minutes over low heat. Add the onions and pepper, and sauté until tender. Turn the heat up to high and brown the chicken pieces on all sides (about 10 minutes). Then lower the temperature, add the blanched milkweed pods, cover the pan, and simmer for 30 minutes or more, until the meat and milkweed pods are very tender. Just before serving, spoon 2 to 3 tablespoons of yogurt into the pan to thicken the sauce. Serve with rice and a bowl of plain yogurt on the table.

GLASSWORT OR SAMPHIRE

Glasswort or **Samphire**, *Salicornia europaea*, a small green or reddish annual herb, grows in salt marshes, along the coast, and occasionally in wet conditions inland. It flowers from August to November.

Found mainly in the West and the East Coast states and in AR, n. FL, GA, s.w. ID, IL, IN, KY, MI, MS, NH, n. NV, NY, OH, s.e. OR, PA, TN, n.w. UT, VT, s. WI, WV. In Canada: BC, NB.

Glasswort is rich in soda and formerly was commonly employed in making both soap and glass, thus giving it its name. Pick during July and August, at low tide. Glasswort should be washed carefully soon after collection and is best eaten raw; older ones should be cooked in boiling, unsalted water.

Glasswort. A European luxury that has gone unrecognized in America.

Pickled Glasswort

Glasswort may be pickled for winter use. Wash it very thoroughly in fresh water and trim off the roots. Then put it into a pan, cover with clean water, and add 2 tablespoons of vinegar. Bring slowly to a boil and simmer, covered, for 10 minutes. Drain and put into preserving jars. Cover with cold vinegar and seal tightly with vinegar-proof lids. It is ready for use straightaway but will keep throughout the winter. The glasswort must not be overcooked or it will lose its lovely, bright green color. It is nicest if pickled in spiced vinegar.

Boiled Glasswort

Wash the glasswort, leaving the roots intact, then tie in bundles and boil in shallow, unsalted water for 8 to 10 minutes. Cut the string and serve the glasswort nice and hot with melted butter and pepper. Each stem contains a woody stalk. Pick the stem up by the root and bite lightly on it, pulling the fleshy part from the woody center. Glasswort is a real delicacy and should be tried at the earliest opportunity.

Wild mint. A variegated form.

Peppermint

MINT

Wild Mint, *Mentha arvensis*, a perennial herb, grows in damp, open soils and on shores. It flowers from July to October.

Found throughout North America.

Peppermint, *Mentha piperita*, a perennial herb, grows in wet meadows and along streams. It flowers from the end of June to October.

Found throughout North America.

Spearmint, *Mentha spicata*, a perennial herb, grows in wet places near settlements and along ditches, roads, and streams. It flowers from late June to October.

Found throughout North America.

Mint is said to be named after the nymph Minthe, a daughter of Cocytus and a favorite of Pluto. Minthe was metamorphosed by Pluto's wife, Proserpina, out of jealousy, into the herb. As Ovid asked,

> Could Pluto's queen, with jealous fury storm
> And Minthe to a fragrant herb transform?

According to M. R. Gilmore (1911–12), wild mint was used by all the Indian tribes to relieve flatulence. The leaves were steeped in water, then sweetened with sugar for the patient to drink. The infusion was also drunk as a beverage because of its pleasant, aromatic flavor. The Dakota Indians used mint as a flavoring when cooking meat and packed layers of mint into their stores of dried meat. The Winnebago boiled their traps in mint to deodorize them so that the animals they wished to catch would not be warned off by the smell of blood.

There is an enormous difference in flavor among different mints, so nibble a little to gauge the strength. Mint can be used to flavor jams, jellies, candy, sauces, and dressings, or steeped in boiling water to make mint tea (see page 45). In the recipes that follow, any of the species of mint may be used.

Mint Julep

Allow 2 ounces of bourbon for each julep. Put tall, thin glasses or silver julep cups on a tray so that they can remain undisturbed while the frost forms. Put the tray in the freezer well in advance of serving time. When that time arrives, bring out the tray and put in each glass a sprig of mint, a lump of sugar, and 1 teaspoon of bourbon. Crush the mint and sugar with a long-handled spoon, being careful not to disturb the frost. Fill the glass with finely shaved ice and tamp it down firmly. Pour in part of the remaining bourbon and stir gently with the spoon. Add more ice, tamp down, add more bourbon, and continue until the glass is full of ice, packed hard. Garnish with a generous bouquet of mint. Serve with or without a straw. From *The All-New Fannie Farmer's Boston Cooking School Cookbook* (1959).

Mint Sauce

MAKES ½ CUP

1 BUNCH MINT
4 TEASPOONS SUGAR
½ CUP MILD VINEGAR

Wash the mint and strip off the leaves. Chop them, then pound them in a mortar and pestle with the sugar. Let the mixture stand for 30 minutes, then stir in the vinegar and serve. Mint sauce is lovely with lamb. Another idea is to insert small bunches of fresh mint into a leg of lamb before roasting it.

Mint Chutney

MAKES 1 QUART

2 CUPS CIDER VINEGAR
2½ CUPS SUGAR
4 TEASPOONS MUSTARD POWDER
4 CUPS FINELY CHOPPED MINT LEAVES
3 CUPS PEELED AND FINELY CHOPPED EATING APPLES
2 MEDIUM-SIZED ONIONS, FINELY CHOPPED
½ CUP SEEDLESS RAISINS
1 TEASPOON SALT

Put the vinegar into a saucepan and add the sugar and mustard. Heat gently, stirring constantly, until the sugar has dissolved. Add the rest of the ingredients, bring to a boil, and simmer for 5 minutes. Pour into sterilized jars and seal tightly with vinegar-proof lids. Delicious served with cold ham.

Wild Mint Sorbet

SERVES 4

½ CUP MINT INFUSION (SEE BELOW)
3 CUPS WATER
¼ CUP SUGAR
1 TABLESPOON CHOPPED WILD MINT
¼ CUP LEMON JUICE

Prepare the mint infusion by pouring 1 cup of boiling water on three large sprigs of mint; set aside to steep and cool for at least 30 minutes. Meanwhile, boil the 3 cups of water and dissolve the sugar in it. Cool, then add the mint, lemon juice, and mint infusion. Cool again, and pour the mixture into a hand-cranked ice cream freezer, if you have one, or into a metal tray in the freezer compartment of your refrigerator. If you use a hand-cranked machine, pack it with ice and keep turning! Excellent for biceps development, or get the children to do it. If you put it in a metal tray in the ordinary freezer, make sure to remove it when it is partially frozen and beat it vigorously before refreezing. Repeat the process at least once before allowing it to harden fully.

We found a glorious hand-cranked ice cream freezer in a junk shop and had great fun using it, but for busy folk the electric ice cream makers that do all the work are undoubtedly much more convenient.

chapter two
TEAS

Sweet fern, *Comptonia peregrina,* page 42

Spicebush

Spicebush Tea

SERVES 1

4–6 SPICEBUSH LEAVES
    OR ¼ CUP FRESH TWIGS OR BARK
1 CUP BOILING WATER

Lightly crush the leaves and steep in the water for 5 minutes (the twigs or bark will need 15 minutes). Serve either hot, with milk and honey to sweeten, or iced.

This fragrant, aromatic tea had a reputation among early settlers as a restorative and stimulant. Gibbons (1962) says the tea is best made with maple sap instead of water, but the sap should first be boiled down to a quarter of its volume, to give it the requisite sweetness.

See page 124 for information about dried spicebush berries.

SWEET FERN

Sweet Fern, *Comptonia peregrina*, a small shrub with aromatic leaves, grows in open sandy woodlands, clearings, and pastures. It flowers from April to June and fruits from August to October.

> Found mainly in n.e. IA, n. IL, n. IN, MA, ME, MI, MN, w. NC, ND, NH, n. NJ, NY, n.e. OH, PA, w. VA, VT, WI, WV. In Canada: s. MAN, NB, NS, s. ONT, PEI, s. QUE, s.e. SASK.

Sweet Fern Tea

SERVES 1

Collect the spicy leaves at any time and use them either fresh or dried. Put 1 teaspoon of dried, or 2 teaspoons of fresh, leaves in a heated cup, pour in boiling water, and steep for several minutes. Strain and serve with milk and sugar, or cool and serve sweetened with a little honey and lots of ice cubes. Very refreshing and not at all bitter.

SPICEBUSH

Spicebush, *Lindera benzoin*, a tall shrub, grows in damp, rich woods and along streams. It flowers from March to May and fruits from September to October.

> Found mainly in AL, AR, CT, DE, n. FL, GA, IL, IN, KY, LA, MA, MD, s. ME, s. MI, MO, MS, NC, NH, NJ, NY, OH, PA, RI, SC, TN, e. TX, VA, VT, WV. In Canada: s. ONT.

YARROW

Yarrow, *Achillea millefolium*, an aromatic, perennial herb, grows in hedgerows, fields, and pastures, and on waysides. It flowers from June to September.

Found throughout North America.

The generic name for yarrow is derived from the name of the Greek hero Achilles. During the Trojan War, he saved the lives of his warriors by healing their wounds with yarrow. In Sweden yarrow has been used as a substitute for hops in the preparation of beer, to which it was supposed to add an intoxicating effect. Yarrow tea can be brewed as a palliative for severe colds.

In England, to learn the reality of her true love's affection a young girl must pluck yarrow on May Day eve and place it under her pillow while she repeats the following rhyme:

> Good morrow, good morrow,
>   sweet yarrow to thee;
> If I see true love in white,
>   his love to me is ever bright.
> If he appears to me in blue,
>   his love to me is ever true.
> If he appears to be in black,
>   his love to me will lack.

Chamomile flowers drying to make Chamomile Tea

Yarrow Tea

SERVES 1

Put 2 or 3 yarrow leaves, fresh or dried, in a heated pot and pour 1 cup of freshly boiling water over them. Cover the pot and keep it hot while the leaves steep for 4 minutes. Strain into a heated cup and serve. Sweeten, if desired, with sugar or honey.

I like yarrow tea served with a slice of lemon and sugar to taste. It is a lovely, soothing drink. Why this tea ever went out of fashion is a mystery to me.

WILD CHAMOMILE

Wild Chamomile, *Matricaria chamomilla*, a low-growing, pineapple-scented annual, grows on roadsides and in waste places. It flowers from May to October.

Found mainly in CT, MA, ME, MI, MN, NH, NJ, NY, OH, PA, RI, VT, WI. In Canada: NB, NFLD, NS, s. ONT, PEI, s. QUE.

Naturalized from Europe, chamomile can be used to make a tea that has a soothing, sedative effect. The tea is absolutely harmless and is considered a certain remedy for nightmares. It is said to be an "herb doctor," with the power of reviving any wilting plant placed near it, and is also reputed to grow better for being trampled, thereby giving rise to the proverb "As the herb chamomile the more it is trodden down the more is spreadeth abroad, so virtue and honesty the more it is spiteth the more it sprouteth.' For use as a tea, the flower heads should be gathered just as the petals begin to run down.

Chamomile Tea

SERVES 1

Put 1 teaspoon of the fresh or dried flowers in a heated pot and pour on 1 cup of freshly boiling water. Cover the pot and keep it hot while the flowers steep for 3 or 4 minutes, then strain into a heated cup. I prefer to drink the tea flavored with a little honey or sugar.

LIME OR LINDEN

Lime or **Linden**, species of *Tilia*, are medium-sized to large trees that grow in rich woods. Their fragrant, cream-colored flowers bloom in June and July.

> Species of lime *(Tilia)* are found throughout eastern North America.

The flowers of the linden have long been used to make a tea that is famous for its delicious taste and soothing effect on the digestive and nervous systems. Honey from linden flowers is regarded as the best-flavored and most valuable in the world, and is used extensively in medicine and liqueurs. The leaves exude a saccharine matter with the same composition as the manna of Mount Sinai, and the sap has been used to make sugar. During the 19th century, Missa, a French chemist, found that the fruit of the lime, ground up with some of the lime flowers in a mortar, furnished a substance much resembling chocolate in flavor.

The flowers, including the wing-like bracts, should be gathered in June or July, when they are in full bloom, and laid out on trays in a warm, well-ventilated room to dry for two to three weeks.

Lime or Linden Tea

SERVES 1

Infuse 1 teaspoon of dried linden flowers in a cup of boiling water for 5 to 10 minutes, then strain and drink the tea as it comes or with a few grains of sugar.

Linden tea has a lovely, honey-like scent, and is often taken last thing at night to help induce sleep.

OSWEGO TEA
OR BEE BALM

Oswego Tea, **Bee Balm**, *Monarda didyma*, a tall herb with beautiful, ragged, red flower heads and leaves that smell faintly of lavender when crushed, grows in rich woods and thickets, and along roadsides and streams. Also called Bergamot, it flowers from the end of June to the end of August.

Found in CT, DE, GA, IN, KY, MD, MI, NC, NJ, NY, OH, PA, SC, TN, VA, WV. In Canada: QUE.

Bee balm

Oswego Tea Tea
SERVES 1

To make a lovely, mildly fragrant tea, reminiscent of mint, dry the leaves in a 140°F oven for 30 minutes. Put six or more broken leaves in a heated pot and pour on 1 cup of freshly boiling water. Cover the pot and keep it hot while the leaves steep for 5 minutes, then strain into a heated cup.

A few grains of sugar help to bring out the flavor rather than sweeten it, and we found milk an unnecessary addition.

Bergamot Tea
SERVES 1

3–6 FRESH BERGAMOT LEAVES
1 CUP BOILING WATER

Steep the leaves in the boiling water for 4 to 6 minutes to infuse the delicate flavor of the plant. Strain and serve in a heated cup. Sweeten with a little sugar or honey if desired.

A soothing alternative for caffeine-frazzled nerves.

MINT

Mint, *Mentha* species. See page 38 for the main mint entry.

Various species of mint were used by both Indians and settlers to make a beverage. The Egyptians and the Romans used mint as a digestive aid. The custom persists in the American habit of having a bowl of mints at the cashier's station in many restaurants.

All varieties of mint make delicious herbal teas, which vary in flavor according to the species. The leaves can be either used on their own or mixed with other tea leaves, as they do in North Africa.

Moroccan Mint Tea

In Morocco delicious mint tea is served without milk but with sugar to taste. To make it, choose a long-leaved Chinese tea with as green a leaf as you can get. Put slightly less tea in the pot than you normally would, add a generous bunch of fresh mint, and infuse for at least 4 minutes.

BIRCH

Sweet Birch or **Black Birch**, *Betula lenta*, a medium-sized tree, grows in mature forests or open, moist woods, especially on north-facing, protected slopes in rich, well-drained soil. It flowers from April to May, and fruits from August to October.

Found mainly in n. AL, CT, n. GA, KY, MA, s. ME, w. NC, NJ, NH, NY, OH, PA, RI, e. TN, w. VA, s. VT, WV.

All the birches were valued by the Indians for their timber, sap, and bark, but the red birch, *Betula rubra*, was particularly prized by colonial cabinetmakers, and the bark of the white or paper birch, *B. papyrifera*, was used by the Indians to make canoes. Hunter (1823) says that the Indians made use of the inner bark as a remedy for colds, coughs, and diseases of the pulmonary organs, and many frontier settlers in the western territories made from it a beverage that they valued highly.

A delicious, spicy tea similar to wintergreen can be made from the young twigs or inner bark. Alternatively, birches can be tapped for their copious flow of thin, sweet sap, in exactly the same way that maples are tapped. Birch sap does not have a strong flavor, but there is a faintly discernible sweetness and an aroma of wintergreen. A syrup can be made from birch sap–the best is from the sweet birch–but it is still only about half as sweet as maple syrup.

Birch Twig Tea

Gather some sweet birch twigs about the size of matchsticks or narrower and cut them into inch-long pieces. Put six or seven into a small pan and add a cup of freshly boiling water or boiling birch sap. Cover and let the twigs steep for several minutes, then strain into a heated cup or mug and serve with sugar and milk to taste. Do not boil the twigs or you will lose the aroma.

chapter three
DANGEROUS
EDIBLE PLANTS

Lamb's-quarters, *Chenopodium album*, page 51

POKE OR POKEWEED

Poke or **Pokeweed**, *Phytolacca americana*, a large, unpleasant-smelling, perennial herb, grows in rich soil on waste ground and roadsides, and at the margins of woods. It flowers from July to October.

Found throughout the United States.

CAUTION: Never eat the root, seeds, berries, mature stems, or mature leaves. All are highly poisonous.

Indians, settlers, and knowledgeable wild food enthusiasts of today have long eaten the young tender shoots of the poke plant when they first appear in early spring. They make a superb vegetable that many have compared to asparagus; but great care must be taken when collecting and eating this plant because the large purple root and the mature stems contain phytolaccin, which is not only slightly narcotic but also a powerful, if slow-acting, emetic.

Peter Kalm, writing in 1748, gives this account of it: "The Phytolacca was called Poke by the English . . . [They and] several Swedes make use of the leaves in spring, when they are just come out, and are yet tender and soft, and eat them partly as green kale, and partly in the manner we eat spinach. Sometimes they likewise prepare them in the first of these ways, when the stalks are already grown a little longer, breaking off none but the upper sprouts, which are yet tender, and not woody; but in this latter case, great care is to be taken, for if you eat the plant when it is already grown up, and its leaves are no longer soft, you may expect death as a consequence, which seldom fails to follow; the plant has then got a power of purging the body to excess. I have known people, who, by eating great full-grown leaves of this plant, have got such a strong dysentery, that they were near dying with it."

Pokeweed as a Potherb

Remember, this plant is dangerous. The mature stems, roots, mature leaves, seeds, and berries are poisonous. Make sure to pick only the young, pale shoots, up to 3 inches high, which you will find at the base of the previous year's dried and dead plants.

Blanch the shoots by plunging them into boiling water for 30 seconds, drain, and repeat, then simmer in more boiling water for 3 minutes. Drain and serve hot with butter, salt, and pepper, or serve cold with vinaigrette dressing or mayonnaise. Its lovely asparagus flavor is delicious either way.

This plant definitely deserves its high culinary reputation.

SASSAFRAS

Sassafras, *Sassafras albidum*, a medium-sized tree with spicy-smelling leaves, grows in moist woods, thickets, and bottomlands. It flowers from April to June.

Found mainly in AL, CT, DE, n. FL, GA, IL, IN, KY, n. LA, MA, MD, s.w. ME, MI, MO, MS, NC, s. NH, NJ, s. NY, OH, s.w. OK, PA, RI, SC, TN, n.e. TX, VA, s. VT, WV.

CAUTION: Sassafras is now thought to be carcinogenic. Do not eat it frequently or in large quantities.

Sassafras leaves. Dry them to make gumbo filé.

When early explorers first discovered America, they were greatly impressed by their discovery of the sassafras tree. Numerous stories circulated about its marvelous medicinal properties as well as its use as a tea or spice, and as an ingredient in stews or salads.

Heriot (1585) gives an account of how one of his captains cured his men of a disease that he does not name but had the following symptoms: swollen knees, shrunken sinews, rotting and stinking teeth and gums. He ordered the bark and leaves of the sassafras tree to be boiled together, and then the men had to drink the decoction every other day and put the dregs upon their swollen knees. They quickly recovered as a result of this treatment, and "there were some had been diseased and troubled with the French pox for four or five years and with this drink were clean healed!"

Kalm, writing in 1748, has a great deal to say about the multifarious uses of the sassafras tree. One passage reads: "The Swedes related, that the Indians, who formerly inhabited these parts made bowls of it. On cutting some parts of the sassafras tree, or its shoots, and holding it to the nose, it had a strong but pleasant smell. Some people peel the root, and boil the peel with the beer which they are brewing, because they believe it wholesome. For the same reason, the peel is put into brandy, either whilst it is distilling, or after it is made.

"An old Swede remembered that his mother cured many people of the dropsy, by a decoction of the root of the sassafras in water, drunk every morning: but she used, at the same time, to cup the patient on the feet. The old man assured me, he had often seen people cured by this means, who had been brought to his mother wrapped in sheets."

Dried sassafras leaves have long been an essential ingredient in Cajun cookery, being the chief constituent of gumbo filé. The filé (powdered sassafras leaves) is added to soups and stews to give them a delightfully thick, smooth texture.

MARSH MARIGOLD
OR COWSLIP

Marsh Marigold or **Cowslip**, *Caltha palustris*, a perennial herb, grows in swamps, wet meadows, and woods, and along streams and ponds. It flowers from early April to June.

Found mainly in AK, CT, DE, IA, IL, IN, e. KY, MA, ME, MI, MN, n.e. MT, ND, NH, NY, OH, RI, SD, e. TN, n.e. VA, VT, WI, WV. In Canada: all provinces.

CAUTION: Do not eat the *raw* leaves and buds. They are poisonous.

Marsh marigolds

One of the traditional uses for marsh marigold is to pickle the flower buds in vinegar and use them as a substitute for capers. As well as this, the Reverend Manasseh Cutler (1785) tells us that "the juice of the flowers boiled, with the addition of alum, stains paper yellow. It has been supposed that the remarkable yellowness of butter in the spring is caused by this plant; but Boerhaave says, if cows eat it, it will occasion such inflammation, that they generally die."

It is true that the raw leaves and buds are poisonous until properly treated. To be eaten as a vegetable they must be blanched for 2 minutes in boiling water, then drained, and the blanching and draining repeated two or three more times, to remove the bitter principle. Then the leaves and buds are cooked like spinach and served with butter or cream.

Although the edibility of this plant is well known and well documented in wild plant books, I have tried it a number of times, in various ways, and personally I consider it to be overrated. If overboiled it is flavorless; if underboiled it is bitter. The food of desperation only, is my verdict.

LAMB'S-QUARTERS

Lamb's-Quarters, *Chenopodium album*, a medium-sized annual herb, grows in cultivated or waste land, in yards, and along roadsides. It flowers from June to October.

Found throughout North America.

CAUTION: Since lamb's-quarters is a nitrate lover, do not eat frequently any you find growing in nitrate-fertilized soil. **NOTE:** This plant is also known as pigweed or goosefoot or wild spinach, depending on where you live. Look it up in your field guide by its Latin name.

Lamb's-quarters

Lamb's-quarters was brought to America by the early explorers, according to Peter Kalm, who traveled around the colonies in the 1740s. He says it soon grew prolifically in gardens and cornhills. The Indians seem to have had no name for it since it was originally unknown to them, but they soon appreciated the numerous uses it could be put to.

Palmer's account (1870) shows that some tribes highly prized this species: "The young tender plants are collected by the Navajo Indians, the Pueblo Indians of New Mexico, all the tribes of Arizona, the Diggers of California, and the Utahs, and boiled as herbs alone, or with other food. Large quantities are also eaten in the raw state. The seeds of this plant are gathered by many tribes, ground into flour after drying, and made into bread or mush. They are very small, of a gray color, and not unpleasant when eaten raw. The peculiar color of the flour imparts to the bread a very dirty look, and when baked it resembles buckwheat in color and taste, and is regarded as equally nutritious. The plant abounds in Navajo Country."

Morrell (1901) says that in Maine it was used to color the curd in making sage cheese; it was also thought to make the curd rich.

Lamb's-quarters have been eaten by man since at least AD 300, having been found in the stomach of the Grauballe Man excavated from the peat bogs of Denmark. It was cultivated as a vegetable all over Eastern Europe and in Russia, and it is said that during times of scarcity, Napoleon lived on the black bread made from its seeds. It was eaten in the Scottish islands until recent times and in Europe in World War II, when the food shortage was acute. Close relatives of *Chenopodium album* have been developed into cultivated plants in the American southern highlands. Two of these crops, quinoa and canahua, are sources of grain, while the third, huauzoutte, is eaten as a vegetable, usually fried in batter.

When picking, gather about three times what you think you are going to need. Use the leaves, flowers, and top inch of the young shoots, and cook them like spinach. The plant contains iron, calcium, and protein and is a valuable addition to the diet.

Zuñi Steamed Dumplings

MAKES 8-10, SERVES 4

½ CUP CORNMEAL
½ CUP COLD WATER
½ TEASPOON SALT
1½ CUPS BOILING WATER
½ CUP GROUND LAMB'S-QUARTERS SEEDS
    (GRIND IN A MORTAR AND PESTLE)

Combine the cornmeal, cold water, and salt, and add slowly to the boiling water. Cover and cook on low heat until the mixture thickens. Remove from the heat, stir in the ground seeds, and form the mixture into small balls. Place them on a rack over boiling water, cover the pan, and steam the dumplings until done (about 15 to 20 minutes).

Add to casseroles and stew gently for half an hour before serving. From Carolyn Niethammer's *American Indian Food and Lore* (1974).

Pigweed Leaves as a Potherb

SERVES 4

Gather 4 cups of young pigweed leaves and wash them thoroughly. In a saucepan with a tight-fitting lid, put ¼ inch of water and the greens. Bring to a boil and allow them to steam for 3 to 4 minutes. Drain and serve with a knob of butter and salt and pepper, or mash the greens with a little cream and add seasonings—either way, they are delicious.

Potage Fit for a King

SERVES 4

4 LARGE POTATOES, PEELED AND CUBED
1 QUART WATER
4 CLOVES GARLIC, CHOPPED
6 SCALLIONS OR 2 ONIONS, FINELY SLICED
2 TABLESPOONS OLIVE OIL
2 CUPS CHOPPED LAMB'S-QUARTERS
    AND/OR PIGWEED LEAVES (SEE BELOW)
1 SMALL BUNCH WILD SORREL LEAVES,
    IF AVAILABLE
SALT AND PEPPER TO TASTE
FRENCH BREAD

Boil the potatoes in as much of the water as is needed to cover them. Meanwhile, fry the garlic and scallions in the olive oil in a large saucepan over low heat until soft and slightly browned. By now the potatoes should be boiled and breaking up. Add the potatoes and their water to the shallots and garlic, and add the rest of the water. Bring the soup to a boil and simmer it, covered, while the wild vegetables are prepared. Wash them and cut the leaves from the stalks. Chop the leaves to fingernail size, add them to the soup, and mix well. Simmer the soup for 20 minutes more and season with the salt and pepper.

Serve the French way with a large crouton in each bowl. Cut French bread into four ½-inch slices and fry them in oil with a tiny touch of garlic.

chapter four
SEAWEEDS

Chonggak, *Codium fragile,* page 54

Sea sac

SEA SAC

Sea Sac, *Halosaccion glandiforme*, an alga comprising several sausage-shaped sacs filled predominantly with water, is attached to a tiny stem and a single holdfast. As the plants age, the end of the sacs disintegrate, dispelling the water and sometimes filling with sand. The plant ranges in color from bleached yellow to purple-red, and grows on rocks, in mussel beds, or in fissures in the mid-intertidal zone. The sacs are best collected when they are young and fresh.

Found along the Pacific coast from AK to MEX.

Known in Russia as *kuschutschitsch*, the fresh young plants are eaten there mixed with berries. Sea sacs can be plucked from the rocks at low tide, washed, and used in salads, vegetable dishes, or stews. One novel idea is to rinse the sacs carefully, and stuff them.

CHONGGAK

Chonggak, *Codium fragile*, a dark green alga that can reach 16 inches in length, has numerous branching "fingers" and a spongy texture. Chonggak grows in sandy bottoms and tide pools in the lower and middle intertidal zones and in the subtidal regions of rocky shores. It's best collected in the spring.

Found all along the Pacific coast from AK to MEX, and along the Atlantic coast from ME to NJ.

Tiny new plants of this alga often fasten themselves to shellfish, which provide a stable attachment for them until they are large enough to sweep away the shellfish from their normal habitats. During recent years this has caused havoc in the New England shellfish industry.

In Korea the fresh plants are cleaned and sun-dried for use as tea, or blanched and chopped into fruit or vegetable dishes. In Japan, the iron-rich *miru*, as it is known, is bleached, soaked, and sugared, or it is boiled and added to soup or used as a garnish.

Chonggak Tea

Collect fresh plants and wash them thoroughly, several times, in lukewarm water to remove grit, sand, and other minute particles. Dry them speedily on rocks in the sun and wind, or on a rack, then grind them into a fine powder with a mortar and pestle and store it in an airtight tin. Use as you would ordinary tea.

Chonggak Salad

SERVES 4

2 CARROTS, CUT INTO FINE MATCHSTICKS
2 ZUCCHINI, CUT INTO THIN ROUNDS
1 GREEN PEPPER, FINELY CHOPPED
1 CUP FINELY SHREDDED WHITE CABBAGE
2 TABLESPOONS WASHED AND CHOPPED
    FRESH CHONGGAK
1 TABLESPOON SOUR CREAM
3 TABLESPOONS OLIVE OIL OR SESAME OIL
SALT AND PEPPER TO TASTE
1 TABLESPOON SESAME SEEDS

Thoroughly mix all the ingredients, except the sesame seeds, in a large salad bowl. Sprinkle with the sesame seeds just before serving.

Stuffed Sea Sacs

SERVES 4

8 LARGE FRESH SEA SACS
    (OR LOTS OF SMALLER ONES)
3 TABLESPOONS OLIVE OIL
1 ONION, CHOPPED
1 CLOVE GARLIC, CHOPPED
1 GREEN BELL PEPPER, FINELY DICED
1 RED BELL PEPPER, FINELY DICED
2 TABLESPOONS CHOPPED FRESH CILANTRO
    OR 1 TEASPOON DRIED CORIANDER
¼ TEASPOON CUMIN SEEDS
1 TABLESPOON RAISINS OR SULTANAS
2 TABLESPOONS PINE NUTS OR SUNFLOWER SEEDS
2 CUPS COOKED WHOLE-GRAIN RICE

Wash the sea sacs carefully to remove any trace of sand and put them aside. Fry all the other ingredients, except the rice, over medium heat for several minutes until golden brown. Then add the rice and cook for 2 minutes, until all the ingredients are thoroughly amalgamated. Fill the sea sacs with this mixture, place them in a greased, ovenproof dish, and bake for 20 to 30 minutes, uncovered, in a preheated 450°F oven.

    This makes an interesting, Japanese-style starter.

Bullwhip kelp

GIANT KELP OR **BULLWHIP KELP**

Giant Kelp or **Bullwhip Kelp**, *Nerecystis luetkeana*, one the largest seaweeds, can grow as long as 163 feet. A long "whip" or stem terminates in a bulb-shaped float with long, thin, trailing blades attached to it. It generally grows on rocks or rocky bottoms in the upper subtidal zone and is best collected in the late summer or early autumn.

    Found along the Pacific coast from AK to CA.

Given the enormous lengths and weights this kelp can grow to—one stem can weigh as much as 24 pounds—it is not surprising that in Scottish folklore children were warned to keep away from "kelpies," the strange sea "creatures," so that they would not be carried away, never to return. Kelps as a whole are considered to have many therapeutic properties, particularly for persons suffering from high blood pressure and poor digestion. Some people living at high altitudes have found that a pinch of kelp powder aids breathing and relieves fatigue.

One tribe of coastal Indians used the oiled stems as fishing line, but generally the stems and bulbs were cleaned, dried, and either candied or pickled. The blades were sun-dried for winter use.

Bullwhip Pickles

MAKES 5 QUARTS

10 BULLWHIP STEMS
4 CUPS WATER, DIVIDED
2 PINTS VINEGAR
3 LARGE ONIONS, CHOPPED
3 POUNDS SUGAR
3 LEMONS, SLICED
6 STICKS CINNAMON
2 TABLESPOONS WHOLE CLOVES
PINCH OF MACE

Cut the bullwhip stems into pieces about 6 or 8 inches long. Bring 2 cups of the water to a boil, add the bullwhip stems, and cook over medium heat, covered, for 5 minutes. Drain, rinse, and slice them into thinner pieces, like pickles. Bring the remaining 2 cups of water to a boil, add the stems, and cook, again over medium heat, covered, for 1 hour or until tender. Then drain and add the pickling ingredients. Cook for 30 minutes, then seal in sterilized jars.

This recipe for tasty, crunchy pickles comes from J. Robert Waaland's excellent book *Common Seaweeds of the Pacific Coast* (1977).

Sea palm

SEA PALM

Sea Palm, *Postelsia palmaeformis*, an olive-green or dark green seaweed, has a firm holdfast from which projects an erect, hollow stem, topped by numerous grooved blades. These give it its palm-like appearance. It grows in groves on exposed rocks or on wind- and wave-battered reefs, and is best collected from early spring to summer. Sea palms that have been washed ashore may be eaten if the stems snap crisply, thus indicating that they are still fresh.

Found along the Pacific coast from BC to c. CA.

Although sea palms are sometimes rather inaccessible, they are well worth collecting if you can do so without undue risk to life and limb. The stems should be washed in cold water, cut into ½ x 2-inch strips, then boiled or steamed. They make a delicious vegetable that may be eaten chilled by itself or with a little sweet soy sauce, or combined with other sea and land vegetables in a stir-fry. Alternatively, they can be made into pickles (see the preceding recipe for Bullwhip Pickles). The sun-dried blades make tasty snacks or can be added to soups and stews to give flavor and beneficial nutrients. This is an excellent, crunchy sea vegetable that adds body to any dish.

DULSE OR NEPTUNE'S GIRDLE

Dulse or **Neptune's Girdle**, *Palmaria palmata*, a bright or purply red dulse, looks like a hand with its tiny, disk-shaped holdfast and short stem from which branch elastic fronds with lobed segments. It grows on rocks, shells, and other seaweeds, often in tight clumps, on exposed and sheltered shores in the lower intertidal zone. It is best collected from late spring into the fall.

Found along the Pacific coast from AK to CA and on the Atlantic coast from NFLD to SC.

A thousand years ago dulse was widely eaten in the Western European islands, but over the centuries its consumption has diminished. Lately, though, it has been enjoying a revival among the health-conscious because it is high in protein, fat, and vitamins, and is particularly rich in iron, potassium, and magnesium.

Freshly picked and washed, dulse can be eaten raw in salads, cooked like spinach, sautéed in butter, or deep-fried in tempura; dried and then reconstituted in water, it can be used in soups or casseroles.

Dulse and Cucumber Salad

SERVES 4

1 CUP FRESH DULSE
1 CUCUMBER, SLICED OR CUBED
¼ CUP VINEGAR
3 TABLESPOONS DARK SOY SAUCE
1 TEASPOON SUGAR
SALT TO TASTE

Wash the dulse thoroughly in cold water and pat dry with paper towels, then cut it into 1½-inch lengths. Put the dulse and the cucumber in a salad bowl. Combine the rest of the ingredients, mix gently into the salad, and serve.

This recipe is adapted from Peter and Joan Martin's *Japanese Cooking* (1972).

Dulse Hash

SERVES 2

1 POUND POTATOES
3 TABLESPOONS OLIVE OIL, DIVIDED
1 TEASPOON MUSTARD SEEDS
2 CLOVES GARLIC, CRUSHED
4 MUSHROOMS, CHOPPED
1 SMALL ONION, CHOPPED
1 SWEET RED PEPPER, CHOPPED
2 TABLESPOONS BITE-SIZED PIECES
   OF DRIED OR FRESH DULSE
CAYENNE PEPPER
PAPRIKA

Wash the potatoes and parboil them for 8 minutes. Allow them to cool, then peel and cube them. In a heavy frying pan, heat 2 tablespoons of the oil, and when it's hot, add the mustard seeds and potato cubes. Fry over medium heat, turning the potatoes as they fry. When they are pale gold, remove them from the pan and put aside. Add the remaining tablespoon of oil, turn the heat to high, and when the pan is hot, stir-fry the garlic, mushrooms, onion, and red pepper for 5 minutes. Add the dulse and potatoes, and cook over medium heat, stirring constantly, for another 10 minutes. Before serving, add a sprinkling of cayenne pepper and paprika. If you have a penchant for hot curries, add extra cayenne pepper to taste. Serve with a mixed or green salad.

This is an excellent recipe, which I have adapted from Sharon Ann Rhoads's *Cooking with Sea Vegetables* (1978).

Laver

are thin and soft to the touch, they have a rubbery texture. Purple laver grows on rocks and the undersides of boulders from the mid- to low-tide mark and is best collected from spring onward.

Found along the Atlantic coast, as are very similar, related species.

Among the most sought-after and consumed sea vegetables, the lavers are extremely nutritious because they contain a high proportion of protein, vitamins (A, C, and B), and minerals (potassium, magnesium, and phosphorus). They decrease cholesterol, aid digestion, and are excellent for dieters because they contain few calories. For centuries the Japanese have collected and dried laver into paper-like sheets called nori and have eaten it as an important constituent in their diet. The Pacific Coast American Indians have either dried and powdered the seaweed or stored it in boxes with chiton juice to make "cakes." The Hawaiians and the British have traditionally collected large buckets of laver, cleaned it thoroughly, and eaten it either fresh in salads or boiled as a vegetable.

LAVER

Laver, *Porphyra perforata*, gray, brown, or purplish in color, is a perennial that forms large, thin, lobed sheets, which are attached to the rocks by a very small disk. It becomes nearly black and rather dry or rubbery when it has been exposed to the air for any length of time.

Growing on rocks, stones, or other seaweeds in the mid- to high intertidal zone, laver is best collected from late spring to summer.

Found along the Pacific coast from AK to MEX.

Purple Laver, *Porphyra umbilicalis*, brown or purplish to olive green in color, is an annual that, when mature, forms large, broad sheets, sometimes with lobed edges. Although the wavy plants

Laver Bread

Collect a good basket of laver, avoiding the very sandy patches. The cleaner it is when you pick it, the less washing you will need to do. Break up the large pieces and wash them thoroughly in cold water. Put them in a large saucepan, add boiling water to cover, and cook them steadily over medium heat, covered, for about 4 hours. Check every half-hour to see that the laver does not boil dry. It is cooked when the sheets have broken up into tiny pieces and have become a smooth puree. (Alternatively, the laver can be cooked much more rapidly in a pressure cooker.) Drain away any excess liquid and store the pureed "laver bread" in the refrigerator. It will keep for about a week. Three cups of fresh laver boil down to about 1 cup of puree. This makes about four servings.

Laver bread is sold in many places in South Wales. Raymond Rees, a fishmonger in Carmarthen who sells it, said that the local people do not make oatcakes out of it as tradition would have it. They heat the mixture for 3 or 4 minutes in a pan and then spread it on fried bread and serve it with bacon. This is an excellent and appetizing way of presenting a food that is very beneficial yet rather unpleasant in texture and appearance. Like black olives, this strange-looking dish is an acquired taste that many grow to love.

Chinese Egg and Laver Soup

SERVES 4

¾ CUP DRIED LAVER
    OR 1½ CUPS CHOPPED FRESH LAVER
3 LARGE SPRING ONIONS
2¼ CUPS CHICKEN STOCK
    OR CANNED CHICKEN BROTH (DILUTED)
2 EGGS, BEATEN
SALT AND PEPPER TO TASTE
1 TABLESPOON SESAME OIL

If you're using dried laver, soak it in cold water for 30 minutes, and then cut it into pieces about ½ inch square. Chop the spring onions into ½-inch-long pieces. In a large saucepan, heat the stock to the boiling point and stir in the laver and spring onions. Simmer, covered, for 3 minutes. Then as you stir the soup, add the eggs in a thin stream so that they form fern-like curds as in egg drop soup. Sprinkle on some pepper and salt if needed. Serve in a tureen or a large bowl with a little sesame oil floating on top (it will break up into attractive globules). This is a really good, thoroughly Chinese dish that is well worth making.

Laver and Sprout Salad

SERVES 4

2-3 SHEETS DRIED LAVER (NORI)
2 CUPS SUNFLOWER SEEDS
2 CUPS ALFALFA SPROUTS
1 CUP MUNG BEAN SPROUTS
1 CUP GRATED CARROT
JUICE OF ½ LEMON
2-3 TEASPOONS SHOYU OR TAMARI SAUCE
1 TABLESPOON FINELY CHOPPED FENNEL
1 TABLESPOON CHOPPED SCALLIONS

Toast the sheets of laver and cut them into 1-inch squares. Toast the sunflower seeds in a hot skillet for 2 minutes. Combine all the ingredients thoroughly for a deliciously crisp and refreshing salad to accompany any rice, fish, or meat dish.

This recipe comes from Gibson, Templeton, and Gibson's *Cook Yourself a Favour* (1983).

CARRAGHEEN OR IRISH MOSS

Carragheen or **Irish Moss**, *Chondrus crispus*, has branched fronds that divide and subdivide from the several blades arising from a single holdfast. The fronds are usually about 6 inches long and reddish purple in color, though they may bleach white or show green tints when exposed to strong light. Carragheen grows on submerged coastal rocks, shells, and wood, and in pools near the low-tide mark. It is best collected in the spring or summer.

Found along the Atlantic coast from NFLD to NJ.

Carragheen has been known for centuries for its marvelous gelling property and so has been used extensively in cooking. High in vitamin A and iodine, as well as in protein, starch, fat, vitamin B, and numerous trace elements, it is particularly nutritious for convalescents because it is so easy on the digestive system. Nutritionists also recommend it for people suffering from pectoral afflictions, kidney and bladder disorders, peptic and duodenal ulcers, and glandular imbalance.

Commonly used to thicken soups, stews, and gravies, or as a base for blancmange, carrageen has a stronger flavor than most seaweeds, so if you're using it fresh, rinse it once or twice (more if you're making a delicately flavored dish) and then soak it for 10 to 20 minutes in cold water. However, it is more commonly collected, washed, and dried, and then reconstituted by soaking in cold water for 10 to 20 minutes. Approximately ½ cup of chopped dried carragheen is needed to gel 4 cups of thin liquid.

Carragheen Soup

SERVES 4

1 CUP DRIED CARRAGHEEN
5 CUPS STOCK OR WATER
3 SLICES LEAN BACON, FINELY CHOPPED
3½ CUPS FINELY CHOPPED CARROTS
3 STALKS CELERY, FINELY CHOPPED
1 TEASPOON FINELY CHOPPED FRESH THYME
SALT AND PEPPER TO TASTE

First, soak the dried carragheen for about 10 to 15 minutes, then pick out any bits of grit or very dry ends and discard them. Drain the carragheen and chop it into dime-sized pieces. In a 2-quart saucepan, heat the stock to the boiling point, add the carragheen, bacon, carrots, celery, and thyme, and simmer, covered, for 45 minutes. Check the flavor and add salt and pepper if needed, then transfer the soup to a blender and puree.

This makes a delicious and nourishing soup. The carragheen gives it a thick body, which creates a most pleasant texture. This is only a basic recipe; carragheen may be added to any soup or stew to thicken and enrich it.

Carragheen Sweet Mousse

SERVES 4

1½ TEASPOONS CHOPPED DRIED CARRAGHEEN
2 STRIPS LEMON RIND
2½ CUPS MILK
1 EGG, SEPARATED
1 TABLESPOON SUGAR
FRESH RASPBERRIES
CREAM

Soak the dried carragheen for 15 minutes in water, then pick out and discard the grit and dried ends, and drain the carragheen. Add it and the lemon rind to the milk, slowly bring to a boil, and simmer, uncovered, for about 10 minutes, or until the mixture is quick thick.

Meanwhile, in a large bowl, beat the egg yolk with the sugar. In a small bowl, beat the egg white until it is stiff. Pour the carragheen mixture through a sieve into the egg yolk and stir until thoroughly blended. Fold in the stiffly beaten egg white and pour the mousse into individual dishes or into a pretty, fluted mold. Turn out when set, in 2 to 3 hours. Serve with raspberries and cream on top.

This makes a delicately flavored mousse that is lovely on its own but even better when served with fresh fruit and cream. If you leave out the egg, the mixture will set just as well and will make a nourishing blancmange, rather plain by itself but excellent with stewed fruit.

Carragheen and Mackerel Savory Mousse

SERVES 4

1½ TEASPOONS FINELY CHOPPED DRIED CARRAGHEEN
2½ CUPS MILK
¾ CUP WATER
2 STRIPS LEMON RIND
1 EGG, SEPARATED
½ POUND SMOKED MACKEREL OR SMOKED TROUT
SALT AND PEPPER TO TASTE
FENNEL, LEMON SLICES, AND BLACK OLIVES,
    FOR GARNISH

Soak the carragheen in water for 10 to 15 minutes, remove any grit or dried ends, and drain off the water. In a 2-quart saucepan, combine the carragheen, milk, water, and lemon zest. Bring to a boil and simmer gently, uncovered, for about 25 minutes, stirring occasionally, until the mixture is really thick. Then strain it through a sieve into another saucepan. Beat the egg yolk and add it to the strained mixture. Break the smoked fish into little pieces and add to the mixture. Flavor to taste with salt and pepper. Beat the egg white until it is stiff and then fold it into the egg yolk mixture. Rinse a mold with cold water, pour in the mousse mixture, and put it in the refrigerator to set (2 to 3 hours). Then turn it out and decorate it with the fennel, lemon slices, and black olives.

ENTEROMORPHA
OR TIGER MOSS

Enteromorpha or **Tiger Moss**, *Enteromorpha intestinalis*, is a bright green seaweed that occasionally bleaches white. It usually grows in masses comprising many long, contorted tube shapes filled with gas. The tubes, which can sometimes be as long as a yard, narrow to a very small stem and a tiny holdfast. Enteromorpha grows on rocks, in pools, and in estuaries in the upper intertidal zone even when the level of salinity is low. For best results, collect it in early spring.

Found along the entire Pacific and Atlantic coasts.

Growing all over the world and tolerant of a wide range of conditions, enteromorpha is very different from the *Porphyra* species, yet it is often dried and made into paper-like sheets called nori. It can also be dried and ground to make *tyau feen* powder, an important constituent in the diet of Chinese Buddhists.

Many species of enteromorpha are similar in appearance and difficult to distinguish from one another, but they are all equally delicious to eat. However, because they can grow quite profusely and happily in very polluted waters, it is important to check carefully before gathering any.

Stir-Fried Enteromorpha

Wash and clean the enteromorpha thoroughly, then heat a light oil, such as sunflower seed oil, in a wok or an ordinary saucepan. Fry the enteromorpha quickly, one small handful at a time, until it is crisp. Serve immediately.

This is a delicious dish very similar to the crispy fried seaweed served in some Chinese restaurants. It is well worth trying, especially as it's so widely available. It can also be added to salads.

SEA LETTUCE

Sea Lettuce, *Ulva lactuca*, is bright green in color with translucent lobed or leaf-shaped fronds attached by a small, disk-shaped holdfast. It grows on rocks or other algae in quiet, shallow waters and on mudflats in the upper intertidal zone. It's best collected in the spring.

Found along the Pacific coast from AK to CA.

Sea lettuce grows so abundantly in many parts of the world that it is used in a variety of dishes and even, where it is sufficiently prolific, by coastal farmers for animal consumption! High in iron, iodine, nickel, protein, starch, fat, and sugar, and containing numerous other vitamins and trace elements, sea lettuce can be used in soups and salads or as a garnish. It can also be made into seaweed balls like those the Chileans make, or it can be brewed to make a tea as the Barbadians do.

Sea lettuce

Sea Lettuce Salad

SERVES 4

4 CUPS FRESH SEA LETTUCE
2 TABLESPOONS BUTTER
1 CUP CREAM
JUICE OF ½ LEMON
1½ TEASPOONS CIDER OR WINE VINEGAR
2 TABLESPOONS OLIVE OIL
4 SCALLIONS, FINELY CHOPPED
SALT AND PEPPER TO TASTE

Thoroughly wash the sea lettuce and chop it into bite-sized pieces. Melt the butter in a saucepan, add the sea lettuce, and toss for 3 minutes over low heat. Cool, and then place a small portion in each individual bowl. Combine the remaining ingredients and pour over the sea lettuce.

Sea Lettuce Soup

SERVES 4

1 PIECE FRESH CHICKEN
3-4 CUPS COLD WATER
1 LARGE CARROT, CUT INTO FINE MATCHSTICKS
1 CUP EGG NOODLES
1 CUP CHOPPED FRESH SEA LETTUCE
SALT AND PEPPER OR SOY SAUCE TO TASTE

Boil the chicken in the water for 30 minutes or more to make a flavorful stock. Remove the chicken, allow it to cool, take the meat from the bone, and cut it in small pieces. Return the meat to the stock and add the carrot. Boil for 5 minutes, then add the noodles, sea lettuce, and seasoning. Simmer for 5 minutes and serve.

chapter five
DESERT PLANTS

Spanish bayonet or datil, *Yucca baccata,* page 68

Saguaro cacti in the beautiful Sonoran Desert

count of the saguaro: "The fruit of the saguaro is borne upon the highest part of the plant, and is usually gathered by means of long, hooked sticks. The interior of the fruit is a beautiful red color, and looks tempting; the rind is pulpy, fibrous, juicy and sweet; the pulp is very palatable, and is full of small black seeds, which are also eaten, reminding one of figs the only difference being that it has more moisture. The seeds are indigestible unless well chewed. The Indians of Arizona, Sonora, and the southern portion of California consider this one of their greatest luxuries and as long as the fruit is obtainable care for nothing else. To dry this fruit as a preserve, the seedy pulp is placed between soft inner corn-husks, the ends of which are tied, and it is then dried in the sun for winter use or trade. It is also put into earthen pots when fresh, secured from the air, and sold in the settlements . . . The Pima Indians of the Gila River annually prepare a wine from this fruit, called by the Mexicans *tiswein* . . . It is highly intoxicating, with the taste and smell of sour beer; but some time elapses after drinking before its stimulating effects are felt."

The fruit of this wonderful cactus is probably best not collected by the amateur, not only to avoid damage to the plant but also because the fruit is extremely difficult to reach. For this reason I am not including specific recipes.

SAGUARO

Saguaro or **Giant Cactus**, *Cereus giganteus*, an enormous succulent, grows up to 55 feet high in gravelly desert soils below 1,600 feet, at the point where the hills ascend from the plain. It flowers in May and June, and fruits in July.

Found mainly in s. AZ, s.e. CA, n.w. MEX.

The saguaro was immensely important in the lives of the Indians of southern Arizona, so much so that the harvest of the saguaro fruit signaled the beginning of the new calendar year for the Pima and Papago tribes.

Edward Palmer (1870) gives the following ac-

AGAVE OR CENTURY PLANT

Agave or **Century Plant**, *Agave* species. There are more than 300 species in the genus *Agave*, so it is hard to describe any particular one. Basically, they are perennials with yellowy purple blossoms or stems, which vary in height from 8 to 26 feet. The name *century plant* arose from the fact that the plant blossoms and seeds only once in its lifetime, and takes 10 to 20 years to store enough food to produce the tall flowering stalk. Once it has bloomed and seeded, which happens between April and August, the plant dies.

Found in various parts of the desert in AZ, CA, NM, TX, UT.

One of the many species of agave

CAUTION: All parts of the agave are poisonous when raw. Never eat agave unless it has been cooked.

The agave formed one of the most useful and versatile articles of diet among the Indians of Arizona, California, and New Mexico, and many early travelers and writers described it. Among them was Father Joseph Baegeart, an 18th-century Jesuit missionary, who wrote: "They make a very palatable dish, which has served me frequently as food when I had nothing else to eat, or as a dessert after dinner in lieu of fruit." Baegeart was amazed by the California Indians' ability to endure hunger longer and more easily than whites.

Palmer (1870) says that the Indians cooked the agave bulbs in a pit for three days, which converted them into a "sweet, juicy article of food . . . resembling pears in taste." They also made a fiery mescal spirit by roasting and then fermenting the heart of the agave.

If the young flower stalks are cut, they yield a sweet liquid that can be fermented to make a drink like pulque, and if this is distilled it makes a sort of tequila.

SUGARBERRY & HACKBERRY

Sugarberry, *Celtis laevigata*, a tall tree that can reach a height of 100 feet, grows in bottomlands and low woods. It flowers in April or May and fruits in October and November.

Found mainly in s. AL, FL, GA, s. IL, s, IN, KY, LA, s. MS, MO, NC, OK, SC, TX, VA, and MEX.

Desert Hackberry or **Spiny Hackberry**, *Celtis pallida*, a small spiny tree or shrub with dense branches, grows on desert foothills and mesas up to 3,250 feet or more. It flowers in April and fruits from September to October.

Found mainly in AZ, s.w. CO, NM, s.e. UT.

Desert hackberry

Many Indian tribes used the fruit of the hackberry in their diet. Certain wild animals also were fond of it, apparently, for Gilmore (1911) says that the Winnebago name for it was *wake-warutsh* (raccoon food). The Omaha ate the berries raw but the Dakota used them, pounded fine, seeds and all, to flavor meat. The Pawnee pounded the berries fine, added a little fat, mixed the puree with parched corn: an excellent combination according to them. C. S. Rafinesque (1828–30) wrote that the bark provides a cooling anodyne and that the berries are useful for treating dysentery.

Either of the two species just described can be used in the following recipe.

Hackberry Jam

MAKES ONE 1-POUND JAR

1½ CUPS HACKBERRIES
1 TABLESPOON LEMON JUICE
½ CUP SUGAR
2 TABLESPOONS WATER

Combine all the ingredients in a saucepan and bring to a boil, mashing the mixture a little to help release the juice. Simmer for about 15 minutes, or until the mixture thickens, stirring continuously to prevent sticking. When the jam is thick, pour it into a sterilized jar and seal.

This recipe has been adapted from Carolyn Niethammer's *American Indian Food and Lore* (1974).

PRICKLY PEAR

Prickly Pear, *Opuntia phaeacantha*, a perennial cactus with jointed pads and bright yellow flowers, grows on rocky desert hillsides and in sandy washes. It flowers from April to June and fruits in August.

Found mainly in s. AZ, CO, NM, UT.

Many species of edible *Opuntia* grow in other parts of the United States, but the desert varieties of the Southwest are the largest and most spectacular. They provided an important article of diet for many Indian tribes, and as we learn from an account of the Yguace Indians written by the Spanish conquistador Cabeza de Vaca in the 16th century, they made a pleasant and longed-for change from normal fare: "Occasionally these Indians kill deer [antelope] and take fish; but the quantity is so small and famine so prevalent that they eat spiders and ant eggs, worms, lizards, salamanders, snakes, and poisonous vipers; also earth and wood—anything, including deer dung and other matter, I omit. I honestly believe that if there were stones in that land they would eat them. They save the bones of fish they consume, of snakes and other animals, so that [they] can afterward pulverize and eat them, too . . . They are a merry people, considering the hunger they suffer. They never skip their fiestas and areitos. To them the happiest time of year is the season of eating prickly pears. They go in no want then pass the whole time dancing and eating, day and night. They squeeze out the juice of the prickly pears, then open and set them to dry. The dried fruit, something like figs, is put in hampers to be eaten on the way back. The peel is beaten to powder.

"Many times while we were among this people and there was nothing to eat for three or four days, they would try to revive our spirits by telling us not to be sad; soon there would be prickly pears in plenty; we would drink the juice, our bellies would get big, and we would be content.

Prickly pears ripening

lecting and don't eat any of the fruit until you have removed the prickly spines.

The chilled fruit pulp is delicious raw, or it can be mashed and strained to make fruit juice, jelly, or preserves. The tender young pads (nopales) of the plant can be gathered in spring, then peeled, sliced, and cooked like green beans, or deep-fried like onions. Alternatively, the nopales can be diced and sprinkled over salad; the roasted seeds can be used as a soup thickener.

Prickly Pear Preserve

MAKES ONE 1-POUND JAR

24 RIPE PRICKLY PEARS
2 CUPS SUGAR
1 CUP WATER
JUICE OF 1 LEMON
JUICE OF ½ ORANGE
½ ORANGE, DICED SMALL
1 PACKET (ABOUT 1 OUNCE) PECTIN

Using a pair of rubber gloves to protect your hands, plunge the prickly pears in boiling water for a few minutes, then remove the thin, outer layer with a sharp knife as you would a tomato skin. Cut the pears in half, scoop out the seeds, and put them aside; then chop the flesh and place it in a saucepan with the sugar and water. Put the seeds into a sieve and mash them vigorously to extract the juice. Add this to the pan along with the citrus juices and the orange pieces. Bring the mixture to a boil, and simmer, uncovered, stirring occasionally, for about 40 minutes, or until the preserve has thickened and the liquid has reduced. If you like your jam very firmly set, add the pectin, but the preserve sets quite adequately without it. Pour the jam into a sterilized jar and seal.

This chunky preserve with its unusual flavor, which my friend Faz described as a cross between blackberry and melon, can be spread on toast, biscuits, or muffins for breakfast, or used to make very pretty pies.

There are many kinds of prickly pear, some very good; they all seemed so to me, hunger never leaving me the leisure to discriminate."

Cabeza de Vaca was probably too hungry to notice, but William Bartram (1791) described what a surprising effect *Opuntia* juice can have on the bladder: "Its pulp is charged with a juice of fine transparent crimson color, and has a cool pleasant taste, somewhat like that of a pomegranate; soon after eating this fruit the urine becomes of the same crimson colour, which very much surprises and affrights a stranger, but is attended with no other ill consequences; on the contrary it is esteemed wholesome, though powerfully diuretic."

Collect the fruit as it ripens in late summer. Usually the dark red ones are the ripest and juiciest, but do wear gloves or use tongs when col-

YUCCA

Spanish Bayonet or **Datil**, *Yucca baccata*, a long-living perennial, grows on mesas and foothills in sandy soil between 3,300 and 4,300 feet. It flowers and fruits from May to September, depending on its elevation.

Found mainly in AZ, s.e. CA, s.w. CO, NM, s.w. TX, UT.

Palmilla, *Yucca elata*, a narrow-leaved perennial, grows in grasslands and deserts between May and July.

Found mainly in AZ, NM, w. TX.

Soapweed, *Yucca glauca*, a short-stemmed perennial, grows on dry plains, sandhills, and roadsides, and in pastures. It flowers in April and fruits between the end of May and July.

Found mainly in e. CO, KS, s.e. MT, s.w. ND, NE, e. NM, n.w. OK, SD, n.w. TX, e. WY.

A yucca in Arizona

The various species of *Yucca* found throughout the southwestern states were highly prized by the Indians who inhabited those regions, not only because they provided a nutritious and plentiful source of food but because they could be used in a number of other ways. Havard (1895) says that the root of the Spanish bayonet, being rich in saponin, was made into an excellent substitute for soap, which the Indians used for washing their hair and clothes.

The ripe fruit is similar in size and shape to the West Indian banana, and its soft pulp is very sweet and palatable. Apparently, when dry, it has a purgative effect: "On one occasion the troops in Northern Arizona captured a quantity of the dried fruit from the Apaches, and, being sweet, it was generally eaten; and for some time neither salts nor castor-oil were needed from the medicine-chest, as this fruit proved to be a vigorous cathartic" (Palmer, 1870).

The ripe fruit can be eaten raw or cooked—baked in the oven or roasted in hot ashes. Alternatively, the "bananas" can be boiled, drained, peeled, and seeded, then thickened with flour and sweetened with honey to make a delicious jam-like filling for pies and pastries. Boil the younger flower stalks for half an hour, peel off the rind, toss in butter and herbs, and serve as a vegetable. Or add boiled flowers or buds to an omelet or fresh salad. Spanish bayonet seeds, roasted and ground into meal, can be used to thicken yucca flower soup.

Yucca Flower Hash

SERVES 4

2 CUPS YUCCA FLOWERS
2 ONIONS, CHOPPED
2 CLOVES GARLIC, FINELY CHOPPED
1 SWEET RED PEPPER, DICED
1 TABLESPOON OLIVE OIL
2 TOMATOES, CHOPPED
1 CUP COOKED PEAS OR GREEN BEANS
SALT AND PEPPER TO TASTE

Discard the flower hearts, as they are bitter. Put the petals in a saucepan, cover with water, bring to a boil, and simmer, covered, for 10 to 15 minutes, then drain. Fry the onions, garlic, and pepper in the oil until well browned, then add the tomatoes and peas, the cooked petals, and the seasonings, and cook for another 5 minutes. Serve with pasta, tortillas, or couscous.

This recipe has been adapted from Carolyn Niethammer's *American Indian Food and Lore* (1974).

Yucca Flower Salad with Apple Dressing

SERVES 4

10 FRESH YOUNG SPINACH LEAVES
1 MEDIUM-SIZED HEAD OF CRISP LETTUCE—
    ROMAINE OR ICEBERG
3 SPRIGS FRESH MINT
3 TABLESPOONS OLIVE OIL
1 TABLESPOON APPLE JUICE
SALT AND PEPPER TO TASTE
3 OR 4 YUCCA FLOWERS

Wash the first three ingredients, dry them with paper towels, and arrange them prettily in a bowl. Put the oil, apple juice, salt, and pepper into a bottle, seal, shake vigorously, and pour over the salad. Just before serving, place a yucca flower in the center of the salad and dot other petals around.

The sharp taste of yucca, which resembles chicory and gives a tang to the salad, is offset by the sweetness of the apple juice (used in the dressing instead of lemon juice).

Unicorn plant or devil's claw

MESQUITE

Screwbean Mesquite, *Prosopis pubescens*, a small spreading tree or shrub, grows on floodplains and in river bottoms, gullies, and washes. It flowers from May to July and fruits in September.

Found mainly in AZ, s.e. CA, NM, s. NV, s.w. TX.

Glandular Mesquite, *Prosopis glandulosa*, a small, spreading tree or shrub, grows in open grazing lands and desert valleys. It flowers from May to August and fruits in September.

Found mainly in w. AZ, s. CA, s.w. KS, s. NM, w. OK, TX, and MEX.

Screwbean mesquite

UNICORN PLANT
OR DEVIL'S CLAW

Unicorn Plant or **Devil's Claw**, *Proboscidea parviflora*, a ground-hugging annual, grows on plains, mesas, and roadsides between 975 and 5,300 feet. It flowers and fruits from April to October.

Found in AZ, s. CA, NM, s. NV, w. TX, and n. MEX.

The seeds contain a high percentage of oil, and when separated from the pods and dried they can be eaten like sunflower seed or ground into mush. The tender young fruits can be scrubbed, then boiled for several minutes and served with butter as a vegetable.

Mesquite, *Prosopis juliflora*, a small tree or shrub, grows below 3,250 feet in washes and wherever there is sufficient water. It flowers from April to June and fruits in September.

Found mainly in AZ, s. KS, NM, OK, TX.

Mesquite

The mesquite bean has been a vital source of food for Indians of the Southwest for centuries. The conquistador Cabeza de Vaca, who traveled in this part of the continent in the 1520s and 1530s, wrote: "The mesquite bean, while hanging on the tree, is very bitter like the carob bean but, when mixed with earth, is sweet and wholesome. The Indian method of preparing it is to dig a fairly deep hole in the ground, throw in the beans, and pound them with a club the thickness of a leg and a fathom and a half long, until they are well mashed. Besides the earth that gets mixed in from the bottom and sides of the hole, the Indians add some handfuls, and pound awhile longer. They throw the meal into a basket-like jar and pour water on it until it is covered. The pounder tastes it. If he thinks it not sweet enough, he calls for more earth to stir in, which is added until he judges the dish just right.

"Then all squat round, and each takes out as much as he can with one hand. The pits and hulls are thrown onto a hide; the pounder puts them back into the 'jar,' where more water is poured on; and again the pits and hulls are savaged. This process is repeated three or four times per pounding. To the partakers, the dish is a great banquet. Their stomachs grow grossly distended from the quantity of earth and water they swallow."

Palmer (1870) confirms that it was a favorite food even when crawling with live bean beetles! "The pods, when in their fresh ripe state, are put into a wooden or stone mortar and bruised, then emptied into an earthen dish, mixed with water and allowed to stand a few hours, the result being a kind of cold porridge or mush . . .

"As the fruit or beanlike pods ripen they are gathered for winter use . . . They are kept in the pulverized state in bags, or stored as pods, but if not thoroughly pulverized so that the seeds are as fine as the pulp they will soon become a living mass, since from every seed will come forth an insect, a species of *Bruchus*. This however, makes little difference to the Indians, who do not pick the insects out, but let them become an ingredient of the bread."

As well as being an important article of food, the gum exuded from the tree is almost identical to gum arabic and is used for medicinal purposes in the preparation of gumdrops and jujube paste. After mixing it with mud, the Indians would cover their heads with it for two or three days to annihilate head lice and dye gray hairs black. The moistened leaves would be rubbed on the Indians' freshly tattooed faces to color them blue, and the bark was used by the women to make skirts, twine, and even baskets.

Grinding mesquite beans in the desert—
the hard way!

Atole

MAKES 2 CUPS

2 CUPS MESQUITE BROTH (SEE BELOW)
2 TABLESPOONS BROWN SUGAR
¼ TEASPOON CINNAMON
¼ TEASPOON CLOVES

Put all the ingredients into a saucepan. Stir over medium heat until the sugar is dissolved. Serve hot or cold. We found this drink to be reminiscent of mulled wine.

Mesquite Pudding

SERVES 4

2 TABLESPOONS WHOLE WHEAT FLOUR
1½ CUPS MESQUITE BROTH (SEE BELOW)
2 TABLESPOONS HONEY
½ CUP RAISINS
½ TEASPOON NUTMEG

Mix the flour with a little cool broth, then add this mixture and the other ingredients to the rest of the broth. Bring to a boil and simmer, stirring constantly, until the mixture is thick. Then cool. It will thicken more as it cools.

This makes a kind of caramel-flavored blancmange.

Mesquite Broth

MAKES 2–3 CUPS

Put 4 cups of mesquite beans in a saucepan and cover them with water. Bring to a boil and simmer, uncovered, for 2 hours, adding boiling water if necessary. Strain the beans, then mash them, and return them to the pan with the cooking water. Again bring them to a boil and simmer for 30 minutes. Strain and pulp them, then return them again to the pan with the cooking water. Cover and simmer for another 30 minutes. Strain for the last time and reserve the thickened liquid.

The pods are so sweet and nutritious that they can be used in many ways. Tender immature pods can be cooked and served as a vegetable or boiled down to make a sweet syrup or beverage. When fresh, the newly opened flowers are deliciously sugary to suck, and the mealy pulp surrounding the seeds can also be eaten raw. Dried and ground, the seeds make a highly nutritious meal that can be used in dumplings, breads, or puddings.

Try some of these genuine Indian recipes, which we have adapted from Carolyn Niethammer's *American Indian Food and Lore* (1974). We thought the screwbean mesquite had the most delicious flavor in the recipes—it was sweeter and more aromatic than the other beans—but all were good.

chapter six
MUSHROOMS

Black morels, *Morchella angusticips,* page 74

Yellow morel

MORELS

Yellow Morel, *Morchella esculenta*, which varies from pale to brownish yellow, has a cap with a wrinkled, ribbed surface that has been likened to a honeycomb. It grows either singly or in groups on burned ground or rotting wood, in old apple orchards, and under ashes, elms, and pines, and occurs from March to June, later in high elevations.

Found throughout North America.

Thick-Footed Morel, *Morchella crassipes*, can grow up to 12 inches high by the end of the season and is just as excellent to eat as the yellow morel. **Black morel**, *Morchella angusticeps* (or *M. elata*), has a black cap and is best known in Michigan, where it is commonly found in broad-leaved woods in association with elms. The Northwest is also a good area for collecting black morels. There they are most frequently found in conifer woods.

CAUTION: All morels are poisonous to some degree until cooked. When collecting morels to eat, check your identification carefully to ensure that you have found true morels. False morels—species of *Gyromitra* and *Helvella*—are similar in appearance to *Morchella* species, but they contain toxins that render most of them inedible.

All true morels—there are many species—are delicious to eat, provided they are cooked properly. Most mushroom gourmets agree that proper cooking must adhere to a basic principle: Don't add anything that will kill the morels' distinctive flavor.

TO PREPARE MORELS FOR COOKING

Morels must be carefully prepared before cooking to make sure that no wood lice, earwigs, or other tiny creatures are lurking in the cavities. Slice the morels in half, top to bottom, and cut the base of each stem. Wash them under cold running water and then drop them into boiling water for 2 to 3 minutes to blanch them.

TO DRY MORELS

Cut the morels in half, remove the base of the stem, and wash them carefully. Dry them with paper towels, thread them on strings, and hang them up to dry in a warm kitchen or over a radiator. When they are dry and crisp, after a day or two, take them down and keep them in a sealed jar in a warm, dry place. To revive, blanch in boiling water for 3 to 4 minutes, then use them as you would fresh ones, without any loss of quality.

Morels à la Crème

SERVES 6–8

PASTRY:
¼ CUP BUTTER
1 CUP ALL-PURPOSE FLOUR
1 TEASPOON SALT
1 EGG
2 TABLESPOONS HEAVY CREAM

MORNAY SAUCE:
2 TABLESPOONS BUTTER
1 MEDIUM ONION, SLICED
1 MEDIUM CARROT, SLICED
1 STALK CELERY, SLICED
SALT AND PEPPER TO TASTE
1 HEAPING TABLESPOON FLOUR
2½ CUPS HOT MILK
3 TABLESPOONS HEAVY CREAM

MUSHROOM FILLING:
APPROXIMATELY 12 LARGE MORELS
    (ENOUGH TO MAKE 7–8 CUPS CHOPPED)
2 TABLESPOONS BUTTER
½ TABLESPOON LEMON JUICE
1 TABLESPOON SHERRY
SALT AND PEPPER TO TASTE
½ CLOVE GARLIC, CRUSHED
¼ TEASPOON PAPRIKA

To make the pastry, rub the butter into the flour, then add the salt and egg. Gently knead into a ball, sprinkle with flour, and roll out. Spread half the cream over it, knead, and roll out again. Add the remaining cream, then knead and roll out yet again. Roll the dough into a ball and chill in the refrigerator for an hour. Preheat the oven to 400°F. Line a flan ring with the pastry and bake the shell for about 10 minutes.

Meanwhile make the Mornay sauce. Melt the butter and fry the vegetables in it until lightly browned, then add the seasonings and flour. Cook gently for 5 minutes, then stir in the hot milk. Simmer for 30 minutes until the sauce is reduced to a consistency somewhat thicker than normal for a pouring sauce. Strain through a fine sieve into a clean bowl and add the heavy cream.

Prepare the morels as directed on page 74. Preheat the oven to 450°F. Chop the morels into inch-square pieces. Melt the butter in a frying pan, add the morels and all the other ingredients, and mix well. Cook over low heat, covered, for 8 minutes. Remove the mushrooms with a perforated spoon, and add them to the Mornay sauce. Pour the mixture into the baked shell and place in the oven for 12 minutes. Keep an eye on it to make sure it does not burn.

This is superb dish that will reward all the effort of preparation. It comes from Jane Grigson's *The Mushroom Feast* (1975), and she believes it is mentioned in *The Alice B. Toklas Cookbook.* I experimented with making individual tartlets in place of the flan and found they were perfect as appetizers.

Mousse Chaude aux Morelles

SERVES 4

FILLING:
4 LARGE MORELS, WASHED VERY THOROUGHLY
3 TABLESPOONS BUTTER, DIVIDED
1½ CUPS WHITE MUSHROOMS

VELOUTÉ SAUCE:
1 TABLESPOON BUTTER
1 TABLESPOON ALL-PURPOSE FLOUR
½ CUP MILK
½ CUP CHICKEN STOCK
1 TABLESPOON MADEIRA

MOUSSE:
BREAST MEAT FROM 1 LARGE COOKED CHICKEN
1 CUP HEAVY CREAM, CHILLED
SALT AND PEPPER TO TASTE

Liberally butter the insides of four teacups. Cut one cleaned and blanched morel into quarters lengthwise, putting aside the stem, and cut each quarter lengthwise into five pieces. Cook the pieces very lightly in a teaspoon of the butter, then place five in each teacup equidistant from one another. If you have no morel large enough, cut up a smaller one similarly and simply place it, star-fashion, in the bottom of the teacup.

To make the velouté sauce, melt the butter in a saucepan and stir in the flour. Cook gently for 2 to 3 minutes, then little by little, stirring constantly, add the mixed milk and chicken stock, then the Madeira. Simmer, uncovered, for 5 minutes, then set aside to cool.

Next, finish the filling. Chop the remaining cleaned, blanched morels (with their stems) and the other mushrooms very finely and cook gently in the rest of the butter until the moisture has evaporated. Season and mix half this mushroom mixture with half the Madeira-flavored velouté sauce. Cool.

Next, make the mousse. Finely chop the chicken breasts, trimmed of all sinew, or put them in a food processor for 20 seconds. Pass this, with the other half of the mushroom mixture, through a sieve into a small bowl. Place over some ice cubes and water in a large bowl and refrigerate for half an hour. Then taste and season the mixture lightly, and little by little beat in the cream. Check for the right degree of seasoning. Divide the mousse into four parts and line each teacup with it to a thickness of ½ inch, making sure the morel pieces remain in place and leaving enough mousse to cover the top of each cup.

Fill the cavities with the chopped mushroom-velouté sauce mixture and spread the remaining mousse over the top. Bake in a bain-marie at 350°F for half an hour, turn out, and serve with the remaining half of the hot Madeira-flavored velouté sauce poured around.

This recipe came to me from Stephen Bull, the chef and proprietor of Lichfields Restaurant in Richmond, England. It is superb.

Morel and Wild Rice Casserole

SERVES 4

¼ CUP WILD RICE
½ CUP LONG-GRAIN WHITE RICE
⅔ CUP CHICKEN BROTH
½ CUP FRESH OR DRIED MORELS
1 TABLESPOON FINELY CHOPPED CELERY
1 TABLESPOON FINELY CHOPPED SCALLIONS
½ TEASPOON BUTTER
1 TEASPOON LEMON
SALT AND PEPPER TO TASTE
1 TEASPOON FINELY CHOPPED FRESH BASIL

Cook the two rices separately, cooking the white rice in the chicken broth. Soak the morels in tepid water for 30 minutes, then drain. Sauté the celery and scallions in the butter until tender, then add the morels, mix thoroughly, and sprinkle with lemon juice. Cover and simmer over low heat for 20 minutes, then blend with the wild rice and the white rice. Season to taste. Place the mixture in a casserole and warm, covered, for 10 minutes in a 300°F oven. Serve sprinkled with basil.

This recipe by Margaret Lewis was printed in the Boston Mycological Club's *Mushroom Recipes* (1979).

Morels on Fried Bread

SERVES 4

8 LARGE MORELS
2 TABLESPOONS BUTTER
¼ CUP STOCK OR WATER
1 TABLESPOON CHOPPED MIXED PARSLEY AND THYME
SALT AND PEPPER TO TASTE
1 EGG YOLK, WHIPPED
3 TABLESPOONS HEAVY CREAM
4 SLICES FRESH BREAD FRIED
    IN 2 TABLESPOONS OLIVE OIL

Prepare the morels according to the directions on page 74. Put them, along with the butter, stock, herbs, and seasonings, into a saucepan, and simmer, uncovered, for 30 minutes. Thicken with the whipped egg yolk and the cream, and serve on fried bread. Divine for a birthday breakfast or brunch.

Ceps

CEPS & BOLETES

Cep or **King Bolete**, *Boletus edulis*, a large mushroom with a brown or red cap, has yellowy white pores and a bulbous stem marked with a network of fine lines. The cep grows under conifers and hardwoods, and occurs from the middle of June to October.

Found throughout North America.

Bay Bolete, *Boletus badius*, has an olive to red-brown cap, which is sticky in wet weather, and white or lemon-yellow flesh that bruises faintly blue when cut. It grows on rotten wood and under conifers and deciduous trees, and occurs from the end of June to November.

Found mainly in the central and northeastern states.

CAUTION: Never eat any mushroom unless you have positively identified it as edible.

Bay boletes

The generic name *Boletus* comes from the Greek word *bolus* (lump). The cep has no gills like a field mushroom, but under the cap is a mass of tubes ending in tiny pores, which give the cep a spongy appearance. In a young, fresh specimen the pores will appear white and can be eaten; they turn yellowish as they age, however, and are then inedible. They must be peeled away from the cap and discarded. Though ceps are delicious fresh, both raw and cooked, they may also be dried and preserved for eating in the barren days of winter. Thoroughly clean them by wiping them with a damp cloth, then cut them into ⅛-inch slices and dry them in the sun if the weather is hot, otherwise in a food dryer.

By the beginning of the 18th century, France was renowned for its superb cuisine, as exemplified in the feasts of Louis XIV's dazzling court. The chief perpetrator of this reputation was one Francois Pierre de la Vareene, a brilliant chef who supposedly learned to cook in the kitchen of Henry IV, Louis's grandfather. In 1651 he published *Le Cuisinier Français*, which revealed, for the first time, the changes that had been taking place in many noble French kitchens and laid the foundations of French cookery that have been with us ever since. One of the recipes he is best remembered for today is Champignons Farcis. Here is a modern version of this rich and superb dish, using ceps.

Colin aux Ceps

SERVES 10–12

1 POUND FRESH CEPS
4 POUNDS FRESH HAKE OR COD
1 BOTTLE MUSCADET
1 ONION, FINELY SLICED
1 CARROT, FINELY SLICED
1 STALK CELERY, FINELY SLICED
2 TEASPOONS CHOPPED FRESH PARSLEY, DIVIDED
1 TEASPOON CHOPPED FRESH BASIL
1 TEASPOON CHOPPED FRESH THYME
1 MEDIUM-SIZED BAY LEAF
SALT AND PEPPER TO TASTE
PINCH OF SAFFRON
2 TABLESPOONS OLIVE OIL
1 TABLESPOON BUTTER
4 SHALLOTS, CHOPPED
4 CLOVES GARLIC (3 CHOPPED, 1 WHOLE)
1 TABLESPOON VINEGAR
1 TEASPOON CHOPPED FRESH TARRAGON
1 TEASPOON CHOPPED FRESH FENNEL
4 EGG YOLKS
½ CUP (1 STICK) BUTTER, SOFTENED
5 TEASPOONS TOMATO PUREE
1 TEASPOON CHOPPED FRESH CHERVIL
½ CUP MILD CHEDDAR CHEESE, GRATED

Wipe the ceps with a damp cloth, remove any yellowish pores, then slice the ceps. Cut the hake into 12 cutlets. In a saucepan, place the Muscadet, onion, carrot, celery, 1 teaspoon of the parsley, the basil, thyme, bay leaf, salt, pepper, and saffron. Bring to a boil and simmer, covered, for 20 to 30 minutes, or until the vegetables are tender, then strain them out and discard them. Pour the liquid into a large, ovenproof pot, add the cutlets, and poach them, covered, in a preheated 350°F oven for 15 to 18 minutes.

Meanwhile, heat the olive oil and the tablespoon of butter in a large frying pan. Add the sliced ceps, the shallots, and the three chopped garlic cloves; sauté over medium to high heat for 5 minutes, stirring constantly. Add the remaining chopped parsley, the vinegar, the whole garlic clove, a pinch of the chopped tarragon, and a pinch of the chopped fennel, and sauté for another 5 minutes. When the fish is done, pour off and reserve the poaching liquid and put the fish aside. Add the liquid to the mushrooms, mix well, and simmer, covered, for another 10 minutes. Strain, reserve the cooking liquid, and set the mushroom mixture aside.

Now prepare the sauce. Put the egg yolks in a bowl, add ¾ cup of the liquid, and beat with a wire whisk over boiling water until the mixture is thick. Stir in the softened butter, the tomato puree, the rest of the tarragon and fennel, and the chervil.

Arrange the fish cutlets in a shallow dish, surround them with the mushroom mixture, sprinkle on the grated cheese, and brown the whole under the broiler. Cover with the sauce and serve.

Shrimp-Stuffed Ceps

SERVES 4–6

6 MEDIUM-SIZED FRESH CEPS
1½ CUPS WHOLE, SHELLED COOKED SHRIMPS
1½ CUPS MINCED CELERY
¼ CUP CATSUP
1 TEASPOON HORSERADISH

Clean the ceps with a damp cloth, removing any pores that are beginning to yellow. Cut off the stems, finely chop enough of them to make ¾ cup, and place them in a medium-sized bowl. Set the caps aside. Reserve 20 shrimps for garnishing and chop those remaining, then add them, with the remaining ingredients, to the chopped stems. Mix thoroughly and spoon a scant 2 tablespoons of the mixture into each mushroom cap. Garnish with the whole shrimps.

Fresh ceps are delicious eaten raw like this.

The recipe was taken from the "Mycophagist's Corner" of the New Jersey Mycological Association's *Newsletter*, December 1975.

Stuffed Ceps

SERVES 4

4 LARGE FRESH CEPS (OVER 6 INCHES)
1 TABLESPOON BUTTER
1 LARGE CLOVE GARLIC, CRUSHED
3 TABLESPOONS CHOPPED ONION
½ POUND BACON, CHOPPED
1½ CUPS FRESH WHITE BREAD CRUMBS
3 TABLESPOONS CHOPPED PARSLEY
¼ CUP HEAVY CREAM

First, prepare each cep by wiping it with a damp cloth. Remove the spongy section carefully, with a spoon, and discard. Cut out the stalk, chop it finely, and put it aside.

Melt the butter in a skillet, add the garlic, onion, bacon, and chopped mushroom stalks, and cook gently, stirring occasionally, until they are well softened but not brown (about 5 minutes). Add the bread crumbs and parsley, and stir thoroughly for 1 minute. Remove the mixture from the heat and let it cool slightly before stirring in the cream. Pile the mixture into the ceps, place them in a greased shallow pan, and bake them in a 425°F oven for about 25 minutes.

Stir-Fried Ceps

SERVES 2–4

½ POUND FRESH CEPS
1 TABLESPOON OLIVE OIL
1 LARGE ONION, CHOPPED
1 GREEN BELL PEPPER, CHOPPED
1 SWEET RED PEPPER, CHOPPED
1½ CUPS SKINNED AND QUARTERED TOMATOES
SALT AND PEPPER TO TASTE
SOY SAUCE

Wipe the ceps with a damp cloth, remove any pore layer that has started to go yellowish, and slice them. Heat the olive oil in a frying pan and sauté the ceps over medium heat for about 5 minutes, stirring frequently. Add the onion, peppers, and tomatoes, and fry for another 10 minutes, stirring continuously. Add the salt, pepper, and soy sauce to taste and serve immediately.

This succulent stir-fry is delicious on its own or as a vegetable with grilled meat.

Ceps with Paprika

SERVES 4

1 POUND CEPS
1 SMALL ONION, CHOPPED
1 SMALL CLOVE GARLIC, CHOPPED
¼ CUP BUTTER
1 LARGE TOMATO, SKINNED, SEEDED,
    AND CHOPPED
1 TEASPOON MILD PAPRIKA
SALT AND PEPPER TO TASTE
¼ CUP SOUR CREAM, AT ROOM TEMPERATURE
1 TEASPOON LEMON JUICE

Wipe the ceps with a damp cloth and remove any pore layer that has started to go yellowish. If the ceps are large, cut them into bite-sized pieces. In a large frying pan, sauté the onion and garlic gently in the butter until they are soft and golden. Stir in the tomato, bring to a boil, and bubble everything together for a moment or two before adding the paprika and then the mushrooms. Mix thoroughly, cover, and simmer for 3 minutes. Remove from the heat and add salt and pepper to taste. Put the pan back on the stove and stir in the sour cream. The mixture should be allowed to boil gently and thicken. Season it with the lemon juice and serve immediately, preferably in the pan.

I got this fabulous recipe from Jan Grigson's *The Mushroom Feast* (1975).

Pickled Boletus

MAKES 1 QUART

14 FRESH YOUNG BOLETUS
3 CUPS WHITE WINE VINEGAR OR CIDER VINEGAR
3 CUPS WATER
2 CUPS OLIVE OIL
2 BAY LEAVES
1 TEASPOON PEPPERCORNS

Wipe the boletus caps and stems carefully with a damp cloth. Discard any mushrooms that are at all buggy. Only very perfect young or button mushrooms are suitable for this recipe. Put the vinegar and water into a saucepan and bring to a boil. Submerge the mushrooms and blanch them for 4 minutes, then remove them with a slotted spoon and pack them tightly into a 1-quart jar. Fill the jar with olive oil, leaving a 1-inch headspace, then add the bay leaves and the peppercorns. Place the jar in a pressure canner and cook according to the manufacturer's instructions. When the jar has cooled down, check the seal and store in a cool place.

Almost any kind of mushrooms can be pickled in this way. We have used boletus, lobster mushrooms, and chanterelles, but the last were so delicious we ate them all before the photograph was taken!

Red-capped scaber stalks

RED-CAPPED SCABER STALK

Red-Capped Scaber Stalk, *Leccinum aurantiacum*, a large mushroom with a broad cap varying in color from orange to red-brown, has white pores that bruise dark red to dark blue. It grows mainly under poplars but also in association with conifers and deciduous trees, and occurs from August to September.

Found in most of North America, except the southernmost states.

Another superb edible in the *Boletus* family.

SLIPPERY JACK

Slippery Jack, *Suillus luteus*, has a slimy red or yellowy brown cap and a sheath-like membrane on the stem. It grows under pine and spruce trees and occurs from late summer into early winter.

Found mainly in eastern North America.

CAUTION: Never eat any mushroom unless you have positively identified it as edible.

The caps of slippery jack and other members of the *Suillus* genus all have a sticky, glutinous coating, which has to be peeled off. If cooked fresh, they tend to be rather soggy and unpalatable, though the flavor is very good. The trick is to do what the Middle Europeans do: Clean, peel, and dry the caps, and then when you come to use them, powder the dried pieces in a mortar and pestle and use the powder to make a soup or add it to casseroles.

Slippery Jack Soup

SERVES 6

¼ CUP BUTTER
2 MEDIUM-SIZED ONIONS,
    PEELED AND ROUGHLY CHOPPED
1 LARGE POTATO, DICED
1–1½ CUPS DRIED SLIPPERY JACK
    MUSHROOM POWDER
4 STICKS CELERY, SLICED
6 CUPS STOCK
SALT AND PEPPER TO TASTE
PINCH OF MIXED HERBS OR THYME
PARSLEY, FOR GARNISH

Melt the butter, add the chopped onions, and sauté over medium heat for 5 minutes. Add the potato, mushroom powder, and celery; continue cooking for another 5 minutes. Add the stock and the seasonings to the vegetables and simmer, covered, for 30 minutes. Blend, reheat, and serve garnished with parsley.

CHANTERELLE

Chanterelle, *Cantharellus cibarius*, is an egg-yellow to orange, funnel-shaped fungus, sometimes smelling mildly of fresh apricots. It grows in all kinds of woodland, particularly under oaks and conifers, and occurs from June to September in the East and from September to February in the West.

Found throughout North America.

CAUTION: Never eat any mushroom until you have positively identified it as edible.

Chanterelles, or *girolles*, as the French call them, are one of the most popular and best-known fungi on the Continent and throughout Scandinavia, where they are served in restaurants and sold in shops and markets. The name is derived from the French diminutive of the Greek *kantharos* (cup).

They keep well for a few days and can also be successfully dried. Clean with a damp cloth, trim away dirty stems, cut in half, and dry in the sun or in a food dryer. Chanterelles are superb when cooked with eggs or potatoes, and make a succulent filling for an omelet, but my favorite way of

Orange chanterelles

serving them is as illustrated here, à la forestière. When cooked, they tend to give off rather a lot of liquid, especially in wet weather. Reduce the excess liquid by simmering for 5 to 10 minutes; if this is inconvenient, discard it.

Chanterelle Pie

MAKES ONE 9-INCH PIE

PASTRY:

1½ CUPS CORNMEAL
3 EGG YOLKS
5 TABLESPOONS BUTTER, MELTED
½ TEASPOON SALT
½ CUP WATER

FILLING:

½ POUND CHANTERELLES, COARSELY CHOPPED
1 CLOVE GARLIC, CRUSHED
1 TABLESPOON BUTTER
3 EGG WHITES
2 TABLESPOONS CHOPPED PARSLEY
1 TABLESPOON CHOPPED FRESH DILL
1 TABLESPOON CHOPPED FRESH CHIVES
SALT AND PEPPER TO TASTE
½ CUP WHOLE OR SHELLED SUNFLOWER SEEDS

To make the pastry, combine the first four ingredients and add enough water to form a soft dough. Press firmly into the bottom and sides of an oiled pie pan and bake at 375°F for 10 minutes.

Meanwhile, make the filling. Lightly sauté the mushrooms and garlic in the butter, then drain off the excess liquid. Whisk the egg whites until frothy, then fold in the mushrooms, herbs, and seasonings. Fill the baked pie shell with the mixture, sprinkle with sunflower seeds, and bake in a preheated 375°F oven for 30 minutes.

By the way, decorating the pie with whole sunflower seeds looks pretty but it makes the eating very slow going! If you are ravenous, use salted, shelled kernels instead. A mixed green salad or a lightly steamed green vegetable makes a good accompaniment.

This recipe was adapted from Virginia Rose's American Indian Mushroom Pie recipe in the Boston Mycological Club's *Mushroom Recipes* (1980).

Girolles à la Forestière

SERVES 4

3 POUNDS CHANTERELLES
½ CUP (1 STICK) BUTTER
¾ CUP LEAN BACON, CUT IN STRIPS
2 MEDIUM-SIZED NEW POTATOES
SALT AND PEPPER TO TASTE
1 TABLESPOON CHOPPED PARSLEY, FOR GARNISH

Clean the mushrooms with a damp cloth and trim off any dirty stem bases. Heat a scant teaspoon of the butter in a large frying pan, add the chanterelles, cook them for 5 minutes, then drain off the liquid. Fry the bacon rapidly in the remaining butter until it begins to brown, then add the chanterelles and simmer them for 20 minutes. Meanwhile, boil the new potatoes and cut them into pieces roughly the size of the mushrooms. Add them to the pan of chanterelles and bacon, and stir everything so that the potatoes color slightly in the juices—this should take about 5 minutes. Season to taste and serve sprinkled with parsley.

This recipe comes from Jane Grigson's excellent book *The Mushroom Feast* (1975).

Chanterelle Schnapps

10 CHANTERELLES
1 BOTTLE SCHNAPPS

Wash the chanterelles, dry them with paper towels, then break them up into small pieces and add them to the bottle of schnapps. Leave for 2 days and then strain out the mushroom pieces. The result will be a lovely golden-yellowish liquid with a faint flavor from the chanterelles. Drink it very cold.

Professor Meinhard Moser of the University of Innsbruck gave me this recipe. He and his students make it in the laboratory.

Chanterelle Bread

MAKES ONE 1-POUND LOAF

½ CUP DRIED CHANTERELLES
½ CUP WATER
½ PACKAGE BREWER'S YEAST
¼ CUP LIGHT BROWN SUGAR, DIVIDED
¼ CUP BUTTER
½ TEASPOON SALT
3 CUPS ALL-PURPOSE FLOUR
1 EGG
⅛ CUP CHOPPED ALMONDS
¼ CUP GOLDEN RAISINS

Reconstitute the mushrooms by simmering them slowly, covered, for 10 to 15 minutes in the water. Let them cool in the cooking liquid, then drain, reserving the liquid. Chop the mushrooms finely. Dissolve the yeast in ¼ cup of the cooking liquid and add 1½ teaspoons of the sugar. Let the mixture stand until it foams. In a saucepan put the remaining ¼ cup of cooking liquid and the butter, and stir over low heat until the butter is melted. Then combine the yeast and butter mixtures in a bowl and add the rest of the sugar, the salt, and 1 cup of the flour. Beat with an electric mixer on high speed for 2 minutes, then beat in the egg. Stir in another cup of flour, by hand, to make a soft dough. Knead until elastic, using the remaining flour, then cover the bowl with a towel and let it rise in a warm place until doubled in bulk (about 1 hour). Punch down the dough, turn out on a floured board, and knead in the chanterelles, almonds, and raisins. Form the dough into a ball and place it in a warm place for about 45 minutes, until the dough "mushrooms" over the top of the pan, then bake in a preheated 375°F oven for 35 minutes. Remove the bread from the pan and cool on a rack.

This recipe was adapted from a traditional Christmas kulich bread by Judith B. Tankard and published in the Boston Mycological Club's *Mushroom Recipes* (1974).

Chanterelle Omelet

SERVES 2

3 SCALLIONS
1 POUND CHANTERELLES
1 TABLESPOON BUTTER
SALT AND PEPPER TO TASTE
4 EGGS

Skin the scallions and chop them very finely. Wash the chanterelles and dry them with paper towels. After cutting off the stem bases, chop the chanterelles into smallish pieces. Melt the butter in a frying pan, add the scallions and mushrooms, and sauté over medium heat for about 5 minutes, then pour off the excess liquid. Flavor the mixture with salt and pepper to taste, cover to keep hot, and set aside. Now prepare a large omelet with the 4 eggs, well beaten. When the outside is cooked but the inside still a bit runny, pour the chanterelles onto one half and flop the other half over the top. Serve piping hot.

BLACK TRUMPET
OR HORN OF PLENTY

Black Trumpet or **Horn of Plenty**, *Craterellus fallax*, is a trumpet- or horn-shaped mushroom, dark gray or black in color with an undulating edge and a fragrant smell. It grows in many habitats, particularly in leaf litter under beech and oak trees, from July to November.

Found throughout North America.

CAUTION: Never eat any mushroom unless you have positively identified it as edible.

Black trumpets

Because they are black, these mushrooms are very difficult to spot, but once you find one you can usually gather quite a few by groveling around on your hands and knees. It is well worth it if you do get a good collection. These inauspicious-looking little fungi have an unmatched flavor. They can be added to stews or soups as a flavoring or supplement and improve the flavor of any other mushroom dish you might be preparing. Black trumpets dry very easily and keep well. Clean them with a damp cloth, slice them in half, cut away the dirty stem bases, and dry the trumpets in the sun or in a food dryer.

Nicky's Black Trumpet Pasta

SERVES 4

2–3 CUPS FRESH BLACK TRUMPETS
    OR DRIED ONES, SOAKED
1 TABLESPOON OLIVE OIL
2 CLOVES GARLIC, CRUSHED
12–16 LARGE BLACK OLIVES, PITTED AND HALVED
1 TABLESPOON FINELY CHOPPED FRESH BASIL
4 SLICES ITALIAN MORTADELLA SALAMI,
    CUT INTO TINY SQUARES
SALT AND PEPPER TO TASTE
1 POUND PASTA SHELLS, COOKED

Wash the black trumpets and dry them with paper towels. (If you are using dried ones, soak them for 15 minutes in cold water and drain.) Heat the olive oil in a large frying pan or saucepan and cook the garlic, olives, and basil over high heat for 1 minute, then add the salami and cook for 3 minutes, stirring constantly. Because the salami is rather fatty, it should give off plenty of oil in which to cook the black trumpets. Add them and fry for another 6 minutes, again stirring constantly. When the mushrooms are tender, throw in the pasta shells and stir thoroughly until all the flavors are well blended. Season and serve immediately.

We personally do not sprinkle grated Parmesan on the pasta because we find its strong taste overshadows the other flavors. Instead, we usually have a pot of sheep's yogurt and a bowl of green salad on the table as accompaniments. The pasta, and a glass of cold Frascati to wash it down, are what we serve friends who come around for lunch on Saturday in the fall.

Black Trumpet Stir-Fry

SERVES 4

6 CUPS BLACK TRUMPETS, FRESH OR DRIED
1½ CUPS BEAN SPROUTS
3 LARGE CARROTS
3 ZUCCHINI
3 TABLESPOONS OLIVE OIL
1 TABLESPOON SOY SAUCE
SALT AND PEPPER TO TASTE
CHOPPED PARSLEY, FOR GARNISH

Wash and drain the black trumpets and trim off the ends. (If you are using dried ones, soak them in cold water for 15 minutes before starting.) Wash the bean sprouts and slice the carrots and zucchini, using a small cookie cutter to give them a decorative edge. Heat the olive oil in a wok or frying pan over high heat until sizzling and add the bean sprouts, carrots, and zucchini. Fry for 2 minutes, stirring continuously. Add the soy sauce, seasonings, and mushrooms, and continue to cook and stir for another 3 minutes. Remove from the heat and serve immediately, sprinkled with parsley.

Black Trumpet Cocktail

5 BLACK TRUMPETS, WASHED AND DRIED
1 BOTTLE (APPROX. 12 OUNCES) SAUTERNE

Open the bottle of sauterne and drink one glass-ful. Remember the taste! Push the black trumpets into the bottle and replace the cork. Leave for 36 hours. Then drink the wine on your own. If you friends come around, you won't even get a taste; it's so good.

This recipe was generously given to us by Gerry Miller.

PARASOL MUSHROOM

Parasol Mushroom, *Lepiota procera,* has a cream- or buff-colored cap covered with large, rough, pink-to-brownish scales and a tall stalk with a movable ring. The parasol grows on paths and lawns and in open woods, particularly under oaks and conifers. It occurs from July to October and as late as December in the extreme Southwest.

Found mainly in DE, FL, GA, IA, IL, IN, MA, MD, ME, MI, MN, NC, NE, NH, NJ, NY, OH, PA, RI, SC, VA, VT, WI. In Canada: NB, NS, ONT, PEI, QUE.

CAUTION: Never eat any mushroom unless you have positively identified it as edible.

Sometimes standing as much as 16 inches high among the grass, with caps 8 inches across, parasols are usually not difficult to spot. A single mushroom can be enough for one person, but for the best combination of size and tenderness, pick when the cap just begins to open. The flesh is very delicate in flavor, so parasols are best cooked rather quickly.

Parasol Fritters and Parasol and Potato Pan Scones. Preparing and cooking this lot kept us busy.

Parasol Fritters

SERVES 4

1 EGG
⅔ CUP MILK
2 TEASPOONS MELTED BUTTER
½ TEASPOON MIXED HERBS
SALT AND PEPPER TO TASTE
8 LARGE FRESH PARASOLS
½ CUP ALL-PURPOSE FLOUR
1 CUP SUNFLOWER OIL, OR OTHER LIGHT OIL

In a bowl, beat together the egg, milk, butter, herbs, and seasonings until the mixture is smooth. Wash the parasols, remove and discard the stems, cut the caps into quarters, and coat them lightly in the flour. Dip each piece in the batter and deep-fry in the oil until golden brown. Drain on absorbent paper.

Serve the parasols hot, with zucchini or broccoli, as a main course, or on their own as a starter. Parasols are unbelievably succulent served like this.

Mushroom and Potato Pan Scones

SERVES 4

3–4 CUPS SLICED FRESH MUSHROOMS
2 MEDIUM-SIZED POTATOES, PEELED AND BOILED
SALT AND PEPPER TO TASTE
1 TEASPOON MIXED HERBS
1 CUP SELF-RISING FLOUR
1–2 TABLESPOONS BUTTER
¾ CUP GRATED CHEDDAR
    OR MONTEREY JACK CHEESE
MILK

Parasols, blewits, and puffballs can all be used, either singly or in combination. Wash them, dry them with paper towels, and chop them finely. Peel and boil the potatoes, then mash them with salt, pepper, and the herbs (do not add milk). Sift the flour, rub the butter into it, and add the potatoes, cheese, and mushrooms. Mix to a firm consistency with a little milk and form into balls. Pat them into circles 2 inches wide and ½ inch thick. Heat a lightly greased frying pan, add the potato-and-mushroom rounds, and cook over medium heat until golden brown (about 3 minutes), then turn and cook the other sides. Serve as a snack or with salad.

SWEETBREAD MUSHROOM OR MILLER'S MUSHROOM

Sweetbread Mushroom or **Miller's Mushroom**, *Clitopilus prunulus*, is white, cream, or grayish in color, with a cap textured like kid leather and white to pink gills that descend the stalk. The smell is strongly mealy. The sweetbread mushroom grows in grassy, open woodlands and occurs from July to September, later in the Southwest.

Found throughout North America.

Sweetbread mushrooms

CAUTION: Never eat any mushroom unless you have positively identified it as edible.

Sweetbread Mushroom Quiche

SERVES 6

PASTRY:
1¼ CUPS FLOUR
¾ TEASPOON SALT
¼ CUP BUTTER
⅓ CUP SHORTENING
1–2 TABLESPOONS MILK

FILLING:
2 CUPS CHOPPED SWEETBREAD MUSHROOMS
    (SEE FILLING DIRECTIONS, PAGE 88)
3 EGGS
1 CUP HEAVY CREAM
1 TABLESPOON BUTTER
1 ONION, THINLY SLICED
1 CLOVE GARLIC, FINELY CHOPPED
1 TABLESPOON ROUGHLY CHOPPED FRESH HERBS
SALT AND PEPPER TO TASTE

First, make the pastry. Sift the flour and salt together, then cut in the butter and shortening with a fork until the mixture resembles small peas. Add enough milk to form a dough and shape into a smooth ball. Chill in the refrigerator for half an hour, then line a greased 10-inch pie pan and bake the shell for 10 to 12 minutes in a preheated 325°F oven.

Now make the filling. Wash the mushrooms, dry them with paper towels, and chop them finely. Beat the eggs in a bowl, add the cream, and mix thoroughly. Heat the butter in a frying pan, add the onion, garlic, herbs, salt, pepper, and mushrooms, and sauté over medium heat until they are well softened. Then stir the mixture into the eggs and cream. Pour this mixture into the pie shell and bake in a preheated 325°F oven for 30 minutes.

BLEWIT

Blewit, *Clitocybe nuda* (synonym *Lepista nuda*), a large-capped mushroom with violet gills, has a mauve cap that becomes tan, and a strongly perfumed smell. It grows in the open under blackberry bushes, on compost, and along paths and open wood borders, especially in deep leaf litter. The blewit occurs from August to December in the East and from November to March in the West.

Found throughout North America.

CAUTION: Blewits may cause stomach upset if eaten raw. Never eat any mushroom unless you have positively identified it as edible.

Blewits can often be found in great profusion during a good season. They make excellent eating.

Blewit and Chicken Pie

SERVES 4

PASTRY:
½ CUP ALL-PURPOSE FLOUR
PINCH OF SALT
¼ CUP BUTTER
1 TABLESPOON WATER

FILLING:
¼ CUP BUTTER
¼ CUP ALL-PURPOSE FLOUR
2 CUPS MILK
SALT AND PEPPER TO TASTE
1 TABLESPOON TARRAGON OR MIXED HERBS
¾ POUND FRESH BLEWITS
2 CUPS COOKED CHICKEN,
    CUT INTO BITE-SIZED PIECES

Make the shortcrust pastry first. Sift the flour and salt together, then rub in the butter until the mixture is like fine bread crumbs. Add the water and gather the mixture gently into a ball. Put it aside while you prepare the filling.

For the white sauce, heat the butter gently, then remove from the heat and stir in the flour. Cook gently for a few minutes over low heat, being careful not to let the mixture turn brown. Remove the saucepan from the heat again and gradually add the milk. Bring the sauce to a boil, stirring constantly, to ensure smoothness as it thickens. Season well with salt, pepper, and herbs.

Wash the blewits, dry them with paper towels, and chop them coarsely. Layer the mushrooms and chicken pieces into a deep pie dish and pour the white sauce over them. Finally, roll out the pastry on a floured board and cover the dish, placing an upturned egg cup underneath it in the center to hold up the crust. Decorate the top of the pie imaginatively and bake in a preheated 400°F oven until the pastry is golden brown (about 45 minutes).

Fairy Ring mushrooms

FAIRY RING MUSHROOM
OR **SCOTCH BONNET**

Fairy Ring Mushroom or **Scotch Bonnet**, *Marasmius oreades*, has a buff- or tan-colored, bell-shaped cap and a tough, hairy stalk. It grows on lawns, in pastures, and in grassy areas; it occurs from May to September, and all year round in California.

Found throughout North America.

CAUTION: Never eat any mushroom unless you have positively identified it as edible. Great care must be taken when picking this particular one. A poisonous *Clitocybe*, similar in appearance and habitat, can be confused with it.

The following tips about serving fairy ring mushrooms comes from C. H. Peck's *Report of the New York State Botanist* (1895): "It has long been esteemed as edible, but owing to its very small size and somewhat tough substance it has not gained the general popularity it deserves. When young it may be eaten in an omelette . . . It has a very agreeable taste and odor and gives a delicious flavor to sauces but it needs cooking a long time . . . It is delicious when broiled with butter. It may be pickled or dried for future use."

One of Peck's correspondents gave him the following recipe: "Throw the clean caps in sufficient boiling water to make a nice gravy when done, and cook them half an hour! Then rub together a small quantity of butter, flour, water, salt and pepper and add to the mushrooms stirring for a moment. Pour on hot toast in a hot dish."

Fairy Ring Peppers

SERVES 4

¼ POUND FAIRY RING MUSHROOMS
4 GREEN BELL PEPPERS
2 TABLESPOONS VEGETABLE OIL
2 ONIONS, FINELY CHOPPED
1 POUND LEAN HAMBURGER
½ TEASPOON MIXED HERBS
½ TEASPOON PAPRIKA
SALT AND PEPPER TO TASTE

Wash the mushrooms and dry them with paper towels, then slice them. Wash the peppers. Remove the tops (set them aside), discard the stems and seeds, and wash them out. Heat the oil in a frying pan and sauté the onions over medium heat until golden brown, stirring occasionally. Add the meat, herbs, paprika, salt, and pepper, mix thoroughly, and continue to sauté until the meat is light brown. Then add the mushrooms and cook for another 3 minutes. Remove the pan from the heat and drain off the excess fat. Fill the pepper cases with the cooked mixture, replace the tops, wrap the peppers in foil, and place them in a shallow baking dish. Bake in a preheated 350°F oven for 1 hour.

HORSE MUSHROOM

Horse Mushroom, *Agaricus arvensis*, a large, white-capped mushroom, has thick, creamy-colored flesh that bruises yellow and smells of aniseed. The horse mushroom grows in fields, meadows, and grassy waste places, often in large fairy rings, and occurs from June to October in the East; November to April in the West.

Found throughout North America.

CAUTION: Never eat any mushroom unless you have positively identified it as edible.

Often growing to an enormous size and sometimes found in great profusion, horse mushrooms are delicious raw or cooked in any mushroom recipe. If you find too many, you can freeze, can, or dry them, and use them throughout the winter.

Horse Mushroom Casserole

SERVES 6

CROUSTADE:
2 CUPS SOFT BREAD CRUMBS
1 CUP FINELY GROUND ALMONDS OR HAZELNUTS
¼ CUP BUTTER
1 CUP SLIVERED ALMONDS, PINE NUTS,
    OR HAZELNUTS
1 CLOVE GARLIC, CRUSHED
½ TEASPOON MIXED HERBS

TOPPING:
1 POUND HORSE MUSHROOMS,
    WASHED AND SLICED
¼ CUP BUTTER
1 TABLESPOON FLOUR
2 CUPS MILK
SALT AND PEPPER TO TASTE
¼ TEASPOON NUTMEG
1–2 TOMATOES, SKINNED AND SLICED
1 TEASPOON CHOPPED PARSLEY

First, preheat the oven to 450°F, and then make the croustade. Mix the bread crumbs and ground nuts, and rub in the butter with a fork. Add the almonds, garlic, and herbs, and mix thoroughly. Grease a round, 10-inch, ovenproof dish and press the mixture into the bottom and sides to make a layer about ½ inch thick. Bake for 15 minutes, or until golden brown.

Meanwhile, wipe the mushrooms with a damp cloth, cut off the stem bases, and slice thinly. Melt the butter in a saucepan and sauté the mushrooms over medium heat until they are tender (8 to 10 minutes). Stir in the flour; when it froths, remove the pan from the stove and stir in the milk. Return the mixture to the heat and cook, stirring constantly, until the sauce has thickened. Then add the salt, pepper, and nutmeg. Spoon the mixture into the baked croustade, top with the tomato slices, and return the dish to the 450°F oven for 10 to 15 minutes. Serve decorated with the parsley.

A tasty and highly nutritious dish.

Shaggy Ink Cap

SHAGGY MANE
OR SHAGGY INK CAP

Shaggy Mane or **Shaggy Ink Cap**, *Coprinus comatus*, has a whitish, cylindrical cap covered with shaggy, fawn-colored scales. The gills turn inky black and gradually disintegrate as the mushroom ages. The shaggy mane grows singly or in groups on either hard or grassy ground and along roadsides. It occurs in May or June, and from September to as late as January in the South.

Found throughout North America.

CAUTION: Never eat any mushroom unless you have positively identified it as edible.

Because the shaggy mane starts to turn black and disintegrate rather quickly, it is important to pick only the young caps and cook them as soon as you get them home. They can often be found in large quantities, even near built-up areas. They are delicious sautéed in butter and simmered in their own inky juice, or cooked with chopped bacon and served on toast.

Baked Eggs and Shaggy Mane Mushrooms
SERVES 4

8 SHAGGY MANE MUSHROOMS
1½ TEASPOONS BUTTER
4 EGGS
1 CLOVE GARLIC
SALT AND PEPPER TO TASTE

Wipe the mushrooms with a damp cloth, discard the stems, and chop the caps coarsely. Heat the butter in a frying pan and sauté the mushrooms over medium heat for 2 minutes, stirring occasionally. Grease four cocotte dishes (individual baking dishes), add an egg to each, then top with the half-cooked mushrooms. Flavor each with a tiny squeeze of fresh garlic and with salt and pepper, and bake in a preheated 400°F oven for 5 to 8 minutes.

The delicate flavor of the shaggy mane benefits from the addition of a smidgeon of garlic.

Shaggy Mane Soup
SERVES 4

2–3 CUPS YOUNG SHAGGY MANE MUSHROOMS
2 TABLESPOONS BUTTER
2¼ CUPS CHICKEN STOCK
SALT AND PEPPER TO TASTE
4 TABLESPOONS LIGHT CREAM
CHOPPED PARSLEY

Wipe the mushrooms with a damp cloth and discard the stems and any caps that have turned black. Heat the butter in a frying pan and sauté the mushrooms over medium heat for 4 to 5 minutes, or until they are tender.

Puree them in a blender or push them through a sieve, then return the puree to the saucepan and add the chicken stock (homemade is best, but it's fine to use a bouillon cube). Simmer for 15 minutes, covered, then check the seasoning. Pour the soup into individual bowls and swirl a tablespoon of cream into each bowl. Top with a generous sprinkling of parsley.

The recipe comes from our daughter Phoebe's grandmother Yvonne Cocking, and is superb. If you find more shaggy mane mushrooms than you can eat, just fry them in butter, let them cool, and freeze them.

MEADOW MUSHROOM
OR **PINK BOTTOM**

Meadow Mushroom or **Pink Bottom**, *Agaricus campestris*, has a smooth cap, which is white when the mushroom is young but turns light to dark brown as it ages. The pink gills also turn brown and are dark chocolate brown when fully mature. The meadow mushroom grows, often abundantly, in meadows, on lawns, and in other grassy areas. It occurs from August to September, later in the West, and at other times if there has been a period of cold, wet weather.

Found throughout North America.

CAUTION: The deadly poisonous amanita (*Amanita phalloides*) may grow in the same places as a meadow mushroom. It is essential to check your identification carefully, and if in doubt take a spore point.

Meadow mushrooms are probably the best-known and most frequently collected wild mushrooms. When I was a child on my grandparents' farm, we picked meadow mushrooms in vast quantities every year.

Meadow mushrooms are very good raw in salads, cooked in soups, or baked in pies.

My Grandmother's Mushroom Soup

SERVES 4

2 POUNDS FRESH MEADOW MUSHROOMS
1 TABLESPOON BUTTER
2 ONIONS, SLICED
4 CUPS MILK
SMALL SPRIG OF THYME
SALT AND PEPPER TO TASTE
1 TABLESPOON CORNSTARCH
2 SLICES WHITE BREAD, CUBED

Clean the mushrooms with a damp cloth, cut away the buggy stems, and chop the mushrooms into bite-sized pieces. Heat the butter in a large saucepan and sauté the onions over medium heat for 3 minutes, stirring frequently. Then add the mushrooms and milk, and bring the mixture slowly to a boil, making sure it does not boil over. Add the leaves from the thyme sprig and a little salt and pepper. Mix well and simmer gently, covered, for about an hour. Mix the cornstarch with a little water to make a paste and add it to the soup as a thickener. Simmer for another 5 minutes, check the seasoning, and serve with croutons that have been sautéed in butter and flavored with a little chopped fresh thyme.

This is how my grandmother Sarah served them day after day in season, and I still love them this way.

Scallops with Mushroom Sauce

SERVES 4

3–4 CUPS FRESH MEADOW MUSHROOMS

8 SCALLOPS (KEEP THE SHELLS)

BREAD CRUMBS

2 TABLESPOONS VEGETABLE OIL

1 CLOVE GARLIC, CRUSHED

1 TABLESPOON BUTTER

1 TABLESPOON CORNSTARCH

SALT AND PEPPER TO TASTE

1–2 TABLESPOONS WHITE WINE

1 EGG YOLK, LIGHTLY BEATEN

1 TABLESPOON CHOPPED FRESH THYME

Wipe the mushrooms with a damp cloth, cut off and discard the stem bases, and chop the mushrooms finely. Clean the scallops by running them under cold water to remove any grit or sand, then roll them in bread crumbs. Heat the oil in a frying pan, add the scallops and garlic, and sauté over medium heat for 4 minutes, turning the scallops occasionally to brown on all sides. In another frying pan, melt the butter and sauté the mushrooms over medium heat for 4 minutes, stirring occasionally. Drain off and reserve the juices. Remove the mushrooms from the pan and set aside. Make a paste of the cornstarch and the juices in the frying pan, season with salt and pepper, and cook the mixture over low heat. As it thickens, add the wine for flavor, stirring constantly to keep the consistency smooth. Add the egg yolk, mix well, and cook for 4 minutes. Then stir in the mushrooms and heat for another 3 minutes. Serve in the scallop shells. In each shell place one scallop, surround it with the sauce, and sprinkle a little of the thyme on top. Put the shells in a shallow pan, pop them under a preheated broiler for a few minutes, and serve bubbling hot.

HONEY MUSHROOM

Honey Mushroom, *Armillariella mellea* (synonym *Armillaria mellea*), has a sticky cap that varies in color from pale, honey yellow to a red or sooty brown with darker, scaly hairs in the middle, and it has a whitish or yellowish ring around the stalk. The honey fungus grows in clusters on old stumps, on and around the base of trees, and in open areas. It occurs from August to November—through to February in California.

Found throughout North America.

CAUTION: Never eat any mushroom unless you have positively identified it as edible. Though the honey mushroom is considered one of the tastiest of the edible mushrooms, it must always be well cooked or it can cause stomach upset in some people. Be sure to cook it at least 5 minutes.

The oldest known cookbook is attributed to a Roman called Apicius. But in fact there were three men called Apicius in Roman times, one in 92 BC, one in AD 14, and one in AD 50, all of whom were famous gluttons.

However, what we do learn from this book is that the Romans were fond of eating mushrooms. There are a number of recipes given both for specific species and for mushrooms in general.

We thought it would be fun to experiment with one of these Roman recipes and try to adapt it for modern consumption. Here is the original version:

"MUSHROOMS, ANOTHER METHOD. Chop the stalks, place in a new shallow pan, having added pepper, lovage, a little honey. Blend with *liquamen*, add a little oil and let it cook."

They key word here is *liquamen*, which was a kind of extract made from salted fish that the Romans appear to have prized highly in their cooking; it took six months to make! We thought that the nearest modern equivalent would be anchovies, so we tried cooking them with honey fungus and found that this seemingly odd combination of ingredients made a really interesting and unusually flavored dish.

Honey Fungus, BC Rome Style

SERVES 4

- 2 CUPS FRESH HONEY FUNGI
- 3 SLICES WHOLE WHEAT BREAD MADE INTO BREAD CRUMBS
- 1 SMALL CAN ANCHOVIES IN OLIVE OIL
- 1 TABLESPOON BUTTER
- 1 CLOVE GARLIC
- 1 TABLESPOON FINELY CHOPPED FRESH LOVAGE

Clean the honey fungi with a damp cloth, or under running water if they are very gritty, then pat them dry with paper towels to remove the excess moisture. Place the bread crumbs, anchovies, and anchovy oil in a blender and puree them. Put the puree aside. Melt the butter in a shallow frying pan, add the mushrooms, garlic, and lovage, and sauté over low heat, stirring occasionally, until the mushrooms are tender (about 8 minutes). Then stir in the bread crumb mixture and heat for 1 minute to allow the flavors to amalgamate. Serve with plain broiled fish or meat.

Hedgehog fungus

HEDGEHOG FUNGUS
OR SWEET TOOTH

Hedgehog Fungus or **Sweet Tooth**, *Hydnum repandum* (synonym *Dentinum repandum*), is a regularly shaped mushroom with a dry, fawn to orange cap and pale cream teeth, or spines, instead of gills. It grows under deciduous trees, conifers, and hardwoods from July to November.

Found throughout North America.

CAUTION: Never eat any mushroom unless you have positively identified it as edible.

Flaming Hedgehogs

1½ POUNDS HEDGEHOG FUNGI
½ POUND SHALLOTS
1 TABLESPOON OIL
1 TABLESPOON BUTTER
1 TEASPOON PAPRIKA
SALT AND PEPPER TO TASTE
2 TABLESPOONS CREAM
¼ CUP CALVADOS

Wipe the mushrooms with a damp cloth and cut off the bottoms of the stems. These mushrooms do not need peeling. Chop both caps and stems into bite-sized pieces. Then peel and chop the shallots finely. Heat the butter and oil in a heavy frying pan that holds the heat well (you will serve the mushrooms in it). Add the mushrooms, shallots, paprika, salt, and pepper, and sauté uncovered over medium heat for 10 to 15 minutes, stirring frequently. Just before serving, heat the calvados in a small pan, stir in the cream, and gently reheat. Take this and the panful of mushrooms to the table. Light the calvados and pour it, flaming, over the mushrooms.

This exotic recipe has been translated and adapted from Marcel V. Locquin's *Mycologie du Gout* (1977).

HEN OF THE WOODS

Hen of the Woods, *Grifola frondosa* (synonym *Polyporus frondosus*), is an enormous mushroom consisting of a large cluster of overlapping, stalked caps with tiny pores and no gills that branches out from a central stem and varies in color from gray to browny gray. It grows near stumps or at the base of oaks and other hardwood trees, and occurs from September to November.

Found in nearly every state east of the Rocky Mountains.

CAUTION: Never eat any mushroom unless you have positively identified it as edible.

Because hen of the woods can grow to an extraordinary size, mycophagists get very excited when they find this delicious edible mushroom, but it also means hard work if it is not to be wasted. Once, Martha Hacker collected 20 pounds of *Grifola* and spent hours preparing it for the freezer. Her method is to sauté it lightly in butter for 2 to 3 minutes and freeze it in meal-sized portions for use throughout the winter.

Gerry Miller and Selena Whitefeather wrote this account of their find for the "Mycophagist's Corner" of the New Jersey Mycological Association's *Newsletter*, February 1980: "It was a bitter cold day last fall after an NJMA foray where we found a few pounds of *Polyporus frondosus*. We were driving back home by way of N.Y.C. where Selena had a meeting . . . when suddenly a pheasant hit the windshield of the car in front of us and fell, intact but dead, to the side of the road. We pulled right over, examined its body and retrieved the pheasant . . . It was way too cold at this point to field-dress the bird outside and also Selena had to get to her meeting so we continued to N.Y.C. . . . Selena went to the meeting and I phoned friends and said, 'Can I use your kitchen to clean and pluck a pheasant?' They said, 'Sure, come up!'

While feathers were flying, they opened some wine and played 'Stereo Chickens,' a Jerry Jeff Walker song. Later back at home we stuffed the pheasant with a mixture of *Polyporus frondosus*, onions, currants, wild rice a friend had given us, sage, rosemary, butter and wine . . . WOW! . . . WOW! . . . WOW! . . ."

Hen of the Woods Mushroom Turnovers

MAKES ABOUT 30 (ALLOW 4 PER PERSON)

PASTRY:
2 CUPS FLOUR
¾ TEASPOON SALT
⅔ CUP SHORTENING
5 TABLESPOONS WATER

FILLING:
1 POUND HEN OF THE WOODS MUSHROOMS
2 TABLESPOONS BUTTER
½ CUP FINELY CHOPPED ONIONS
½ POUND BACON, THINLY SLICED
1 TEASPOON CHOPPED FRESH THYME
SALT AND PEPPER TO TASTE
1 TEASPOON FLOUR
1 EGG YOLK BEATEN WITH 1 TABLESPOON WATER

Make the pastry first. Combine the flour and salt in a bowl, cut in the shortening, and form into a ball by adding the water. Cover and chill in the refrigerator for at least 30 minutes.

Wipe the mushrooms with a damp cloth and chop them finely. Heat the butter in a skillet, add the onions and bacon, and sauté over medium heat until the onions are tender. Add the mushrooms, thyme, salt, and pepper, and cook over low heat for about 5 minutes or until the mushrooms are soft. Blend in the flour and allow the mixture to thicken slightly, then set aside.

Roll out the pastry to ⅛-inch thickness and cut it into rounds with a 2½-inch cooker cutter. Place a teaspoon of the mushroom mixture on one side of a round, fold over, and seal the edge by pressing it down with a fork. When all the turnovers are made, place them on an ungreased baking sheet and brush the tops with the egg yolk and water mixture. Bake for 25 to 30 minutes in a preheated 400°F oven.

These delicious little turnovers were made by our friend Sue Kibby and eaten in large quantities by me.

GIANT PUFFBALL

Giant Puffball, *Calvatia gigantea*, a huge white ball with a smooth, kid-like surface that cracks a little in age, is attached to the ground by a sort of root rather than a stalk. It grows in a wide variety of habitats, particularly on the edge of wet meadows, along streams, and in open woods and urban areas. It occurs from the end of May to October.

Found mainly in CT, DE, IL, IN, KY, MA, MD, ME, MO, NC, NH, NJ, OH, PA, RI, TN, VA, VT, WV.

CAUTION: Never eat any mushroom unless you have positively identified it as edible.

As its name applies, the giant puffball can grow to vast proportions—one weighing 47 pounds was once reported—but more generally they are between 10 and 20 inches in diameter.

The American Indians used various species of puffballs, eaten in their early stages of growth, either raw, boiled, or roasted. The Zuñi dried them for winter use; the Iroquois fried them and added them to soups. The Omaha cut the giant puffball into chunks and fried them like meat. When picked for consumption, the flesh must still be pure white. As puffballs age, the flesh turns yellowish. A good young specimen can be kept in the refrigerator for a few days.

Crunchy Puffball

SERVES 4

**4 SLICES FRESH WHITE OR
WHOLE WHEAT BREAD, CRUMBED**
1 EGG
1 TABLESPOON WATER
½ CUP FLOUR
SALT AND PEPPER TO TASTE
YOUNG PUFFBALL
8 SLICES BACON

Toast the bread crumbs under the broiler. Make a batter by beating the egg lightly with the water and gradually mixing in the flour. Season with salt and pepper, and leave for 20 minutes so the flour can swell. Wipe the puffball clean with a damp cloth, then cut it into slices about ¼ inch thick. Start frying the bacon. Then dip the puffball slices first in the batter, then in the bread crumbs, and fry them in the bacon fat, along with the bacon, until they are a lovely, golden brown. Serve with the bacon, for breakfast.

This is a very traditional recipe, enhanced by Jacqui Hurst's idea of the toasted bread crumbs.

CHICKEN MUSHROOM
OR SULPHUR SHELF

Chicken Mushroom or **Sulphur Shelf**, *Laetiporus sulphureus*, has a series of smooth-fleshed, over-lapping caps, which are a bright red or orangey yellow when young and turn dull yellow to white when old. It grows on the roots, stumps, or trunks of dead or living trees, particularly hardwoods or conifers, and occurs from May to November.

Found throughout North America except in the very hot southern areas.

CAUTION: Never eat any mushroom unless you have positively identified it as edible. Old specimens of chicken mushroom or those that have grown on such trees as eucalyptus can cause stomach upset in some people. Be sure to pick young, fresh specimens.

This mushroom has long been a favorite of Americans and German-speaking Europeans. In both color and taste it is reminiscent of chicken meat. If you gather more than you can use right away, keep the extras in the refrigerator for 3 to 4 days, or sauté them in butter for a few minutes, then freeze them for later use.

Chicken Casserole
SERVES 4

3 TABLESPOONS OIL
8 PIECES CHICKEN, SKIN LEFT ON
3 CLOVES GARLIC, CRUSHED
1 STRIP LEMON PEEL, ½ X 2 INCHES
1 TABLESPOON CHOPPED FRESH GARDEN HERBS
SALT AND PEPPER TO TASTE
1–1½ POUNDS POTATOES, PEELED AND SLICED THINLY
2–3 SLICES LEMON
2 TABLESPOONS CORNSTARCH,
    DISSOLVED IN 1 CUP WATER
1–2 POUNDS CHICKEN MUSHROOMS,
    WIPED WITH A DAMP CLOTH AND CUBED

Heat the oil in a large saucepan, add the chicken pieces, garlic, lemon peel, herbs, and seasonings, and fry over medium heat for several minutes, turning the pieces so they brown evenly. Transfer the chicken and juices to a large casserole, add the potatoes in a layer, and put the lemon slices on top of the potatoes. Pour in the cornstarch-and-water mixture to cover (add more water if necessary). Bake for 45 minutes, covered, in a preheated 400°F oven, then add the mushrooms, lower the heat to 350°F, and bake for another 30 minutes.

The chicken mushrooms add a really lovely flavor and texture to this or any casserole. They are equally good with beef or pork.

Chicken mushrooms or sulphur shelves

LOBSTER MUSHROOM

Lobster Mushroom, *Hypomyces lactifluorum*, is a large orange or orange-red parasite that grows in woods on other mushrooms, usually on species of *Russula* or *Lactarius*. It occurs from July to October.

Found throughout North America.

CAUTION: Never eat any mushroom unless you have positively identified it as edible. With the lobster mushroom it is equally important to identify the host mushroom it is growing on. If the host is edible, then the lobster mushroom is safe to eat. If you are unable to identify the host, it is best to avoid eating the lobster mushroom.

This strange, parasitic plant derives its name from its bright color and is highly praised as one of our great edible mushrooms.

Lobster Mushroom Stirabout with Noodles

SERVES FOUR

½ POUND FRESH LOBSTER MUSHROOMS
½ CUP OLIVE OIL
1 LARGE CLOVE GARLIC, FINELY CHOPPED
1 LARGE RED ONION, FINELY SLICED
1 INCH FRESH GINGER, PEELED
1 LARGE BROCCOLI HEAD, BROKEN INTO FLORETS
2 STALKS CELERY, CHOPPED
1 MEDIUM-SIZED RED BELL PEPPER, DICED
1 MEDIUM-SIZED GREEN BELL PEPPER, DICED
SALT AND PEPPER TO TASTE
1 (12-OUNCE) BOX SPINACH FETTUCCINE
    OR OTHER PASTA
1 TABLESPOON CHOPPED PARSLEY
¼ CUP GRATED SMOKY CHEESE

Wipe the mushrooms clean with a damp cloth and chop them coarsely. Heat the olive oil in a large frying pan or wok. Add the garlic, onion, and ginger, and fry over high heat for 5 minutes, stirring constantly. Add the broccoli and fry for another 5 minutes. Then stir in the celery, peppers, mushrooms, and seasonings. The rest of the cooking time depends on how crunchy you like your vegetables, but lengthy frying spoils the appearance of the dish. In all, 15 to 20 minutes should be enough. While the vegetables are frying, cook the pasta.

To serve, make a bed of noodles on each

person's plate, pour the sauce over them, and sprinkle with the parsley and cheese.

This recipe comes from Jill Bryan.

SAFFRON MILK CAP

Saffron Milk Cap, *Lactarius deliciosus*, an indented, orange-capped mushroom, becomes slimy when wet and turns green if bruised or as it ages. If broken or damaged, *Lactarius* exudes a bright orange, milky substance. It has a slightly fruity smell, grows in moss or under conifers, and occurs from August to October.

Found throughout North America.

CAUTION: Never eat any mushroom unless you have positively identified it as edible.

This mushroom is highly esteemed by Europeans for its edibility, although some Americans find it not as good as its name implies. Possibly they are put off by the orangy green juice it exudes when cooking, but in fact it is a delicious edible and they are missing out on a treat if they let such things influence them.

Lactarius and Beans

SERVES 4

¾ CUP DRIED LIMA BEANS
1 POUND *LACTARIUS* MUSHROOMS
1 TABLESPOON OIL OR DRIPPINGS
1 ONION, CHOPPED
2 CLOVES GARLIC, CHOPPED
1 GREEN BELL PEPPER, CHOPPED
1 TEASPOON CHOPPED WILD THYME
SALT AND PEPPER TO TASTE

Soak the beans overnight, then boil them gently, covered, for 2 hours, or until they are thoroughly soft. Wipe the mushrooms clean with a damp cloth and chop them coarsely, stalks included, unless they are woody. Heat the oil in a frying pan, add the onion, garlic, and green pepper, and fry over high heat, stirring constantly, until they are brown. Add the mushrooms and continue to fry for 3 minutes, adding a little more oil if necessary. Then simmer gently until the mushrooms are soft and the liquid is somewhat reduced (milk caps give off a lot of liquid during cooking). Stir in the beans, thyme, and seasonings, and simmer the mixture for another 10 to 15 minutes.

OYSTER MUSHROOMS

Oyster Mushrooms, *Pleurotus ostreatus*, a fan-shaped or oyster-shell-shaped fungus, varies in color from a beautiful blue-gray to a fawn or flesh brown and has virtually no stem. It grows in overlapping clusters on old or damaged trees and stumps, usually on those of deciduous trees such as the willow or the aspen but occasionally on conifers. The oyster mushroom occurs at any time of the year but is most common from the end of summer through to winter.

Found throughout North America.

CAUTION: Never eat any mushroom unless you have positively identified it as edible.

Oyster mushrooms

Ragout of Beef, Sausage, and Oyster Mushrooms

SERVES 8

2 POUNDS OYSTER MUSHROOMS
¼ CUP BUTTER
3 TABLESPOONS OLIVE OIL
2 POUNDS BEEF TENDERLOIN, CUBED
2 POUNDS HOT ITALIAN SAUSAGE, ROUGHLY CHOPPED
2 LARGE ONIONS, CHOPPED
2 CLOVES GARLIC, CRUSHED
4 CELERY STALKS, CHOPPED
4 CARROTS, THINLY SLICED IN ROUNDS
2 CUPS BEEF BROTH
2 CUPS DRY WHITE WINE
2 CUPS TOMATO PUREE
2 GREEN BELL PEPPERS, WASHED, SEEDED,
    AND COARSELY CHOPPED
1 BOUQUET GARNI
SALT AND PEPPER TO TASTE
1½ CUPS STUFFED GREEN OLIVES, CHOPPED
2 TABLESPOONS CORNSTARCH
    MIXED WITH ¼ CUP COLD WATER
½ CUP CHOPPED PARSLEY, FOR GARNISH

Wipe the mushrooms carefully with a damp cloth and check them for beetles, then chop them coarsely. Heat the butter in a 7-quart casserole, add the mushrooms, and sauté them over medium heat until they are tender. Transfer them, with any remaining butter, to a bowl. Heat the olive oil in the casserole, brown the beef cubes on all sides over high heat, then transfer them with a slotted spoon to another bowl. Similarly, brown the sausage in the casserole and transfer it with the slotted spoon to a third bowl. Turn the heat down to medium, add the onions, garlic, and celery, and sauté them until they are soft. Then add the beef, sausage, carrots, beef broth, wine, tomato puree, peppers, bouquet garni, and salt and pepper to taste. Stir well, cover the casserole, and cook over low heat, stirring occasionally, for 3 or 4 hours. Refrigerate overnight and remove the excess fat. Reheat the casserole, add the mushrooms and olives, and cook for 1 hour over low heat. Half an hour before serving, add the cornstarch and water mixture and cook to thicken the ragout. Check the seasoning, garnish with the parsley, and serve with noodles or steamed rice.

This recipe comes from Pallonji Bhiladvala.

Oyster Mushrooms à la Provençale

SERVES 2–4

¾ POUND OYSTER MUSHROOMS

2 TABLESPOONS OLIVE OIL

1 ONION, FINELY CHOPPED

1 SMALL CLOVE GARLIC, PEELED

4 MEDIUM-SIZED, RIPE TOMATOES, SKINNED, SEEDED, AND CHOPPED

¾ CUP WHITE WINE

SALT AND PEPPER TO TASTE

1½ TABLESPOONS CHOPPED PARSLEY

Wipe the mushrooms clean with a damp cloth and check carefully for small, burrowing beetles. Chop the mushrooms coarsely. In an iron casserole put the oil, onion, garlic clove, and mushrooms, and fry furiously for 1 to 2 minutes, stirring constantly. Now add the tomatoes, wine, salt, and pepper, and parsley. Cover and simmer gently for 30 minutes. Remove the garlic clove, check the seasoning, and serve.

I have drawn this recipe from Marcel V. Loquin's *Mycologie du Gout* (1977), but I think it is the standard recipe from Escoffier. For those who like garlic, add a clove of garlic, crushed, a few minutes before serving.

Oyster Mushrooms with Okra

SERVES 4

1½ POUNDS OYSTER MUSHROOMS

1 SCALLION, INCLUDING GREEN PART, FINELY CHOPPED

2 TABLESPOONS OIL

1 SLICE BROILED HAM, 1 INCH THICK, CHOPPED

½ CUP ½-INCH-SLICED OKRA

PINCH OF DILL

SALT AND PEPPER TO TASTE

1 TEASPOON CHOPPED FRESH PARSLEY, FOR GARNISH

Wipe the mushrooms and check them carefully for beetles, then chop them into large bite-sized pieces. Sauté the scallions in the oil over high heat, then add all the other ingredients except the parsley. Cook over medium heat for 15 minutes, stirring frequently. Check the seasoning, sprinkle with the parsley, and serve with boiled rice.

The okra releases a gelatinous liquid that brings out the oyster flavor of the mushrooms.

This recipe was given to me by Bob Peabody, mycophagist extraordinaire.

chapter seven
BERRIES & FRUITS

Serviceberries, *Amelanchier laevis,* page 113

MULBERRIES

White Mulberry, *Morus alba*, a medium-sized tree, grows along roadsides and hedgerows, in waste places and woodlands. It flowers in April and fruits in June and July.

Found throughout North America.

Red Mulberry, *Morus rubra*, a medium-sized tree, grows in rich, moist woods, river valleys and floodplains, and on the slopes of low hills. It flowers from April to early June and fruits from the end of June to July.

Found mainly in AL, AR, DE, FL, GA, e. IA, IL, IN, e. KS, KY, LA, MD, s. MI, MO, MS, NC, NJ, OH, e. OK, PA, SC, TN, e. TX, VA, s. WI, WV.

CAUTION: The raw shoots and unripe fruits contain hallucinogens.

From the accounts of early explorers it is clear that the mulberry grew abundantly in many parts of the United States and that its fruit was highly prized by the Indians. Several of the accounts suggest that it would have been very easy to develop a silk industry in areas where there were great quantities of mulberry trees, but the settlers did not take up the idea. In a diary entry of 1748, Peter Kalm explains their reluctance as follows: "It would not be worthwhile to erect any silk manufacturers here, because labor is so dear. For a man gets from eighteen pence to three shillings [fifteen to twenty cents in present-day currency] and upwards, for one day's work, and the women are paid in proportion. They were therefore of opinion, that the cultivation of all sorts of corn, of hemp, and of flax, would be of greater advantage, and that at the same time it did not require near so much care as the feeding of silkworms."

Despite their abundance, mulberries are, generally speaking, a very underrated fruit and frequently ignored; yet when fully ripe they are mouthwateringly delicious eaten directly from the tree or served with cream. If they are squeezed through a jelly bag or put through an electric juicer, the juice can be used to make a long, cool, bubbling drink with sugar, ice, lemon juice, and soda. The fruit is also excellent for jams, jellies, and pies, and in breads, muffins, and cakes. The tender young shoots can be boiled to make a surprisingly tasty vegetable. Some people find the white mulberry too sweet, but the white mulberry tree has one advantage: It sometimes produces berries that are almost seedless.

Mulberry Sorbet

SERVES 4

6 CUPS RIPE MULBERRIES
1¼ CUPS SUGAR
1 CUP WATER
JUICE OF 1 LEMON
2 EGG WHITES, STIFFLY BEATEN

Wash the berries gently in a sieve under running water, then put them in a saucepan with the sugar and water, and simmer them for 20 minutes, or until the fruit is soft. Cool, add the lemon juice, then press the mixture through a fine sieve. The smooth puree should be just liquid enough to pour, but if it is too thick, add a little water. Pour the puree into a shallow metal container and freeze until the mixture starts to get mushy in the middle. Remove the container from the freezer and scrape the partially frozen sorbet into a chilled bowl. Beat it briskly with a whisk until smooth, then fold in the egg whites. Return the sorbet to the container and refreeze until firm (about 2 hours).

Pour some freshly squeezed mulberry juice over the sorbet to accentuate the wonderful flavor of the fruit.

WILD STRAWBERRY

Wild Strawberry, *Fragaria virginiana*, a small, perennial herb, grows in fields, open spaces, and woodlands. It flowers, then fruits, from April to June.

Found mainly in AK, AL, AR, CT, DE, GA, e. IA, ID, IL, IN, KY, n. LA, MA, MD, ME, MI, MN, MO, MS, MT, NC, ND, NH, NJ, NY, OH, PA, RI, SC, TN, VA, VT, n.e. WA, WI, WV. In Canada: ALTA, BC, NB, NS, ONT, PEI, QUE.

Many of the early explorers were amazed by the quantity of wild strawberries to be found across the land. William Bartram (1791) delightfully describes riding through knolls in the Cherokee Mountains where the profuse and fragrant strawberries dyed his horse's feet and ankles with their rich juice. On another occasion he landed on the bank of a fine meadow and gives us the following poetic description:

"I immediately alighted and spread abroad on the turf my linen books and specimens of plants etc. to dry, turned out my stud to graze and then advanced into the strawberry plains to regale on the fragrant delicious fruit, welcomed by communities of the splendid meleagris, the capricious roe-buck and all the free and happy tribes which possess and inhabit these prolific fields, who appeared to invite and joined with me in the participation of the bountiful repast presented to us from the lap of nature."

For medical purposes, the leaves were frequently used for various "spring drinks," which were taken with ground ivy, to stimulate the system after a winter diet that would, by our standards, have been deficient in vitamins and mineral salts. Strawberries contain very high levels of vitamin C, in both the leaves and the fruit, so steeping the leaves in boiling water makes a very healthful drink.

The wild strawberry has a flavor and fragrance so delicate and delicious that it is universally claimed as one of the finest products of the wild and well worth the trouble of gathering.

Sir Kenelm Digby (1669) suggest soaking them in a little kirsch and sugar for an hour before serving with cream, but personally I prefer to savor their distinctive flavor unadulterated.

Wild Strawberry Tea

MAKES 1 QUART

**2 CUPS FRESH STRAWBERRY LEAVES
OR ½ CUP DRIED
1 QUART BOILING WATER**

Put the leaves in a heated pot and pour the boiling water over them. Cover the pot and keep it hot while the leaves steep for 4 to 5 minutes. Strain into heated cups and serve either plain or with milk and sugar.

Wild Strawberry Dessert

**1 QUART WILD STRAWBERRIES
1 PINT WATER
1 CUP SUGAR
1 TABLESPOON BUTTER
4 EGGS, SEPARATED
3 TABLESPOONS POWDERED SUGAR**

"Cook the berries in water until tender, add sugar, butter and egg yolks beaten light. Mix well. Pour into serving dish. Add powdered sugar to stiffly beaten egg whites, heap on berries and chill."

Another winner quoted from *Mrs. Rorer's Philadelphia Cook Book* (1886).

CURRANTS

Currants and **Gooseberries**, *Ribes* species. Since more than 100 species are found in the United States, it is impossible to list them all. Most are edible, although some are rather spiny, so be careful about those you eat raw.

Golden Currant, *Ribes aureum*, a tall, open shrub, grows on mountain slopes, in ravines and washes, and along streams, usually between 2,500 to 8,200 feet. It flowers in April and May and fruits between June and September.

> Found mainly in CA, CO, ID, NM, NV, OR, s.w. SD, UT, e. WA, WY. In Canada: s. ALTA, s. SASK.

Wax Currant or **Squaw Currant**, *Ribes cereum*, an open, spreading shrub, grows in ravines and canyons, on prairies, in open woodlands, and on hillsides. It flowers in May and June and fruits in July or August.

> Found mainly in n. AZ, e. CA, CO, ID, MT, s.w. ND, w. NE, n. NM, OR, w. SD, WA, WY. In Canada: s. BC.

Subalpine Prickly Currant, *Ribes montigenum*, a many-branched, spreading shrub, grows along streams and washes, wet forests, and ravines, usually between 7,000 and 12,500 feet. It flowers between April and June and fruits in July and August.

> Found mainly in n. AZ, e. CA, w. CO, ID, w. MT, NV. n. NM, e. OR, UT, e. WA, w. WY. In Canada: s. ALTA, s. BC.

On July 17, 1805, Captain Meriwether Lewis recorded his amazement at the quantity of currants he and his men found as they traveled up the Missouri River: "There are a great abundance of red yellow purple and black currants, and serviceberries now ripe and in great perfection. I find these fruits very pleasant particularly the yellow currant which I think vastly preferable to those of our gardens." The Swedish traveler Peter Kalm, writing in 1748, also commented on their profusion: "The ladies make wine from some of the fruits of the land. They principally take white and red currants for that purpose, since the shrubs of this kind are very plentiful in the gardens, and succeed very well."

Wax currants

Prickly currants

The species of currants mentioned above are among the sweetest and best to eat raw. They can also be used to make wines, jams, jellies, puddings, pies, and pemmican. No species of currant is poisonous.

Currant Wine

"Currants four pounds; sugar three pounds; water one gallon. Place the currants, stems and all, in a tub, and mash them well; add the water; set in a cool place, and stir occasionally; continue stirring for three days, then drain the liquor through a sieve, squeeze the pulp in a cloth, add the sugar (stirring until it is all dissolved), and put into a barrel or cask, which should stand in a dry, cool cellar. When fermentation is over, bung up tight, and leave all winter. Rack off in spring before second fermentation, and bottle after second fermentation."

From *Mrs. Winslow's Family Album and Domestic Receipt Book for 1866.*

Currant Jelly

"Currants should not be over-ripe, nor gathered after a rain, as then they are too watery. In New England currants are in the best condition about the 10th July. Equal parts of red and white currants, or currants and raspberries, make a delicately colored and flavored jelly. Pick over and remove the leaves and poor fruit, and if gritty wash and drain them, but do not stem them. Mash them in a porcelain kettle with a wooden pestle, without heating, as that makes the jelly darker. Let them drain in a flannel bag over night. In the morning measure a bowl of sugar for each bowl of juice, and heat the sugar carefully in an earthen dish in the oven. Stir it often to prevent burning. Boil the juice twenty minutes, and skim thoroughly. Add the hot sugar, and boil from three to four minutes, or till it thickens on a spoon when exposed to the air. Turn at once into glasses, and let them remain in the sun several days, then cover with paper dipped in brandy, and paste paper over the top of the glass.

"One who is an authority of this subject recommends covering with melted paraffine, or putting a lump of parrafine on the jelly while still hot; then no paper is needed. If one can be sure of several sunny days, and a perfectly dry place in which to keep jellies, they may be made without boiling. Mix the sugar with an equal weight of currant juice, and stir until dissolved. Fill the glasses and keep in the sun till dry.

"After draining the juice the currants may be squeezed, and a second quality of jelly made. It may not be clear, but answers for some purposes."

From *Mrs. Lincoln's Boston Cook Book* (1896).

Pemmican

2 CUPS FINELY GROUND DRIED BEEF
¼ CUP BROWN SUGAR
½ CUP DRIED BERRIES OR 1 CUP FRESH BERRIES
2 CUPS MELTED SUET

Mix the meat, sugar, and berries thoroughly, then add the melted suet. Pour it all into a blender and whirl on low speed to make a paste. Pack the mixture in small cans or plastic containers and freeze until needed.

This highly concentrated, nourishing food was used by the Indians whenever they needed to make a long journey and travel light.

Colorado Currant Salad

SERVES 4–6

1 CUP WAX CURRANTS OR OTHER WILD CURRANTS
2 TABLESPOONS KIRSCH
1 LARGE SLICE PINK-FLESHED WATERMELON, SEEDED
1 LARGE SLICE YELLOW-FLESHED WATERMELON, SEEDED
2 RIPE NECTARINES, PEELED AND SEEDED
2 CUPS BLACK CHERRIES (PITTED IF DESIRED)

Wash the currants and cut away the tails (the remains of the flower) with a pair of kitchen scissors. Place the currants in a small bowl with the kirsch and set aside while you prepare the rest of the salad. Cut the melon flesh into bite-sized chunks and almost fill a large bowl. Cut the nectarines into thinnish slices and place them and the cherries decoratively on top of the melon, pouring any excess fruit into the bowl. Finally, sprinkle the soaked currants over the top of the salad just before serving.

The flavor of the wax currants gives an exotic, slightly spicy taste to this refreshing salad–ideal for a scorching summer's day.

BLACKBERRIES & OTHER *RUBIS* BERRIES

Common Blackberry, *Rubus allegheniensis*, an upright or spreading shrub with straight spines, grows in old fields, hedgerows, thickets, and the margins of woods. It flowers from May to July and fruits in late July or August.

Found mainly in n. AR, CT, DE, e. IA, s.e. KS, KY, MA, MD, ME, MI, e. MN, MO, w. NC, NH, NJ, NY, OH, PA, RI, TN, w. VA, VT, WI, WV. In Canada: s. NB, NS.

Black Raspberry, *Rubus occidentalis*, a spreading shrub with stout spines, has young shoots that are turquoise in color. It grows in rich thickets, ravines, and fields, on the edges of woods, and in disturbed areas, flowers in May and June, and fruits in June or July.

Found mainly in CT, DE, IA, IL, IN, KS, KY, MA, MD, ME, MI, MN, MO, NC, ND, NE, NH, NJ, NY, OH, PA, RI, n. SC, SD, TN, VA, VT, WI. In Canada: NB, NS, s. ONT, PEI, s. QUE.

Thimbleberry, *Rubus odoratus*, a thornless shrub with large, maple-like leaves, grows in thickets, moist and rocky wood margins, and ravines. It flowers from June to September and fruits from July to September.

Found mainly in CT, DE, GA, IN, KY, MA, MD, ME, MI, NH, NJ, OH, PA, RI, SC, TN, VA, VT, WV. In Canada: NB, NS, s. ONT, s. QUE.

Raspberry, *Rubus strigosus* (synonym *R. idaeus* var. *strigosus*), a low shrub with trailing prickly branches and stiff hairs, grows in thickets, wood borders, clearings, and roadsides. It flowers from

Allegheny blackberries

Black raspberries

Thimbleberries. Cleanest and easiest of the raspberries to pick.

Raspberries

the end of May to July and fruits from June to October.

Found mainly in AL, n. AZ, w. CO, CT, DE, n. IN, MA, MD, ME, MI, MN, MO, NE, NH, NJ, n.w. NM, NY, OH, PA, RI, UT, w. VA, n.e. WA, WI, WY. In Canada: all provinces.

Wineberry, *Rubus phoenicolasius*, a tallish, spreading shrub, densely covered with grandular hairs, grows in thickets and open woods, along streams and roads, and in disturbed areas. It flowers from late May to July and fruits from June to September.

Found mainly in CT, DE, IN, KY, MA, s. ME, NH, NJ, NY, OH, PA, RI, s. VT, WV.

Salmonberry, *Rubus spectabilis*, a branching shrub, grows in damp, woody areas below 1,000 feet. It flowers from March to June and fruits from June to August.

Found mainly in AL, n. CA, ID, MO, OR, WA. In Canada: ALTA, BC.

Wineberries

The ripe berries of many of the *Rubus* species were a great favorite of the Indians and settlers. In 1870, Palmer wrote that the Indians of the Northwest Coast would consume quantities of salmonberries or thimbleberries "to serve as an alternative to the system which has become loaded with humors from the winter's diet of dried fish and oil." He also wrote that the young sprouts were sometimes cooked by being "tied in bundles and steamed over hot stoves, in which manner they were highly relished." Morrell (1901) describes how an old woman of Irish descent prepared for him a strange dish of greens, consisting of dandelions, thistles, hog brake (braken), and the young shoots and leaves of the red raspberry.

Mrs Child (1836) says that blackberries are extremely useful in cases of dysentery, and a tea made of the roots or leaves is beneficial. Traditionally, in England, the village midwife encouraged her patients to drink an infusion of raspberry leaves to make childbirth easier, but as time went on, this old-fashioned aid was largely superseded by imported drugs. However, when these

Salmonberries

were unobtainable at the beginning of World War II, research revealed that raspberry leaf tea was no old wives' tale but contained a valuable principle, fragarine, which acted very beneficially on the pelvic muscles of the mother in childbirth.

Most of the species in the *Rubus* group have edible fruits, and many of these are delicious eaten fresh or served with a little sugar and cream. They can be used cooked or fresh in pies, tarts, desserts, ice creams, water ices, jams, jellies, and sauces. The tender growth tips can be cooked with greens or used raw in salads, and the fresh or dried leaves make a refreshing tea.

Blackberry Sherbet

SERVES 4

⅔ CUP SUGAR
½ CUP WATER
1 POUND FRESH WILD BLACKBERRIES
1 SMALL EGG (WHITE ONLY)

Turn the refrigerator to its coldest setting. Make a syrup by boiling the sugar and water for 4 minutes. Allow it to cool. Put the blackberries through a sieve or a food mill and mix the pulp with the

Blackberry Sherbet and Scots Cream Crowdie

syrup. Beat the egg white until it forms soft peaks and fold it thoroughly into the blackberry mixture. Put it into a freezer container, cover, and freeze to a mush. Then beat the sherbet and freeze it for another half hour. Beat again and freeze until set—about 2½ to 3 hours altogether.

Adapted from Susan Campbell and Caroline Conran's *Poor Cook* (1981). A super recipe that everyone I know loves.

Scots Cream Crowdie

SERVES 4

⅔ CUP COARSE OATMEAL
2 CUPS HEAVY CREAM
⅓ CUP GRANULATED SUGAR
1 TABLESPOON RUM
1½ CUPS FRESH WILD BLACKBERRIES

"Put the oatmeal in a thick-bottomed saucepan and shake it over the heat until crisp. Beat the cream to a thick froth in a separate bowl and stir in the toasted oatmeal, sugar, rum and fruit. Serve at once. Very rich but scrumptious."

From Barbara Hargreaves's *The Second Country Cookbook* (1974).

Wild Blackberry and Apple Pie

MAKES ONE 10-INCH PIE

3 CUPS FLOUR
¼ TEASPOON SALT
1 CUP (2 STICKS) BUTTER
½ CUP ICE WATER
3 CUPS RIPE, WILD BLACKBERRIES
2 LARGE COOKING APPLES
¼ CUP SUGAR

Preheat the oven to 375°F and grease a 10-inch pie pan.

Sift the flour into a large bowl, add the salt and butter, and work them into the flour with your fingertips until the mixture resembles bread crumbs. Add the ice water and quickly mix into a dough. Wrap the dough in waxed paper or foil and put it into the refrigerator for 30 minutes while you prepare the pie filling.

Wash the blackberries, then peel, core, and dice the apples (you should have about 2 cups in all). Divide the pastry into two portions, one somewhat larger than the other. Roll out the bigger portion and line the bottom of the pie dish. Place the blackberries and apples on the pastry, heaping the fruit a little higher in the center, then sprinkle with the sugar. Roll out the remaining pastry, cover the pie, and brush with a little beaten egg or milk. Crimp the edge of the crust with a fork. If you have any pastry left over, use it to decorate the top of the pie. Bake for 30 to 35 minutes, until the pastry is golden brown. Serve hot or cold, sprinkled with sugar.

This recipe comes from Jacqui Hurst.

Sour Cream Soufflé Flan with Wild Blackberry Sauce

MAKES ONE 10-INCH SOUFFLÉ

FLAN:
¼ CUP BUTTER
⅓ CUP FLOUR
1 TABLESPOON SUGAR
1½ CUPS MILK
4 EGGS, SEPARATED

SOUR CREAM FILLING:
1 TEASPOON VANILLA EXTRACT
1 TABLESPOON SUGAR
1½ CUPS SOUR CREAM

BLACKBERRY SAUCE:
2 CUPS WASHED RIPE BLACKBERRIES
½ CUP SUGAR
1½ TEASPOONS LEMON JUICE
2 TEASPOONS CORNSTARCH
1 TABLESPOON COLD WATER

Preheat the oven to 400°F. Butter a 10-inch flan dish and dust with flour. Melt the butter in a saucepan, add the flour and sugar, and stir to a smooth paste. Gradually stir in the milk, bring the mixture to a boil, and cook for 1 minute, stirring continuously. Beat the egg yolks and add them to the pan a little at a time, continuing to stir. Cook the mixture for 1 more minute but do not allow it

Wild Blackberry and Apple Pie and Sour Cream Soufflé Flan with Wild Blackberry Sauce

to boil. Set it aside and let it cool to room temperature.

Beat the egg whites until stiff and fold them into the cooled flan mixture. Don't worry if the mixture seems to have formed a skin–this disappears when the egg whites are added. Pour it into the flan dish, trying to spread a little more of the mixture around the edge, and bake for 25 minutes, until the soufflé has risen and browned. Don't be alarmed at how high it rises; it soon flops down to manageable proportions when it comes out of the oven.

To prepare the filling, simply stir the vanilla extract and sugar into the sour cream and set the mixture aside while you make the blackberry sauce.

Put the blackberries, sugar, lemon juice, and water into a saucepan, bring to a boil, and allow the mixture to cook for 2 minutes. Dissolve the cornstarch in the cold water, add it to the cooked berries, and boil for 2 minutes, or until the sauce has thickened. Put it aside to cool.

To serve the flan, fill the center of the soufflé with the sour cream filling and swirl into it 3 or 4 tablespoons of the blackberry sauce. Pour the rest of the sauce into a jug and everyone can help themselves. This makes a super dessert for those who like puddings but don't like heavy pastry.

Bramble Jelly

MAKES TWO 1-POUND JARS

4 POUNDS WILD BLACKBERRIES
⅔ CUP WATER
JUICE OF 2 LEMONS
SUGAR
¼ TEASPOON MACE (OPTIONAL)
¼ TEASPOON NUTMEG (OPTIONAL)
¼ TEASPOON CINNAMON (OPTIONAL)

The jelly sets better if slightly underripe berries are used. Wash and de-stalk the fruit and drain well. Put it into a large saucepan with the water and lemon juice, bring to a boil, and simmer, covered, for about an hour, until the berries are soft. Strain the mixture through a jelly bag—but do not squeeze the pulp, or the jelly will be cloudy. Measure the juice into a saucepan and for each pint of juice add a pound of sugar. Heat the juice gently, stirring the sugar until it is dissolved, then boil vigorously, uncovered, for 10 to 15 minutes, stirring frequently. Test if it has reached the setting point by dripping two drops of jelly on a cold saucer. If it sets, the jelly is ready to be bottled into sterilized jars and covered.

If you like, the jelly may be flavored by adding the spices.

Wild Raspberry Vinegar

"Put two quarts of ripe fresh-gathered raspberries into a stone or china vessel, and pour on them a quart of vinegar. Let it stand for twenty-four hours, and then strain it through a sieve. Pour the liquid over two quarts of fresh raspberries, and let it again infuse for a day and a night. Then strain it a second time. Allow a pound of loaf sugar to every pint of juice. Break up the sugar, and let it melt in the liquor. Then put the whole into a stone jar, cover it closely, and set it in a kettle of boiling water, which must be kept on a quick boil for an hour. Take all the scum, and when cold bottle the vinegar for use.

"Raspberry vinegar mixed with water is a pleasant and cooling beverage in warm weather; also in fevers."

From Miss Eliza Leslie's *Directions for Cookery, in Its Various Branches* (1837).

Wild Raspberry Wine

7 CUPS WILD RASPBERRIES
5 QUARTS WATER
2 CAMPDEN TABLETS
JUICE OF 2 ORANGES
5 CUPS SUGAR
1 PACKET BREWER'S YEAST

CAUTION: Campden tablets may be detrimental to some asthma sufferers.

Pick over the raspberries, removing any unripe fruit, and place them in a plastic bucket. Pour in 3 quarts of boiling water and mash the berries well with a wooden spoon. Then add one crushed Campden tablet, stir thoroughly, and cover the bucket with muslin or cheesecloth. Let the berries sit for 2 days, then strain off the juice through a jelly bag, pressing well to get all the fruit juice through, and stir in the orange juice. Boil the remaining 2 quarts of water with the sugar and add the syrup to the juices. Mix well. Now start the yeast and add it when the mixture has cooled down. Cover the bucket with a cloth and leave the must to ferment for 3 days, then transfer it to a fermenting jar with an air lock. Let it ferment until all working has stopped, then filter it and add the second Campden tablet, crushed. Taste the wine—it may be too dry. If so, you can sweeten it with a very small amount of sugar syrup. Bottle in sterilized bottles and store them in a cool place.

This is a very special wine with a sharp, distinct flavor, ideal for drinking after a meal. I have found that it is delicious as soon as it has finished working, and I have inevitably run out of it in a few months.

SERVICEBERRIES

Serviceberry, *Amelanchier laevis*, a shrub or small tree, grows in thickets, woods, and swamps, along rivers, and on rocky slopes, often with oak, hickory, or sweet birch. It flowers in February in the South, in May in the North, and fruits from June to August.

> Found mainly in AL, n. AR, CT, DE, GA, s.e. IA, IL, IN, KY, MA, MD, ME, MI, e. MN, MO, w. MS, NC, NH, NJ, NY, OH, PA, RI, n.e. SC, TN, VA, VT, WI, WV. In Canada: NB, NS, s. ONT, PEI, s. QUE.

Saskatoon Serviceberry, *Amelanchier alnifolia* (synonym *Amelanchier florida*), a deciduous shrub, grows as high as 10 feet on mountain slopes, hillsides, prairies, and the moist banks of lakes and streams. It flowers in February or March, and the large berries ripen to purple from black from June to September.

> Found mainly in AK, CO, ID, w. MN, w. MT, ND, OR, SD, UT, WA, w. WY. In Canada: ALTA, BC, MAN, SASK.

Serviceberries (also called juneberries and shadberries) were eaten both fresh and dried by all the Indian tribes and by many white settlers, who called them shadberries, according to Palmer (1870). The dried berries could be used for seasoning meat or soups, and when boiled in a broth of fat meat or with dog salmon were considered a dainty for feasts.

On August 13, 1805, Captain Meriwether Lewis and his party came upon some Indians and were invited to their camp: "After the ceremony of the pipe was over . . . it was late in the evening and we had not tasted any food since the evening before. The Chief informed us that they had nothing but berries to eat and gave us some cakes of *serviceberries* and *Choke cherries* which had been dried in the sun; of these I made a hearty meal." But two days later Lewis was complaining: "I had ate nothing yesterday except one scant meal of the flour and berries except the dried cakes of *berries* which did not appear to satisfy my appetite as they appeared to do those of my Indian friends."

Besides the berries, the wood of the serviceberry was put to use by a number of tribes. The Swindmish made spreaders of it for their fish lines—not even a halibut could split it—and the Indians of Mendocino County, California, often used it to make arrows.

Palmer (1870) gives excellent directions for preserving the fruit: "In preparing the fruit for future use a favorite plan is to take a tub holding twenty or thirty gallons, on the bottom of which bark of the spruce tree is placed; upon this bark a quantity of berries is laid; stones nearly red hot are next laid on; then another layer of berries; then hot stones, and so on until the tub is filled. The whole is then allowed to remain untouched for six hours, when the fruit will be thoroughly cooked. It is then taken out, crushed between the hands, and spread on splinters of wood, tied together for that purpose, over a slow fire, and while it is drying the juice which was pressed out in cooking in the tub is rubbed over the berries. After two or three days' drying they will keep a long time, and are very palatable more so when a few huckleberries are mixed with them."

Not all species of serviceberries produce equally good fruit, but most of them make good eating. They can be picked and eaten fresh or used like blueberries or huckleberries, in pies, cakes, bread, and muffins, or to make jams and jellies.

Serviceberry and Banana Bread

MAKES 1 LOAF

2 CUPS FRESH RIPE SERVICEBERRIES
¾ CUP (1½ STICKS) BUTTER
1¼ CUPS SUGAR
3 LARGE, VERY RIPE BANANAS, WELL MASHED
3 LARGE EGGS, WELL BEATEN
1½ CUPS ALL-PURPOSE FLOUR
1½ CUPS WHOLE WHEAT FLOUR
1½ TEASPOONS BAKING SODA
¾ TEASPOON SALT
7 TABLESPOONS HOT WATER

Wash and drain the berries, preheat the oven to 325°F, and grease a 10 x 5-inch loaf pan. Cream the butter and sugar together in a large bowl, then stir in the bananas, then the eggs. Beat or whisk the mixture thoroughly. Sift the dry ingredients in another bowl, then stir spoonfuls of water and spoonfuls of flour into the banana mixture until they have all been incorporated and the mixture has a lovely, smooth consistency. Last, stir in the serviceberries. Pour the batter into the loaf pan and bake on the middle shelf of the oven. After an hour, insert a skewer into the center of the loaf. If it comes out clean, the bread is ready; if not, give it another 10 minutes or so.

The addition of serviceberries gives a deliciously moist, fruity texture to this standard banana bread recipe.

BLUEBERRIES

Bog Bilberry or **Tundra Bilberry**, *Vaccinium uliginosum*, a low shrub, grows in the tundra of the Arctic, in bogs and rocky or peaty barrens, and on high mountain slopes. It flowers from June to July and fruits from late July to September.

Found mainly in AK, n. CA, ME, n. MI, n. MN, NH, w. OR, VT, WA, n. WI. In Canada: ALTA, BC, MAN, NFLD (including LAB), ONT, QUE, SASK.

Highbush Blueberry, *Vaccinium corymbosum*, a tallish shrub, grows in swamps and bogs, in low, wet woodlands, and sometimes in dry uplands. It flowers from May to June and fruits from late June to early September.

Found mainly in CT, DE, s.e. GA, e. KY, MA, MD, ME, MI, NC, NH, NJ, OH, PA, RI, SC, e. TN, VA, VT, e. WI, WV. In Canada: s. NB, NS, PEI, s. QUE.

Lowbush Blueberry, *Vaccinium vacillans*, a low shrub, grows in dry, open woods, thickets, and clearings. It flowers from May to June and fruits from late June to September.

Found mainly in n. AL, CT, DE, GA, IL, IN, n.e. IA, MA, MD, s. ME, MI, MO, n. MS, NC, s. NH, NJ, NY, OH, PA, RI SC, TN, VA, VT. In Canada: NB, w. NS, e. ONT, PEI, s. QUE.

Blueberries and cranberries are the United States' world-famed wild fruits, and blueberry muffins and cranberry sauce, along with hamburgers and pecan pie, probably symbolize typical American food in a way that no other dishes can. They have always been firm favorites. On January 26, 1806, William Clark of the Lewis and Clark expedition wrote: "The Shat-lun [*Vaccinium ovatum*] or deep purpleberry is in form much like the huckleberry . . . The natives eate those berries ripe immediately from the bushes, or either in the Sun or by means of the Swetting Kiln; very frequently they pound them and bake them in large loaves of 10 to 15 pounds weight; this bread keeps verry well dureing one Season and retains the moist jouicies of the frute Much better than any other

Highbush blueberries

If you go picking berries in the wild, it is back-breaking work to gather a large basketful. One day we drew onto a grassy verge near Graham Lake in Maine, where the wild blueberries were rampant, and started painstakingly to gather the tiny fruits. Suddenly three men drew up in an old van and produced three implements that, they explained, were the traditional tools for gathering blueberries. A sort of cross between a dustpan and a rake, the blueberry picker made light work of the task.

I was fascinated to find an account, written well over a century ago, that obviously describes the same method. Elizabeth Ellet (1853) says: "Another distinctive feature of the St Croix region [of Minnesota] . . . is its marshes and swamps . . . From the cranberry marsh the farmer not only gathers a supply of fruit for his own family use, but finds a crop of which he can always dispose at good prices. These berries . . . are gathered with rakes so constructed as to let the vines pass between the teeth while retaining the fruit, and a single person may . . . gather two or three barrels in a day."

method of preparation. The bread is broken and stured in coald water until it be sufficiently thick and then eaten, in this way the nativ's most generally use it."

Half a century earlier Peter Kalm, the Swedish traveler, described their popularity among both Indians and Europeans: "The Indians formerly plucked them in abundance every year, dried them either in the sunshine or by the fire-side, and afterwards prepared them for eating, in different manners. These huckle-berries are still a dainty dish among the Indians. On my travels through the county of the Iroquese, they offered me, whenever they designed to treat me well, fresh maize-bread, baked in an oblong shape, mixed with dried Huckleberries, which lay as close in it as the raisins in a plumb-pudding, of which more in the sequel."

But there are so many delicious muffins, pies, tarts, jams, sauces, fritters, and puddings you can make from these berries that it seems a shame, when they are available in abundance, to confine yourself to eating them only in their natural state.

Blueberry Grunt

MAKES ONE 9-INCH PIE

FILLING:
3 CUPS BLUEBERRIES
SCANT ⅓ CUP SUGAR
¼ TEASPOON CINNAMON
¼ TEASPOON NUTMEG
¼ TEASPOON GROUND CLOVES
¼ CUP MOLASSES
2 TABLESPOONS LEMON JUICE

TOPPING:
1 CUP FLOUR
1½ TEASPOONS BAKING POWDER
¼ TEASPOON SALT
3 TABLESPOONS BUTTER
1 TABLESPOON VEGETABLE SHORTENING
1 EGG, LIGHTLY BEATEN
½ CUP MILK

Preheat the oven to 375°F. Wash and pick over the berries and spread them in a deep 9-inch pie pan.

Combine the sugar and spices and sift over the berries. Drizzle the molasses over all and sprinkle with the lemon juice. Bake for 5 minutes, or just until the berries begin to release juice. Remove the pan from the oven and increase the temp to 425°F. Mix the flour, baking powder, and salt, and blend in the butter and shortening. Stir in the egg and as much of the milk as needed to produce a soft dough. Drop the dough by tablespoons over the berry mixture and spread evenly to cover. Bake for 20 minutes, or until the biscuit is well browned. Serve either hot or cold.

Adapted from James Beard's *American Cookery* (1972).

Blueberry Muffins and Blueberry Grunt—
two great traditional favorites.

Blueberry Muffins

MAKES 6 GIANT OR 12 AVERAGE-SIZED MUFFINS

2 CUPS ALL-PURPOSE FLOUR
1 TABLESPOON BAKING POWDER
3 TABLESPOONS SUGAR
¼ TEASPOON SALT
1 LARGE EGG
¾ CUP MILK
½ CUP (1 STICK) BUTTER, MELTED
1½ CUPS FRESH BLUEBERRIES, WASHED
    AND MIXED WITH 2 TABLESPOONS SUGAR

Butter and flour a 12-cup muffin tin or six tin jelly molds. Sift the flour, then sift it again with the baking powder, sugar, and salt. Beat the egg and milk together and mix into the dry ingredients. Pour in the melted butter and stir until all ingredients are evenly moistened. Do not beat or the muffins will be grainy and holey. Lightly fold in the blueberries and fill each cup or mold two-thirds full of batter. Bake in a preheated 400°F oven for about 25 minutes, until the muffins are brown and puffy.

Adapted from Martha Lomask's *The All American Cookbook* (1981).

The two recipes that follow come from Susan Brown's *Book of Forty Puddings* (1882).

Baked Blueberry Pudding with Yellow Pudding Sauce

"Mix one cup of sugar with a piece of butter the size of a large egg. Add one cup of sweet milk with half a teaspoonful of soda in it. Stir in one pint of flour, with a teaspoonful of cream tartar mixed in it. Add one coffee cup of ripe blueberries well sprinkled with flour. Bake in a round dish and eat with Yellow Pudding Sauce.

"[The Sauce:] One third of a cup of butter, beaten light, two thirds of a cup of sugar, and the yolk of an egg. Mix well, and pour on it one cup of boiling water. When it cools a little, add the beaten white of the egg, stirring in a spoon at a time."

Blueberry Steamed Pudding with Egg Sauce

"One cup of sweet milk with half a teaspoon of soda dissolved in it; one cup of molasses, one pint of blueberries; flour enough to make pretty thick batter. Steam two hours. Serve with Egg Sauce . . .

"[The Sauce:] The white of 2 eggs beaten to a stiff froth; one and a half cups of sugar; four table-spoons of sweet milk."

Summer Pudding

SERVES 6

8-10 SLICES THIN, DAY-OLD WHITE BREAD
2-3 TABLESPOONS WATER
¾ CUP GRANULATED SUGAR
2 POUNDS WILD BILBERRIES

Rinse a 3-cup pudding bowl with cold water. Trim the crusts from the bread. Cut a circle of bread to fit the bottom of the bowl and some wedge-shaped pieces to fit around the sides. Press the bread firmly to line the bowl and see that there are no gaps. Reserve a few pieces to cover the top.

Place the sugar and water in a saucepan and stir over low heat to dissolve the sugar. Add the bilberries and cook for a few minutes only. Remove from the heat and strain off about ½ cup of fruit juice.

Turn the fruit and the rest of the juice into the lined pudding bowl and cover the top with the re-maining bread slices. Place a saucer on top of the pudding and press it down with a weight. Leave overnight. Boil up the reserved fruit juice until syr-upy and let it cool.

The next day, remove the weight and saucer from the pudding, then place a serving plate over it and invert it onto the plate. Pour the fruit syrup over the top and serve with cream.

This recipe comes from Katie Stewart, who suggested trying this traditional dish with wild fruit. I think the result is superb, better even than when made with the more traditional summer fruits.

Black huckleberries

BLACK HUCKLEBERRY

Black Huckleberry, *Gaylussacia baccata,* a thicket-forming shrub, grows in dry or moist woods and clearings. It flowers from May to July and fruits from August to September.

Found mainly in n.e. AL, CT, DE, n. GA, IL, IN, KY, MA, MD, ME, MN, w. NC, NH, NY, OH, PA, RI, TN, VA, VT, WI, WV. In Canada: s. MAN, NB, NS, s. ONT, PEI, s. QUE.

The Indians were fond of huckleberries and ate them fresh or dried, often as part of a feast. John Long (1791) mentions them when describing an Indian adoption ceremony: "A feast is prepared of dog's flesh boiled in bear's grease with huckle-berries of which it is expected every one should heartily partake."

Mrs. Child (1836) also recommends huckle-berries for sick children: "Made into bread and sweetened with molasses, they are very beneficial, when the system is in a restricted state, and the digestive powers out of order."

Huckleberry Cake

"Spread a quart of ripe huckleberries on a large dish, and dredge them thickly with flour. Mix together half a pint of milk; half a pint of molasses; half a pint of powdered sugar, and half a pound of butter. Warm them by the fire till the butter is quite soft; then stir them all together, and set them away till cold. Prepare a large table-spoonful of powdered cloves and cinnamon mixed. Beat five eggs very light, and stir them gradually into the other ingredients; adding, by degrees, sufficient sifted flour to make a thick batter. Then stir in a small tea-spoonful of pearl-ash or dissolved salaratus. Lastly, add by degrees the huckleberries. Put the mixture into a buttered pan, or into little tins, and bake it in a moderate oven. It is best the second day."

A rather large but tasty cake from Miss Eliza Leslie's *Directions for Cookery, in Its Various Branches* (1837).

Partridgeberries

PARTRIDGEBERRY

Partridgeberry, *Mitchella repens*, a small, creeping herb, grows on dry or moist knolls in woods and forests. It flowers from June to July and fruits from July into the winter.

Found mainly in AR, CT, DE, FL, GA, IA, IL, IN, KY, LA, MA, MD, ME, MI, MN, MO, NC, NH, NJ, NY, OH, PA, RI, SC, TN, TX, VA, VT, WI, WV. In Canada: NB, NFLD, NS, s. ONT, PEI, s. QUE.

Indian women made tea from the leaves and drank it during labor to ease delivery pains. Although the bright red berries are dry and tasteless, they are quite edible and make a pretty addition to fresh salads.

WINTERGREENS

Wintergreen or **Checkerberry**, *Gaultheria procumbens*, a low, evergreen plant, grows in sterile woods and clearings in poor soil. It flowers from July to August and fruits from August until the following June.

Found mainly in CT, DE, n. IL, n. IN, KY, MA, MD, ME, n.e. MN, NC, NH, NJ, NY, OH, PA, RI, s.e. TN, VA, VT, WI, WV. In Canada: s.e. MAN, NB, NS, s. ONT, PEI, s. QUE.

Salal or **Western Wintergreen**, *Gaultheria shallon*, an upright shrub with numerous spreading branches, grows in woods, bushy areas, and clearings below 2,100 feet. It flowers, then fruits, from April to July.

Found mainly in w. CA, w. OR, w. WA. In Canada: s.w. BC.

Wintergreen

Wintergreen is one of the best known of all American wild plants, and the spicy, aromatic flavor of the leaves and berries was appreciated by the Indians and early settlers long ago.

On December 9, 1805, William Clark of the Lewis and Clark expedition described the hospitality he received from 12 families of the Clatsop nation: "These people appeared much Neeter in their dress than Indians are Comonly, and frequently wash their faces and hands. in the eve[ni]ng an old woman presented [in] a bowl made of light colored horn a kind of surup made of Dried berries which is common to this countrey which the natives Call Shele wele [the fruit of *Gaultheria shallon*, a shrub allied to the common wintergreen] this Surup I thoudh was pleasant, they gave me Cocke Shells to eate a kind of Seuip [soup] made of bread of the Shele well berries Mixed with roots."

Fresh wintergreen leaves are best for making tea. The dried leaves lose their flavor. Both young leaves and berries are refreshing when eaten raw, though the latter become plumper and juicier if frozen and are delicious added to pancakes, muffins, or salads. The leaves and berries contain a compound similar to aspirin and can be taken to soothe minor aches and pains.

Wintergreen Tea

SERVES 4

Pick a quart of fresh young leaves and cover them with boiling water. Cover and allow them to steep for 1 to 2 days to extract the aromatic wintergreen oil. Strain, then gently reheat and serve with a little sugar to sweeten if desired.

Mountain cranberries

Small cranberries, not quite ripe.

CRANBERRIES

Large Cranberry, *Vaccinium macrocarpon*, a low, trailing shrub, grows in open bogs and swamps and on wet shores. It flowers from June to August and fruits from September to November.

Found mainly in CT, n.e. IL, n.e. IN, MA, ME, MN, NH, NY, n.w. OH, RI, VT, WI. In Canada: NB, NFLD, NS, s. ONT, PEI, s. QUE.

Mountain Cranberry, *Vaccinium vitis-idaea*, a small, creeping plant, grows in subarctic conditions, in bogs, and in rocky or dry, peaty soils. It flowers from June to July, fruits from the end of August to October, and holds over the winter.

Found mainly in AK, ME, n. NH, VT. In Canada: all provinces.

Small Cranberry, *Vaccinium oxycoccos*, a slender, creeping shrub, grows in bogs and peaty soil. It flowers from May to July, fruits from August to October, and holds over the winter.

Found mainly in AK, ME, MI, MN, NC, NH, NJ, NY, n. OH, OR, PA, VA, VT, WA, WI, WV. In Canada: all provinces.

Cranberry Sauce

"Wash a quart of ripe cranberries, and put them in a pan with about a wine-glass of water. Stew them slowly, and stir them frequently, particularly after they begin to burst. They require a great deal of stewing, and should be like a marmalade when done. Just before you take them from the fire, stir in a pound of brown sugar.

"When they are thoroughly done, put them into a deep dish, and set them away to get cold.

"You may strain the pulp through a cullender or sieve into a mould, and when it is in a firm shape send it to table on a glass dish. Taste it when it is cold, and if not sweet enough, add more sugar. Cranberries require more sugar than any other fruit, except plums.

"Cranberry sauce is eaten with roast turkey, roast fowls, and roast ducks."

From Miss Leslie's *Directions for Cookery, in Its Various Branches* (1837).

Buckingham Pies

PASTRY:
3½ CUPS ALL-PURPOSE FLOUR
¾ CUP LARD, DIVIDED
⅓ CUP WATER
1 TEASPOON SALT

FILLING:
¾ CUP TURKEY
½ CUP HAM
¾ CUP PORK
2 TABLESPOONS SAGE-AND-ONION STUFFING
1 EGG, BEATEN
2 TEASPOONS SALT
1 TEASPOON PEPPER
2 TABLESPOONS WATER

TOPPING:
1 TABLESPOON GELATIN
⅔ CUP WATER
PINCH OF SALT
PINCH OF PEPPER
3 CUPS FRESH, WHOLE CRANBERRIES

First, make the pastry. Put the flour in a bowl, and using two knives or a pastry blender, cut into it ½ cup of the lard, until the mixture resembles coarse bread crumbs. Place the rest of the lard, the water, and the salt in a saucepan and bring to a boil. Immediately add the boiling liquid to the flour-and-lard mixture and stir with a fork. When the liquid has been completely absorbed, shape the dough into a ball, wrap it in waxed paper, and let it cool in the refrigerator for at least 20 minutes.

Meanwhile make the filling. Mince or finely chop all the meats, then mix them thoroughly with the other ingredients, adding the water last.

Then, thoroughly grease an 8-cup muffin tin and preheat the oven to 375°F. Roll out the cooled pastry and cut into eight circles 5 inches in diameter and ⅛ inch thick, or mold it into flat rounds with your hands. Cut a radius line in each of the circles to facilitate fitting them into the cups of the muffin tin. Fill each pastry case two-thirds full of the meat mixture and press it down firmly. Bake the pies for 30 minutes, then remove them from the oven and immediately run a knife around the edge of each pie. This makes it easier to remove the pies later. While they are cooling, make the gelatin, following the instructions on the gelatin packet. When it is ready, pour it on the top of each pie, then put the muffin tin into the refrigerator for 20 minutes, or until the gelatin has set. Decorate the top of each pie with cranberries, then glaze with more topping and again cool until set.

We had bought some of these wonderful pieces at the famous Harrods food hall in London, and they very kindly sent us the recipe to put in the book. Although the pies take time to make, they are so superb it is well worth the effort for a special occasion, like Thanksgiving.

Four people ate the pies we photographed. Two of them loved the slightly tart topping of fresh cranberries and ate every one. The other two found that one or two berries were all they could manage, so you will have to decide for yourself which you prefer.

Wild plum brandy

Klamath plums

Chokecherries

PLUMS & CHOKECHERRY

American Plum or **Wild Plum**, *Prunus americana*, a coarse shrub or tree with spiny branches, grows in thickets, on the borders of woods, and along streams, fencerows, and the margins of fields. It flowers from late April to early June and fruits from late August through September.

Found mainly in n. AL, w. GA, IA, IL, IN, KS, KY, MA, s.e. MI, MN, MO, e. NC, ND, NE, NH, n. NJ, NY, OH, PA, SD, TN, e. VA, s. WI, WV. In Canada: s. MAN, s. ONT.

Flatwood Plum, *Prunus umbellata*, a small tree, grows on coastal plains, along rivers, and in swamps. It flowers in April and fruits between June and September.

Found mainly in AL, s. AR, FL, GA, n.w. LA, s.w. MS, SC, e. TX.

Beach Plum, *Prunus maritima*, a low, straggling shrub, grows in sandy soil near the coast. It flowers from April to June and fruits in September and October.

Found mainly in DE, MA, ME, NJ, e. PA.

California, **Klamath**, or **Sierra Plum**, *Prunus subcordata*, a shrub or small tree, grows on dry, rocky, or moist slopes below 6,500 feet. It flowers from March to May and fruits from June to September.

Found mainly in CA, NV, OR.

Common Chokecherry, *Prunus virginiana*, a large shrub or small tree, grows in dry woods, thickets, and fencerows. It flowers from the end of April to June and fruits from July to September.

Found mainly in CA, w. CO, CT, IA, ID, IL, IN, KS, MA, ME, MN, n. MO, MT, ND, NE NH, NJ, w. NV, NY, OH, OR, PA, RI, SD, n. UT, VT, WA, WI, WV, WY. In Canada: all provinces.

According to Valery Havard (1895), several authorities have agreed that the wild plum was planted by New England and Canadian natives, and some 45 species have developed from it. The fruits of the wild plum and wild cherry were highly prized as food by Indians and settlers, though it is important to be sure they are ripe if they are to be enjoyed raw.

Captain John Smith, writing in 1606, tells us: "Plums there are of three sorts. The red and white are like our hedge plums, but the other which they call Putchamins, grow as high as a Palmeta: the fruit is like a Medlar; it is first green, then yellow, and red when it is ripe; if it be not ripe, it will draw a mans mouth awry, with much torment, but when it is ripe, it is as delicious as an Apricot."

Peter Kalm, in a diary entry of 1749, agrees: "The wild Plumb-trees grow in great abundance on the hills, along the rivulets about the town. They were so loaded with fruit, that the boughs were quite bent downwards by the weight. The fruit was not yet ripe, but when it comes to perfection, it has a red color and a fine taste, and preserves are sometimes made of it."

Captain Meriwether Lewis, on May 12, 1805, describes some of the ways the Indian prepared and ate chokecherries: "The Indians of the Missouri make great use of this chokeberry which they prepare for food in various ways, sometimes eating when first plucked from the trees or in that state pounding them mashing the seed boiling them with roots or meat, or with the prairie beans and white apple; again for their winter store they geather them and lay them on skins to dry in the sun; when thus dryed they fold them in skins or put them in bags of parchment and keep them through the winter either eating them in this state or boiling them as before mentioned. The bear and many birds also feed on these berries."

Wild plums and cherries can be used in any recipe calling for plums, although the amount of sugar will need to be adjusted depending on the species used. Those that are too tart to be enjoyed raw make excellent jellies, jams, and sauces. Or try an 18th-century prescription from the traveler Jonathan Carver: Add them to brandy to give it "an agreeable flavor . . . and turn it the colour of claret."

Beach Plum Jelly

MAKES 4–6 SMALL JARS

12 CUPS RIPE BEACH PLUMS, RINSED
4 CUPS GREEN (UNRIPE) BEACH PLUMS, RINSED
1 CUP SOUR CRAB APPLES
    OR 1 LARGE GRANNY SMITH APPLE,
    CORED AND QUARTERED
2 CUPS WATER
SUGAR

Put the first four ingredients into a 6- or 9-quart enamel pot, bring to a boil, and simmer for about 15 minutes, or until the plums are softened. Stir and bruise the fruit, and simmer for another 5 to 10 minutes. Ladle this mixture into a damp jelly bag and let the juice drip *undisturbed* overnight. The next day measure the number of cups of juice you have collected and pour it into the enamel pot. Stir in ⅔ cup of sugar for each cup of juice and bring the mixture to a boil over moderate heat, stirring continuously. Then increase the heat to medium high and boil the mixture until it reaches the jelly stage (place a little water on a saucer and, if it sets, it has reached the jelly stage) or until a candy thermometer reads 222°F. Pour the jelly into small, sterilized canning jars, filling them to within ¼ inch of the rim, put on lids, screw down the bands, and process in boiling water. For processing instructions, see http://nchfp.uga.edu/publications/uga/using_bw_canners.html.

This recipe was given to me by Bob Hosh. We collected several baskets of beach plums on the shore down near Sandy Hook, and he made this absolutely scrumptious jelly with them. It set perfectly and was beautifully transparent. But when he gave us the recipe, he said his efforts were not always so successful and he asked us to add this warning: "This recipe can be a bitch! A lot depends on Mother Nature—like how much rain got into the fruit at harvest; how much water you add when cooking, etc., etc. Also the greennees of the plums comes into play and one must be very careful and watch the pot. Needless to say, I've made some very good beach plum syrup this way!"

WILD CHERRY

Wild Cherry, *Prunus avium*, a common deciduous tree in its range, is found in woods and hedges. It flowers in late April or May and the fruit ripens in early July. Wild cherries can be substituted for cultivated cherries in any recipe but the amount of sugar must be adjusted to compensate, as the wild crop is normally very sour.

Found in CA, CT, DC, DE, ID, IL, IN, KY, MA, MD, ME, MI, MT, NC, NH, NJ, NY, OH, OR, PA, RI, SC, TN, UT, VA, WA, WI, WV, WY. In Canada: BC, NB, NS, ON, QC.

Wild Cherry Soup

5 CUPS CHERRIES, WASHED AND PITTED
1¼ CUPS WATER
1 INCH CINNAMON BARK
ZEST OF 1 LEMON
1¼ CUPS RED WINE, PREFERABLY HOMEMADE
A LITTLE DRIED MASHED POTATO

Place the cherries, water, cinnamon, and lemon zest in a saucepan, bring the mixture to a boil, and cook over high heat, covered, for 10 minutes. Then transfer the lot to a blender and puree. Combine the wine and the cherry mixture, and thicken to taste with the mashed potato. Sweeten as necessary, reheat, and serve at once.

This recipe comes from Barbara Hargreaves's *The Second Country Book* (1974).

Wild Cherry Wine

MAKES 1 GALLON

1 GALLON WATER, DIVIDED
10 CUPS CHERRIES
6 CUPS SUGAR
GRATED RIND AND JUICE OF 1½ LEMONS
1½ TEASPOONS BREWER'S YEAST

Pick the cherries when they are really ripe, then de-stem and wash them. If you cannot find enough, add shop fruit, but remember that this will make a much sweeter wine. Bring 3 quarts of the water to a boil, place the cherries in a bucket, and pour the boiling water over them. When they have cooled, mash them with your hands. Allow them to stand, covered with a cloth, for 3 days, then squeeze them through a wine bag. Place the liquid in a fermentation jar. Make up a syrup with the remaining quart of water and the sugar, then add it to the cherry juice in the fermentation jar, along with the lemon juice and rind. Start the yeast and add it to the wine. Fit an air lock and leave for 3 months, then siphon the wine into a clean jar and keep it for another 3 to 4 months. Now it will be ready to drink.

This recipe was given to me by Geoff and Jenny Stone. It makes a delicious, sharp, dry wine.

SPICEBUSH

Spicebush, *Lindera benzoin*, a tall shrub, grows in damp, rich woods and along streams. It flowers from March to May and fruits from September to October.

Found in AL, AR, CT, DE, n. FL, GA, IL, IN, KY, LA, MA, MD, s. ME, s. MI, MS, MO, NC, NH, NJ, NY, OH, PA, RI, SC, TN, e. TX, VA, VT, WV. In Canada: s. ONT.

NOTE: See page 42 for spicebush tea.

Oliver Medsger (1939) says that at the time of the American Revolution, spicebush berries were dried and used as a substitute for allspice. Our friend Bob Peabody decided to revive the custom. He collected a bowl of berries, dried them slowly in his oven, and used them in any recipe that called for allspice. He assured us that they were every bit as good.

BUNCHBERRY

Bunchberry, *Cornus canadensis,* a perennial herb, grows in cold wet woods and bogs, and on mountain slopes. It flowers from May to July and fruits from late July to October.

Found mainly in AK, n. CA, ID, ME, MI, n. MN, w. MT, NH, NY, OR, PA, VT, WA, WI. In Canada: all provinces.

Bunchberry Syrup with Yogurt

SERVES 4

4 CUPS BUNCHBERRIES
¼ CUP SUGAR
2 TABLESPOONS WATER
2 CUP PLAIN YOGURT

De-stem and wash the berries, then put them in a saucepan with the sugar and water; bring to a boil. Simmer for 2 minutes, then strain through a cloth.

This syrup looks very pretty poured over plain yogurt and is just one way of using these berries, which can be found in such profusion in the North.

PAWPAW

Pawpaw, *Asimina triloba,* a large shrub or small tree, grows in rich, moist soils in woods, river valleys, and bottomlands. It flowers in April and May and fruits between August and October.

Found mainly in AL, AR, DE, FL, GA, s. IA, IL, KY, LA, MD, MO, MS, NC, s.e. NE, NJ, w. NY, OH, PA, SC, TN, e. TX. In Canada: s. ONT.

CAUTION: Handling pawpaw can cause contact dermatitis in some people.

The pawpaw, also known as custard apple or false banana, provokes very contradictory responses: Some people love it, others find it a taste that has to be acquired. Rafinesque (1828–30) describes it as "sedative, laxative, and healthy," and feels that all the shrubs of this family deserve cultivation. He also points out that the Indians made strong ropes with the bark.

The ripe, sweet yellow pulp of the fruit can be eaten raw or baked in the oven, or used to make puddings and ice creams. We tried making a bread with it as one would banana bread, but the slightly fetid taste was not enjoyed by any of our family or friends. We found it much more successful served fresh with slices of Parma ham or salami as an hors d'oeuvre, or sliced thinly and alternated with Chinese gooseberries for a light dessert. Another idea we all voted a success was pawpaw crepes.

Pawpaw Crepes

SERVES 4 (12 SMALL CREPES)

FILLING:
1 TEASPOON BUTTER
6 RIPE PAWPAWS, SKINNED AND CUBED
1 TABLESPOON SUGAR
JUICE OF 1 LEMON OR LIME
1 CUP FRESH WHIPPED CREAM

CREPES:
1 CUP FLOUR
PINCH OF SALT
2 EGGS PLUS 1 EGG YOLK
1¼ CUPS MILK
1 TABLESPOON MELTED BUTTER OR OIL
⅓ CUP WHITE VEGETABLE SHORTENING

First, make the filling. Heat the butter in a small saucepan, add the pawpaw cubes, sugar, and citrus juice, and toss them in the butter for a minute or two, until they are just warm. Set aside.

To make the crepes, sift the flour and salt into a mixing bowl. Make a hollow in the center and into it put the eggs, egg yolk, and half the milk. Stir, using a wooden spoon, and gradually draw in the flour to make a smooth batter, then add the rest of the milk and the melted butter or oil. Mix thoroughly. Pour the batter into a jug with a pouring spout.

Melt the vegetable shortening in a small saucepan. Heat a crepe pan, pour in a little of the hot fat, and follow it quickly with about 2 tablespoons of batter, poured into the center of the hot pan. Tip the pan so that the batter runs over the surface to make a thin crepe, top with a dollop of whipped cream, fold, and serve with lemon quarters (optional).

Honey locust

HONEY LOCUST

Honey Locust, *Gleditsia triacanthos*, a thorny tree, grows in rich woods and fields and cultivated areas, and flowers in May and June. The pods ripen from September to February.

Found mainly in AL, AR, CT, DE, FL, GA, e. KS, IA, IL, IN, LA, MA, MD, ME, MI, MS, NC, e. NE, NH, NJ, NY, OH, e. OK, PA, RI, SC, e. SD, TN, e. TX, VA, VT, WV. In Canada: NS.

The pulp of the unripe seedpods is deliciously sweet (thus giving rise to the common name of the plant) and can be eaten instead of candy when hiking in the country. Occasionally, the quality of the pulp is not as good as its name implies and may be slightly bitter. The Mediterranean relative of the honey locust, called Saint John's bread, also has pods containing sweet, fleshy pulp; these are thought to be the "locusts" eaten by John the Baptist in the desert.

PERSIMMON

Persimmon, *Diospyros virginiana*, a large shrub or tree, grows in dry woods, old fields, and rich bottomlands, on rocky hillsides, and along highways. It fruits from August to October.

Found mainly in AL, AR, DE, FL, GA. s. IL, s. IN, KY, LA, MD, MO, MS, NC, NJ, s. OH, e. OK, SC, TN. e. TX, VA, WV.

Both Palmer (1870) and Rafinesque (1828–30) say the Indian tribes consumed ripe persimmons in large quantities and preserved them in various ways. In a diary entry of 1748, Peter Kalm gives instructions for making what he claims is a very palatable liquor from persimmons: "Persimmon apples are put into a dough of wheat or other flour, formed in cakes, and put into an oven in which they continue till they are quite baked and sufficiently dry, when they are taken out again; then, in order to brew the liquor, a pot full of water is put on the fire, and some of the cakes are put in: these become soft by degrees as the water grows warm, and crumble in pieces at last; the pot is then taken from the fire, and the water is well stirred about, that the cakes may mix with it; this is then poured into another vessel, and they continue to steep and break as many cakes as are necessary for a brewing: the malt is then infused, and they proceed as usual with the brewing. Beer thus prepared is reckoned much preferable to other beer."

Alas, when we tried to follow Kalm's instructions, all we got was a bucket of stinking mush!

With persimmons it is essential to wait until they are absolutely ripe before eating them; otherwise their strange astringent quality will cause your lips to purse unbearably.

Kalm illustrates this point with an amusing anecdote: "Hesselius [a Swedish painter Kalm was visiting] gathered some of them, and desired my servant to taste of the fruits of the land; but this poor credulous fellow had hardly bit into them, when he felt the qualities they have before the frost has penetrated them. For they contracted his mouth so that he could hardly speak and had a very disagreeable taste. This disgusted him so much that he was with difficulty persuaded to taste of it during the whole of our stay in America."

Persimmons are meltingly sweet to eat fresh, or the strained pulp can be used to make jams, pies, puddings, or breads.

Bob and Genia's Persimmon Pudding

SERVES 8

2 CUPS PERSIMMON PULP
3 EGGS
1¼ CUPS SUGAR
1½ CUPS FLOUR
1 TEASPOON BAKING POWDER
½ TEASPOON SALT
½ CUP MELTED BUTTER
1 CUP MILK
2 TEASPOONS FRESHLY GROUND NUTMEG
½ CUP RAISINS OR CURRANTS OR NUTS (OPTIONAL)

Preparing the persimmons can be tricky if you don't have a food mill. If you do, it is simple: Just put the ripe persimmons through the mill to separate the fresh fruit from the skin and seeds. But if, like us, you are vacationing in a rustic cabin without all the modern conveniences, you have to improvise. We blanched the fruits in boiling water to remove their skins and cut them in half to pick out the seeds. Then we boiled the flesh for a few minutes to break down the fibers, chopped it as finely as we could with a sharp knife, and pressed it through a sieve with the back of a wooden spoon. It was hard work!

Anyway, once you've got the pulp the rest is plain sailing. Put all the ingredients into a big bowl and combine thoroughly. Pour the mixture into a large, well-greased, 11 x 13-inch baking pan and bake in a preheated 325°F oven until the pudding is firmly set (about an hour). Serve with whipped cream.

When we stayed with Bob and Genia Hosh, they got the last of their previous year's persimmon puddings out of their freezer, in our honor. It was so scrumptious, we immediately asked them if we could put the recipe in this book.

KUDZU VINE

Kudzu Vine, *Pueraria lobata*, a long trailing or very high-climbing vine with a hairy stem, grows on the edges of woods and fields. It flowers from late July to September.

Found mainly in AL, AR, CT, DE, FL, GA, HI, IL, IN, KS, KY, LA, MA, MD, MO, MS, NC, NE, NJ, NY, OH, OK, OR, PA, SC, TN, TX, VA, WA, WV.

This exceedingly fast-growing weed was introduced into North America from East Asia and it has spread rapidly, sometimes totally covering a whole row of trees and shrubs at the edge of a wood. Its common name comes from Japan, where the plant is valued not only as an ornamental but also for its fiber and its starchy, tuberous roots, which are edible. Starch can also be extracted by peeling and cutting the root branches, crushing them in water, and letting the starch separate out. Numerous washings in cold water refine the starch.

Squawbush

SQUAWBUSH & SUMAC

Squawbush, *Rhus trilobata*, a shrub with very hairy twigs, grows in washes, in dry, rocky canyons, and on dry, rocky slopes, usually below 3,600 feet. It flowers in April and fruits in August.

Found mainly in n.e. AZ, CA, w. CO, ID, w. MT, n.w. NM, n. NV, s.e. OR, w. WY. In Canada: s. ALTA.

Staghorn Sumac, *Rhus typhina*, a small tree or shrub with very hairy twigs and branches, grows in dry, rocky soil on roadsides and streambanks, in upland fields, and on the margins of woods. It fruits from June to September.

Found mainly in IN, MA, MD, ME, MI, NH, NY, OH, PA, TN, n.w. VA, VT, WI, WV. In Canada: NB, NS, s. ONT, PEI, s. QUE.

Smooth Sumac, *Rhus glabra*, a shrub or small tree with smooth branches, grows in dry soil on abandoned farmland, in old fields and fencerows, and along streams. It fruits from June to October.

Found mainly in the eastern states, though locally throughout the West (exceptions: AZ, CA, NM, NV).

Kudzu vine

CAUTION: Avoid swamp sumac (*Rhus vernix*), poison oak (*R. toxicodendron*), and poison ivy (*R. radicans*), all of which have white fruit and are very poisonous. When touched, they cause severe blistering and swelling, with nasty itching.

Sumac is prolific in many parts of the United States and has long been used by Indian tribes for food and medicine, and as a material for making baskets. Palmer (1870) says that the western Indians used the young twigs for basketry because they were more durable than willow. "The mode of preparation is as follows: The twigs are soaked in water to soften them, and to loosen the bark, which his scraped off by the females. The twigs are then split, by the use of the mouth and both hands. Their baskets are built up by a succession of small rolls of grass stems over which these twigs are firmly and closely bound. A bone awl is used to make the holes under the rims of grass for the split twigs. Baskets thus made are very durable."

Gilmore (1911–12) says that in the fall, when the leaves of the smooth sumac had turned red, they were gathered and dried for smoking by all the tribes; the roots were further used to make a yellow dye. Kalm, in a diary entry of 1748, records that "the branches and berries boiled together make a black ink-like tincture."

Medicinally, the sumac seems to have been put to a number of uses. Chesnut (1902) says that a Yoki Indian told him of a treatment for smallpox: "70 or 80 years ago when smallpox was prevalent in Anderson valley, and few, if any, white men were around, the fruit, which is rather viscid and acid in taste, was used as a remedy. The ripe berries were dried and then finely powdered. While the pox was still dry, water was added to the powder, which was then applied as a lotion. When the sores were open and moist, the powder was dusted on the surface."

Despite their rather sour taste, the fruits of the sumac make a refreshing thirst quencher either when sucked fresh or when made into a beverage. Pick the entire, ripe fruit clusters, preferably before heavy rains remove some of the acid, and use them to make jams, jellies, syrup, or lemonade.

Sumac Lemonade

MAKES 2 QUARTS

4 CUPS SUMAC BERRIES
4 QUARTS NEARLY BOILING WATER
2 CUPS SUGAR

De-stalk the berries, put them in a saucepan, pour the near-boiling water over them, and let them steep, covered, for about 15 minutes. Strain through a cloth into a large jar, add the sugar, and stir until it dissolves. Allow the liquid to cool, then seal the jar tight and refrigerate. Serve the lemonade diluted to half strength with water and lots of ice.

This is a very refreshing summer drink. You can also make this recipe with squawbush berries. Although the squawbush version is much paler in color and has a rather strange flavor difficult to describe, it has the same refreshing quality as the sumac version.

COMMON APPLE

Common Apple, *Malus sylvestris*, a small, familiar, round-headed tree, grows along roadsides and in woods and hedgerows. It flowers from March to May and fruits from September to November.

Found throughout North America.

This is the Eurasian wild apple, which was introduced into America by the early settlers in various cultivated forms and was spread through the hedgerows by birds carrying and dispersing the seeds. The trees then quickly reverted nearly to the wild form, and nowadays they can be found all over the country. The apples are much smaller and harder than their cultivated counterparts, and they vary greatly in sweetness. A useful rule of thumb when making jams or jellies with wild apples is that the more bitter they are, the more pectin they contain.

Indians, explorers, and settlers obviously relished wild apples when they were in season. Captain Meriwether Lewis wrote in his journal on December 1, 1805: "There is a wild crab apple which the natives eat. This growth differs but little in appearance from that of the wild crab of the Atlantic contour, and when the fruit has been touched by the frost is not unpleasant, being an agreeable asset."

In Europe the history of the apple goes back to the dawn of time. The charred remains of small apples have been found in prehistoric Swiss lake dwellings, and there are references to apples in all the early books on food and medicine. The ancient Britons cherished the apple for both food and beverage purposes. Crab apples are the ancestor of all cultivated varieties and are still used as a rootstock. Because the apple is such an ancient and valued fruit, there are many traditions and customs connected to it.

It has always been a symbol of fruitfulness and plenty, and of all fruit trees, apples were considered the most magical. To sleep under an apple tree rendered one liable to be carried off by the fairies. A single spray of apple blossoms flowering among ripe apples portended the death of one of the family. The oldest tree in the orchard con-

Wild apples

tained the Apple Tree Man, who was responsible for the fruitfulness of the orchard and was customarily left the last apple of each year's crop.

The crab apple has also been the subject of several proverbs and expressions. Its sourness led to calling an ill-tempered person a crab or crabby. Other characteristics of the crab apple tree are described in the following verse:

> The crab of the wood
> Its sauce very good
> For the crab of the sea;
> But the wood of the crab
> Is sauce for a crab
> That will not her husband obey

It is said that the older the crab tree, the more crabs it bears. Verjuice is a fermented brew made from either crab apples or sour grapes. It keeps in the bottle, like wine, and was used by medieval cooks in many dishes, as we would use lemon juice. Crab apples have long been used in drinks. Four thousand years ago cider made from crab apples and mead made from wild honey were probably the most common drinks of our ancestors. Another ancient drink is the Wassail Bowl. The chief ingredients were strong ale, sugar, spices, and roasted crab apples. Traditionally, people kept wassail on Twelfth Night and Christmas Eve, as in *Hamlet*:

> The king doth wake-to-night,
>   and takes his rouse
> Keeps wassail, and the swaggering
>   up-spring reels.

Verjuice

Gather some ripe crab apples and lay them in a heap to sweat, then throw away the stalks and decayed fruit, and—having mashed the apples—express the juice. A cider or wine press is useful for this purpose. Strain it, store it in a jar in the refrigerator, and in a month it will be ready. It is the best simple substitute for lemon juice that can be found and answers still better in place of sorrel. The French, for many dishes, prefer verjuice to lemon. (Four pounds of apples will make about a quart of juice.)

Wild Apple Jelly

MAKES 2 OR 3 SMALL JARS

4 POUNDS CRAB APPLES
WATER
GRANULATED SUGAR

Wash, de-stem, and cut up (or chop) the apples. Place them in a 1-gallon pot with water just to cover—about 1 quart. Bring slowly to a boil, then simmer the fruit gently, uncovered, for about 1 hour. Stir occasionally and mash the apples once or twice with a potato masher to break up the fruit thoroughly and extract the pectin.

Ladle the softened fruit and juice into a scalded jelly bag and allow the juice to drip for several hours into a large bowl. Measure the strained juice back into the rinsed pot, and for each pint of juice add 2 cups of sugar. Stir over low heat until the sugar has dissolved, then bring to a boil. Boil rapidly, uncovered, until the setting point is reached—about 10 to 15 minutes. Test by dripping two drops of the jelly onto a cold plate. If it's ready, it will set. At that point, take the pot off the heat and skim it, then quickly pour the jelly into small, sterilized jars. Wild apple jelly generally sets very fast.

This makes a beautiful pink jelly with a lovely flavor—great on biscuits or toast, and excellent served with meat or game.

Apple Butter

MAKES TWO 1-POUND JARS

3 POUNDS WILD APPLES
1 CUP APPLE CIDER
1 CUP WATER
BROWN SUGAR
½ TEASPOON EACH CINNAMON, CLOVES, ALLSPICE

Wash the apples, drain them well, and cut them into pieces without peeling or coring. Put them into a large saucepan with the water and cider, and bring to a boil. Simmer, covered, until the fruit is very soft, then press it through a sieve. Allow 1 cup of sugar to each cup of puree. Return the puree to the pan, stir in the sugar with a wooden spoon, and cook over low heat until the sugar has dissolved. Add the spices, bring the mixture to a boil, and simmer it, stirring constantly, until it's smooth and thick. Pour into straight-sided, sterilized jars and seal.

When we stayed in Shenandoah National Park in the Appalachian Mountains, we listened to a talk by one of the park rangers about some of the traditions of the area. Making apple butter was an annual ritual. At the end of the summer, just as the leaves were starting to turn, all the family would go out and pick huge basketfuls of apples, which would then be cooked outdoors in a big cooper kettle over an open fire. The children would make sure that the woodpile was constantly replenished so that the person who was stirring the apple butter with the specially curved stirring stick or paddle would be able to keep the fire blazing at an even temperature. Sometimes night came before the apple butter had attained the correct shade of golden brown and the perfect consistency. Whoever was in charge would then mount a nighttime vigil and continue to stir the pot until the apple butter was ready to be put into jars.

COMMON BARBERRY

Common Barberry, *Berberis vulgaris*, a thorny shrub, grows in thickets, pastures, and old fields, and along roadsides. It flowers from May and June and fruits in August and September.

Found mainly in IA, IL, IN, MA, s.e. ME, MI, MN, n.e. MO, NH, n, NJ, NY, OH, PA, RI, VT, WI. In Canada: s.e. NB, NS, s. ONT, PEI, s. QUE.

The Reverend Manasseh Cutler (1785) comments on both the edible qualities of the barberry and its usefulness in dyeing: "The berries are used for pickles. Boiled with sugar, they form a most agreeable jelly. An infusion of the bark in white wine is purgative. The roots boiled in lye dye wool yellow. In Poland, they dye leather of the most beautiful yellow with the bark of the root. However, it is said, that rye and wheat will be injured by this shrub at the distance of three or four hundred yards; but only when it is in blossom, by means of the *Farina foecundans* being blown upon the grain which prevents the ears from filling."

Barberries were obviously popular with cooks in the 19th century because they are mentioned in biscuit, ice cream, and even catsup recipes in a number of the old cookbooks. They were also used to make jellies or conserves, as we learn from the following quotation from Thomas Tusser in Julia Andrews's *Breakfast, Dinner and Tea* (1859):

*Good housewife provides, ere a
    sickness do come,
Of sundry good things in her house
    to have some;
Conseves of barberry, quinces and
    such.
With sirops, that easeth the sickly
    so much;*

*Good broth and good keeping do much
    now and then,
Good diet with wisdoms best
    comforteth man.*

Barberry Conserve
MAKES 3 PINTS

4 CUPS CRUSHED BARBERRIES
2 WHOLE ORANGES
2 CUPS WATER
1½ CUPS SUGAR
1 (1 OUNCE) PACKET PECTIN

Pick the berries in the fall when their red color is intense. Put them in a saucepan with the oranges and water, and bring to a boil. Simmer, covered, for about 20 minutes, or until the fruit is tender, then strain the juice through a jelly bag or cloth. Return the juices to the saucepan, add the sugar, and bring to a rolling boil. Add the pectin and boil over high heat for 2 minutes. Then put the conserve into hot, sterilized jars and seal.

Barberry Catsup
to Serve with Venison
MAKES FIVE OR SIX 8-OUNCE JARS

10 CUPS RIPE BARBERRIES
½ CUP WATER
1 TABLESPOON FINELY MINCED ONION
1 CUP BROWN SUGAR
⅓ CUP CIDER VINEGAR
1½ TABLESPOONS BUTTER
1 TEASPOON SALT
¼ TEASPOON CAYENNE
**½ TEASPOON EACH GROUND ALLSPICE,
    CLOVES, AND GINGER**

First, make a puree with the fruit. Put the barberries in a large saucepan, barely cover with water, and cook over medium heat, covered, until the fruit is soft. Press the berries through a sieve to separate the pulp from the skin and seeds. There should be about 3 cups of pulp. Put into a saucepan with the rest of the ingredients, bring to a boil, and simmer gently, covered, for 30 to 40 minutes, or until the mixture has thickened. Pour into sterilized jars and seal.

Roast Venison with Wine Sauce

SERVES 10 OR MORE

1 (5-POUND) VENISON ROAST
16 SLICES THICK-CUT BACON

SAUCE:
3 TABLESPOONS FAT FROM THE VENISON
1 TEASPOON SALT
1 TEASPOON PEPPER
½ TEASPOON THYME
½ TEASPOON ROSEMARY
3 CLOVES GARLIC, CRUSHED
3 TABLESPOONS FINELY CHOPPED ONION
1 TABLESPOON FINELY CHOPPED FRESH MINT
1½ CUPS RED WINE

Preheat the oven to 500°F. Place several length of string horizontally on a large board and cover them vertically with eight slices of the bacon. Place the venison on top of the bacon, then put the remaining bacon slices vertically on the meat. Pull up the strings and tie them securely, so that the venison is completely wrapped in bacon. Roast the meat for 15 minutes, remove it from the oven, and turn the heat down to 425°F. Combine 3 tablespoons of the melted fat from the roasting pan with the other sauce ingredients and coat the meat with sauce. Cover the roast loosely with a piece of foil, return it to the oven, and let it roast for 2 to 2½ hours, or until a meat thermometer registers 130°F. Baste it every half hour with the juices in the pan.

Serve with creamed potatoes or parsnips or rutabagas and barberry catsup. The slightly tart, spicy tang of the catsup is the perfect accompaniment to venison, especially for those who don't like their sauces sweet.

ELDERBERRIES

Common Elder, *Sambucus canadensis*, an upright shrub, grows in wet, damp, or rich soil at the edges of the woods, in fencerows, and on riverbanks. It flowers from June to July, and fruits between August and October.

> Found mainly in AL, AR, CT, DE, FL, GA, IA, IL, IN, KY, LA, MA, MD, ME, MI, s. MN, MO, MS, NC, NH, NJ, NY, OH, PA, RI, SC, TN, VA, VT, WI, WV. In Canada: NB, NS, s. ONT, PEI, s. QUE.

Blue Elder, *Sambucus caerulea*, a small tree or large shrub, grows in woodlands and pastures at the edges of fields, on riverbanks, and in gullies. It flowers from May to June, and fruits from August to September.

> Found mainly in AZ, CA, CO, ID, w. MT, OR, WA, and dotted around other western states. In Canada: s. BC.

Black-Berried Elder, *Sambucus melanocarpa*, a large shrub or small tree, grows along washes and streams and on moist slopes. It flowers in March and April, and fruits from July to August.

> Found mainly in AZ, CA, CO, ID, MT, NV, NM, OR, UT, WY.

Gilmore (1911–12) says that the larger stems of the elderberry bush were used by small boys for making popguns. That they could be quite dangerous weapons is confirmed by a reference in Shakespeare's *Henry V*: "a perilous shot out of an elder-gun." The California Indians hollowed out the pithy stems and used them as flutes.

Medicinally, the elder has been used in a variety of ways. Richer in vitamin C than orange juice, elderberry cordial is an effective treatment for coughs or colds, and a hot tea made from the blossoms induces perspiration and is especially useful in cases of bronchitis and similar troubles. In 1899 an American sailor informed a physician of Prague that getting drunk on genuine old dark red port was a sure remedy for rheumatic pains.

Elderberries make terrific jellies, syrups, and wines.

This observation started a long series of investigations ending in the discovery that genuine port wine has practically no anti-neuralgic properties. But the cheap stuff, faked to resemble tawny port by the addition of elderberry juice, often banished the pain of sciatica and other forms of neuralgia, although it is of no avail in genuine neuritis. The dose recommended is 4 tablespoons of elderberry juice mixed with 1 to 2 tablespoons of port wine.

John Evelyn (1699) recommends that the blossoms be infused in vinegar as a salad ingredient, and in Victorian times every household kept a bottle of elderflower water for removing freckles and sunburn.

Mrs. Child (1836) recommends that elder buds be gathered in early spring and mixed with new butter or sweet lard as a healing and soothing ointment.

Ripe elderberries can be eaten raw or dried like raisins, and used in pies or in muffin recipes. The flower clusters can be dipped in batter and deep-fried, or a cup of blossoms can be added to a pancake batter or a fresh, mixed salad. Delicious wines and soft drinks can be made from the fruits and blossoms, and elderberry jelly is an unusual accompaniment to turkey or game.

Elderflower Fritters

SERVES 4

1 CUP FLOUR
1 EGG
1¼ CUPS TEPID WATER
PINCH OF SALT
12 ELDERFLOWER HEADS
COOKING OIL OR FAT

Make a batter of the first four ingredients. Hold the flower heads by their stalks and dip them into the batter until thoroughly coated. Deep-fry them in very hot oil or fat until golden brown. Drain on paper towels and trim off the excess stalks. Serve hot, sprinkled with sugar.

Elderflower Champagne

MAKES 5 QUARTS

3½ CUPS SUGAR
1 LEMON
4 ELDERFLOWER HEADS IN FULL BLOWN
2 TABLESPOONS WHITE VINEGAR
5 QUARTS COLD WATER

Dissolve the sugar in a little warm water and allow the mixture to cool. Squeeze the juice of the lemon and cut the rind in quarters. Then put the juice and pieces of peel with the elderflowers in a large jar or basin, add the vinegar and dissolved sugar, and pour on the cold water. Mix and let the must steep for 4 days. Strain off and bottle the champagne in screw-topped bottles. It should be ready to drink in 6 to 10 days, but test after 6 days anyway, to see that it does not get too fizzy. If it fails to work, leave it for another week; sometimes the natural yeast of the flowers is very slow to get going, and occasionally you will get a batch that fails altogether. Some people say you should pick the flowers on a sunny day, though I have picked them in the rain and had success with them.

I advise everyone to make this fragrant champagne. It is a very refreshing summer drink served chilled or with ice and lemon.

Elderflower Water Ice

SERVES 4

1¾ CUPS WATER
⅓ CUP SUGAR
¾ CUP LEMON JUICE
2 TABLESPOONS GRATED LEMON RIND
2 TABLESPOONS DRIED ELDERFLOWERS

In a heavy pan, bring the water and sugar to a boil over moderate heat, stirring constantly, and wash down any sugar crystals clinging to the sides of the pan with a brush dipped in cold water, until the sugar has dissolved. Boil the syrup for 5 minutes, then stir in the lemon juice and rind. Put the elderflowers in a double thickness of cheesecloth and tie the ends with string. Add to the syrup mixture and heat for 5 minutes. Remove the pan from the heat and cool. Remove the elderflowers and squeeze out the excess liquid. Pour the mixture into freezing containers and freeze, stirring every hour for 4 hours, or until the ice is well blended and firm.

This recipe is adapted from Pamela Harlech and was first published in *Vogue* (1975).

Light Elderberry Wine

MAKES 5 QUARTS

2½ CUPS ELDERBERRIES
WATER
2 CAMPDEN TABLETS
1 PACKET BREWER'S YEAST
5 CUPS SUGAR
1 OUNCE PECTIC ENZYME

CAUTION: Campden tablets may be detrimental to asthma sufferers.

Pull the berries off the stalks with a dinner fork, put them in a strong polyethylene bag, and crush them thoroughly with a rolling pin to break the skins. Then put them in a 2-gallon crock, or similar container, and add 2½ quarts of boiling water and the Campden tablets. Mix well, cover, and leave overnight. The next day, activate the yeast by following the instructions on the packet. Boil 2½ quarts of water, add the sugar, and allow it to dissolve. Let the sugar water cool, then add it, along with the pectic enzyme and the activated yeast, to the crock. Stir well. Put the must in a gallon jar, fit an air lock, and leave for 3 days. The color will return to normal at this stage. Strain through a dampened jelly bag and pour the liquid into a clean jar. Insert an air lock and leave in a warm place (75° to 80°F) to ferment out (approximately 6 weeks). Siphon off the wine into a clean jar, leaving the sediment, and let it stand until clear. Repeat this process if necessary. Bottle and store in a cool place. The wine will be ready to drink in a year.

Elderberry Syrup

RIPE ELDERBERRIES
WATER
SUGAR
CLOVES

Pick the berries on a dry day. Strip them from the stems, then wash and dry them thoroughly. Put them in a saucepan, add just enough water to cover, and bring to a boil. Simmer, covered, for 30 minutes, or until the berries are soft. Strain them through a dampened jelly bag or cloth and measure the juice as you return it to the pan. For each pint of juice add 2½ cups of sugar and 10 cloves, and mix well. Heat the mixture gently, stirring until the sugar has dissolved, then bring to a boil and simmer, covered, for 10 minutes, stirring occasionally. Remove from the heat and allow to cool. The syrup may be frozen in small quantities, or it may be refrigerated after being packed into small, screw-topped, soft-drink bottles that have been sterilized.

Elderberry syrups of this kind have been used since Tudor times to relieve colds and chest troubles and bring on a sweat. They are normally diluted. Allow 2 tablespoons of syrup to a tumbler of hot water and a squeeze of lemon juice. A little whiskey may be added if you like. A few drops added to a glass of wine makes an excellent aperitif.

Elderberry and Apple Jelly

MAKES THREE 1-POUND JARS

RIND OF 1 ORANGE
½ STICK CINNAMON
10 COOKING APPLES
1½ CUPS ELDERBERRIES, WASHED
3 PINTS WATER
SUGAR

Tie the orange rind and the cinnamon stick together with cotton thread. Wash the apples well, then chop them roughly and put them in a pan with the elderberries. Add the water, bring to a boil, and simmer, covered, until the apples are a pulp. Turn the pulp into a dampened jelly bag and let it drip overnight. Measure the juice as you pour it back into the pan. Add 1 cup of sugar for each cup of juice, and heat gently, stirring constantly, until the sugar has dissolved. Then add the orange rind and cinnamon, and boil rapidly until the setting point is reached. Test by dripping two drops of the jelly onto a cold plate. If they set, the jelly is ready. Remove the orange rind and cinnamon, pour the jelly into small, warmed jam jars, and seal.

This soft-jelly recipe comes from Liz Roman's *Fenland Village Cookery Book* (1977).

WILD ROSES

California Rose, *Rosa california*, a tall shrub with stiff, curved spines, grows along streams, in marshes, and in moist canyons below 6,500 feet. It flowers from May to July, and fruits between September and November.

Found mainly in CA and s. OR.

The hips of the California rose

The hips of the wrinkled rose

Wrinkled Rose, *Rosa rugosa*, a large, spiny shrub with dark green, wrinkled leaves, grows on roadsides and sand dunes, and in seashore thickets. It flowers from June to September, and fruits from September to November.

Found mainly in CT, IL, MA, ME, n. MI,
n.e. MN, NH, w. NY, n. OH, RI, n. WI.
In Canada: NB, NS, s. ONT, PEI, s. QUE.

Wild Rose, *Rosa carolina*, a low slender shrub with broad-based, straight spines, grows in dry, sandy woodlands, in fields, and on rocky outcrops. It flowers from May to July, and fruits between September and October.

Found mainly in AL, AR, n. CT, DE, FL, GA, IA,
IL, IN, s.e. KS, KY, LA, MA, MD, s. ME, MI, MN,
MO, MS, NC, NH, NJ, NY, OH, e. OK, PA, RI,
SC, TN, e. TX, VA, VT, WI, WV.

Eglantine or **Sweetbrier Rose**, *Rosa eglanteria*, a tallish shrub with broad-based and recurved spines, grows in thickets and clearings, on roadsides, and in abandoned pastures and fencerows. It flowers from May to July, and fruits between September and October.

Found throughout North America.

The Indians ate the berries (rose hips) in times of food scarcity. Although they did not know that the berries were 20 times richer in vitamin C than oranges, they prepared a tea from the leaves, which they drank for colds, and some tribes ground the dried petals and mixed them with grease to make a mouth salve.

Rose hips can be used in jams, jellies, and sauces.

Dried and ground they make a vitamin- and mineral-rich tea. The young leaves can also be used for tea or in salads, and the crystallized flower petals make pretty candy.

Rose Hip Soup (Nyponsoppa)
SERVES 6

5 CUPS ROSE HIPS
5 PINTS WATER
¾ CUP SUGAR
1 TABLESPOON CORNSTARCH
   MIXED WITH 1 TABLESPOON WATER
¼ CUP SLIVERED ALMONDS

Rinse the rose hips, put them in a saucepan with the water, bring to a boil, and simmer them, covered, until they are soft. While cooking, stir the soup vigorously now and again. Strain, add the sugar and the cornstarch/water mixture, and bring to a boil again. Serve in individual bowls with the almonds sprinkled on top.

This recipe came to me from Sweden, where it is a popular winter dish.

Rose Hip Syrup
MAKES 2-3 PINTS

10 CUPS ROSE HIPS
3 QUARTS WATER
1½ CUPS SUGAR

De-stalk and wash the rose hips, then chop or mince them. (Don't leave the rose hips lying about once they are prepared or the valuable vitamin C content will be lost.) Bring 2 quarts of the water to a boil, add the rose hips, and bring to a boil again. Remove the pan from the heat, cover it, and let the rose hips infuse for 15 minutes. Ladle the rose hips and liquid into a scalded jelly bag and allow the bulk of the juice to drip through. Then transfer the pulp from the jelly bag to the saucepan. Bring the remaining quart of water to a boil and add it to the pulp. Bring to a boil and infuse as before, this time for 10 minutes. Again, strain the pulp though the jelly bag. Combine the juices from the two infusions into a clean saucepan and simmer until the amount of liquid is reduced to about 1 quart. Add the sugar, bring the mixture to a boil, stirring constantly, and cook over high heat, uncovered, for 5 minutes. Immediately pour the syrup into hot, scalded jars. Leave ¼ inch of headroom and adjust the lids. Process in a hot-water bath at 190°F for 30 minutes. Then remove the jars and complete the seals if needed.

Rose Hip Wine

MAKES 1 GALLON

10 CUPS ROSE HIPS
5 QUARTS BOILING WATER
5 CUPS SUGAR
1 QUART COLD WATER
JUICE OF 1 LEMON
JUICE OF 1 ORANGE
2 TEASPOONS BREWER'S YEAST

Be sure to pick the rose hips after the first frost and use them immediately to conserve the vitamin C content. Mince them, place them in a bucket, and cover them with the boiling water. Stir with a long-handled spoon or a rolling pin. Allow the must to stand, covered with a cloth, for 3 days. Stir daily—it will be quite stiff to stir—then strain it through a wine bag into another bucket. Prepare a syrup by combining the sugar, cold water, and citrus juices in a saucepan and bringing the mixture to a boil to dissolve the sugar. Add the syrup to the wine juice and pour the mixture into a fermentation jar. Activate the yeast according to the directions on the packet, then add it to the must. Top up the amount of liquid with boiled, cooled water to within 1 inch of the top of the jar and fit with an air lock. Leave to work until clear, then siphon the wine into a clean container and keep for 3 months. By then it should be ready to drink, but it improves if allowed to keep for a few more months.

VIBURNUMS

Nannyberry, *Viburnum lentago*, a large shrub or small tree, grows on the borders of woods, along streambanks, and in swamps. It flowers in May and June, and fruits from August to October.

Found mainly in CT, IA, n. IL, n. IN, MA, s. ME, MI, MN, e. ND, NH, NY, n. OH, PA, RI, VT, WI, e. WV. In Canada: MAN, ONT.

Highbush Cranberry, *Viburnum trilobum*, a coarse shrub or small tree, grows in cool woods and thickets, and on rocky slopes, shores, and streambanks. It flowers from the end of May to July, and fruits in September and October.

Found mainly in n.e. IA, n. ID, n. IL, n. IN, ME, MI, MN, MT, ND, NH, NY, n. OH, PA, w. SD, VT, WI, n.e. WY. In Canada: all provinces.

There are more than 20 species of *Viburnum* commonly found growing throughout the United States, and many have fruits that, even if rather tart or bitter when raw, can be cooked and made into jellies, jams, sauces, and beverages. The fruits should be picked late in the summer, and in some cases during the winter, to ensure that they are fully ripe. Highbush cranberry is no relation to the store-bought variety, but its fruit can be

Nannyberries

made into a sauce similar to cranberry sauce and is used as such in some parts of the country. The sweetened juice can be diluted to make a drink rich in vitamin C or, with pectin added, used to make a beautifully flavored, clear jelly.

AMERICAN MOUNTAIN ASH

American Mountain Ash, *Sorbus americana*, a small tree or shrub with smooth, grayish bark, grows in moist or rocky soils on hillsides or ridges. It fruits from August to October.

Found mainly in n. MA, ME, n.e. MN, NH, NY, n. PA, VT, WI. In Canada: NB, NFLD, NS, ONT, PEI, QUE.

American mountain ash

Traditionally, in Britain, the fruit was distilled into a wine, spirit, or ale, but in recent times its most common use has been as a tart but agreeable jelly to accompany venison, game, or fowl. The berries are very bitter to eat raw but are more palatable if picked after several frosts.

Mountain Ash Jelly
MAKES ABOUT FOUR 1-POUND JARS

2 POUNDS JUICY APPLES
5 CUPS WATER
3 POUNDS MOUNTAIN ASH BERRIES
BROWN OR WHITE SUGAR

Peel, slice, and core the apples. Put them and the water in a saucepan, bring to a boil, and boil until soft (20 minutes). Add the berries and simmer until the mixture is a pulp. Strain through a jelly bag into another pan and measure. You will need 1 pound of sugar for each pint of juice. Warm the sugar in a separate pan. Boil the juice, uncovered, for 10 minutes and then add the warmed sugar. Stir until dissolved, then boil for another 10 minutes, skimming constantly. Pour into jars and tie down at once.

Adapted from Lyndsay Shearer's recipe, which came from May Buchan's "Common Place Book." This is a lovely old recipe, but I found that the brown sugar tends to make too strong a taste, so I prefer to use white.

HAWTHORN

Hawthorn, *Crataegus* species. The hawthorns are easy to recognize. Whether shrubs or small trees, they all have long, sharp thorns, most of them bear white flowers, and they all have yellow-to-red or black berries that usually ripen in the fall. But the individual species are a subject of academic debate and are extremely difficult to separate.

Found throughout North America.

Almost all hawthorn fruits are edible, but some are dry and flavorless. One species, *Crataegus tomentosa*, was praised by Peter Kalm in 1749 for its fragrant white flowers and fruit, which, he wrote in his diary, "is very good eating when it is ripe."

Palmer (1870) says the fruit of *Crataegus coccinea* was eaten by the Indians either fresh or mixed with chokecherries and serviceberries, then bruised, pressed into cakes, and dried for winter use. A century earlier, Manasseh Cutler (1785) wrote that an ardent "spirit" could be distilled from the juice of the hawthorn.

The berries are most commonly used to make excellent jams and jellies, or they can be steeped to make a tea, or dried and stored for winter use.

Haw Wine

MAKES 1 GALLON

- 4 POUNDS HAWTHORN BERRIES
- 5 QUARTS BOILING WATER
- JUICE AND THINLY PEELED RIND OF 1 LEMON
- JUICE AND THINLY PEELED RIND OF 2 ORANGES
- 5 CUPS SUGAR, BROWN OR GRANULATED
- 1 PINT COLD WATER
- 2 TEASPOONS BREWER'S YEAST

Put the berries in a large bowl and pour the boiling water over them. Let them stand, covered with a cloth, for a week. Stir daily. Then put the lemon and orange rinds and juices in a bucket and strain the berries over them. Make a sugar syrup by putting the sugar and cold water into a saucepan and heating until the sugar is completely dissolved. Stir thoroughly, then cool for 5 minutes. Add to the bucket. Activate the yeast, add it to the bucket, cover with a cloth, and leave for 24 hours. Then transfer the mixture to a fermentation jar and ferment to finish.

This makes a very delicate pink wine that seems to benefit from keeping. If you find it hazy, use pectic enzyme to clear it (follow the directions on the packet).

Haw's Turkish Delight

- 5 CUPS HAWTHORN BERRIES
- 2 CUPS WATER
- JUICE OF 1 LEMON
- SUGAR

De-stalk the berries, put them in a saucepan with the water and lemon juice, and bring to a boil. Simmer, covered, for 45 minutes, stirring from time to time. Put the pulp and liquid in a jelly bag and let them drip into a large bowl overnight. The next day, discard the pulp and measure the juice. Stir in 2½ cups of sugar for every 2 cups of juice, then heat gently until it comes to a boil. Boil the juice rapidly until a really firm setting point is reached. Test by dripping two drops of the jelly onto a cold saucer; if the jelly sets, it's ready. Pour the jelly into small molds (an ice cube tray is good) and leave it to set. The result is a stiff, delicately flavored jelly that can be cut with a knife, dusted with confectioners' sugar, and served with coffee after dinner.

California grapes

Riverbank grapes

WILD GRAPES

California Grape, *Vitis californica*, a large, climbing, woody vine, grows along streams and in canyons and forest clearings, often twinning around trees or dead stumps. It flowers in May to June, and fruits from August to October.

Found mainly in CA and s. OR.

Riverbank Grape, *Vitis riparia*, a pithy, high-climbing vine, grows on riverbanks in rich thickets. It flowers from May to July, and fruits in August and September.

Found mainly in AL, AR, DE, n.w. GA, IA, IL, IN, KY, LA, MA, MD, s.w. ME, MI, MN, MO, MS, ND, NH, NJ, NY, OH, e. OK, RI, n. SD, TN, e. TX, n. VA, VT, WI, WV. In Canada: s. MAN, s. ONT.

Frost Grape, *Vitis vulpina*, a high-climbing vine, grows along riverbanks and in bottomlands and thickets. It flowers from May to June, and fruits from September to October.

Found mainly in AL, AR, CT, DE, n. FL, GA, s. IL, IN, KY, LA, MD, MO, NC, NJ, OH, PA, RI, SC, TN, e. TX, VA, WV.

Northern Fox Grape, *Vitis labrusca*, a trailing or high-climbing vine with a few purply black grapes, grows in wet or dry thickets on the edges of woods. It flowers from May to July, and fruits from September to October.

Found mainly in CT, DE, GA, IN, KY, MA, MD, s. ME, MI, NC, NH, NY, OH, PA, RI, SC, TN, VA, VT, WV.

NOTE: It is from this grape that many horticultural varieties have been bred, including the Concord grape.

Frost grapes

Northern fox grapes

Silverleaf or **Blueleaf Grape**, *Vitis argentifolia*, a high-climbing vine with bluish black grapes, grows in dry woods and thickets. It flowers from the end of May to the end of July, and fruits from September to October.

Found mainly in AL, CT, DE, IL, IN, KS, KY, MA, MD, MI, s. MN, MO, NH, OH, PA, RI, s.e. VA, VT, WV.

Jacques Cartier in 1535, Peter Kalm in 1748, and William Clark in 1804 all commented on the profusion of wild grapes they saw as they traveled through the American interior. The various species of wild grape were a useful article of food for pioneers and Indians in all parts of North America. William Bartram (1791) says the Indians prepared them for keeping "by first sweating them on hurdles over a gentle fire and afterwards they dry them on their bunches in the sun, and air, and store them up for provisions." According to Palmer (1878), the Utah Indians would grind up grape seeds and eat them, or grind up dried grapes and cook them. A Pawnee told Gilmore (1911–12) that his tribe sometimes tapped large vines in the spring and collected the sap to drink fresh.

Most species of wild grape are too acid to eat in quantity in their fresh state, unless they are really ripe, but nearly all varieties, or a mixture of them, make fine juice, jellies, pies, preserves, and wines. The unripe fruit is very rich in vitamin C and an excellent source of pectin. You can also collect tender young leaves in June and cook them as a vegetable, or use them to wrap around meat and rice to make stuffed vine leaves.

Wild Grape Conserve

MAKES FOUR 1-POUND JARS

12 CUPS GRAPES
STRIP OF ORANGE PEEL, ½ X 2 INCHES
JUICE OF 1 ORANGE
4 CUPS SUGAR, OR 8 CUPS IF MUCH OF THE FRUIT
    IS UNRIPE
1 CUP FINELY CHOPPED NUTS OF CHOICE (OPTIONAL)

Put the grapes and orange peel in a large saucepan, cover with water, and bring to a boil. Simmer, covered, for 30 minutes, stirring occasionally, then strain through a coarse sieve. Return the juice to the pan, add the sugar, and simmer for about 1 hour, or until the mixture sets when a few drops are put on a cold saucer. Stir in the nuts (if used) and simmer for another 5 minutes, then pour the jelly into sterilized jars and seal.

I like to pick the fruit when about 20 percent of the grapes are still green. This gives a slightly tart flavor to the conserve, which I prefer.

Frosted Wild Grapes

Take individual ripe grapes and cut off half the stalk. Have ready in one dish some beaten egg white, and in another, some granulated sugar. Dip each grape into the egg white, then roll it in the sugar. Put a cake rack on the kitchen stove or some other warm surface, and lay a sheet of white paper over it; then spread the grapes on the paper and leave until the "icing" hardens.

This recipe is adapted from one in Miss Leslie's *Directions for Cookery, in Its Various Branches* (1837). It makes a beautiful dessert for an outdoor summer feast.

chapter eight
NUTS & SEEDS

American Chestnut, *Castanea dentata*, page 154

WILD RICE

Wild Rice, *Zizania aquatica,* a tall annual grass, grows in quiet waters—in marshes, lakes, streams, and the mouth of rivers, and in bays of fresh or brackish water. It flowers from July to September, and the seeds ripen at the end of this period.

Found mainly in AL, e. AR, CT, DE, n. FL, GA, IA, ID, IL, IN, KY, LA, MA, MD, ME, MI, MN, e. MO, MS, MT, NC, ND, NH, NJ, NY, OH, n. OR, PA, RI, SC, n.e. SD, TN, s.e. TX, VA, VT, WA, WV. In Canada: s. ALTA, s. MAN, NB, NS, s. ONT, s. QUE, s. SASK.

Wild rice can be very common on riverbanks and along estuaries.

Indian rice, *wild oats, folle avoine,* and *manomin* are all names for wild rice, which has, throughout the centuries, been such an important article of diet among the Indians who live in the areas where it grows in profusion. In his *Voyages . . . Among North American Indians, 1652-1684,* the explorer Pierre Esprit Radisson describes a feast he shared with the Dakota: "Our songs being finished, we began our teeth to worke. We had there a kind of rice, much like oats . . . that is their food for the most part of the winter, and due dresse it thus: for each man a handful of that they putt in the pott that swells so much that it can suffice a man."

The explorer Jonathan Carver (1766) explains the Indian method of harvesting wild rice: "This grain, which grows in the greatest plenty throughout the interior parts of North America, is the most valuable of all the spontaneous productions of that country. Exclusive of its utility, as a supply of food for those of the human species who inhabit this part of the continent . . . the sweetness and nutritious quality of it attracts an infinite number of wild fowl of every kind, which flock from distant climes to enjoy this rare repast; and by it become inexpressibly fat and delicious . . . The natives gather the grain in the following manner: nearly about the time that it begins to turn from its milky state and to ripen, they run their canoes into the midst of it, and tying bunches of it together just below the ears with bark, leave it in this situation three or four weeks longer, till it is perfectly ripe. About the latter end of September they return to the river, when each family, having its separate allotment and being able to distinguish their own property by the manner of fastening the sheaves, gather in the portion that belongs to them. This they do by placing their canoes close to the bunches of rice, in such position as to receive the grain when it falls, and then beat it out, with pieces of wood."

Indians being particularly fond of soup, their most common dishes were soups or mushes of wild rice with meat or game or fish, and a soup made of wild rice and blueberries was, apparently, eagerly sought after by those who had been living on salt food for several weeks. The Sandy Lake Indians esteemed wild rice a luxury when boiled with rabbit excrement! Although, according to the trader John Long, an Indian mother suckled her child until it was four or five years old and sometimes older, the Indians valued wild rice as a dietary supplement for their children. (Actually, wild rice is richer in carbohydrates than any of our common cereals and very rich in crude protein, or albuminoids.) They made a pap from wild rice and oats, "which being cleansed from the husk, and pounded between two stones, are boiled in water with maple syrup: this food is reckoned very nourishing." We made this dish and gave it to our year-old daughter, Phoebe, for breakfast, and she walloped it down far faster than her normal cereal.

In fact, wild rice is not a rice but a kind of grass seed that swells up just as grains do when cooked in water. It can be used instead of ordinary rice in any dish. It can also be ground into flour and substituted in part for ordinary flour in baking. Following the Indian tradition, we like it best served with game or fish, although rather than stuffing the game birds, which you can do, we serve the rice separately.

Wild Rice with Quail

SERVES 2

2 CUPS WILD RICE
1⅓ CUPS WATER
2 TABLESPOONS FINELY CHOPPED AND MIXED
    CHERVIL, DILL, AND PARSLEY
2 QUAILS, PLUCKED AND GUTTED
SALT AND PEPPER TO TASTE
1 TEASPOON BUTTER

SAUCE:
1 TABLESPOON WINE VINEGAR
½ TEASPOON MUSTARD
SALT AND PEPPER TO TASTE
2 TABLESPOONS OLIVE OIL

Wash the rice thoroughly in cold, running water and drain. Bring the water to a boil in a saucepan with a tightly fitting lid, add the rice, cover, and steam over low heat for 45 minutes, or until the water is absorbed. Remove the pan from the heat and allow the rice to cool, then combine it thoroughly with the herbs and spread the mixture on a warm serving platter.

While the rice is cooking, roast the quails. Preheat the oven to 450°F, season the quails inside and out with salt and pepper, and anoint them with the butter. Place them in a small roasting pan and roast for 20 minutes. Check to see how tender they are after 15 minutes, then baste them and return them to the oven for another 5 minutes. When they are done, put them on a plate in the bottom of the oven to keep warm while you make the sauce.

Pour off the butter in which the quails were cooked and add the wine vinegar to the roasting pan. Simmer briefly, scraping up the juices and caramelized deposits. Pour immediately into a bowl and add the mustard, salt and pepper, and olive oil. Mix well and check the seasoning. Place the quails on the rice and pour the sauce over the whole dish.

A fitting repast for an Indian chief.

Wild Rice and Fish Soup

SERVES 4

4 SLICES BACON
1 ONION, FINELY CHOPPED
1 CLOVE GARLIC, CRUSHED
1 CUP MILK
1 CUP WATER
1 TEASPOON MIXED FRESH HERBS
1 TEASPOON SALT
½ TEASPOON PEPPER
1 MEDIUM-SIZED BASS, GUTTED AND CLEANED
    (OR USE ANY OTHER FISH YOU CAN CATCH)
1 CUP WILD RICE, THOROUGHLY WASHED
    AND DRAINED
CREAM OR BUTTER, FOR SERVIING

Put the cold bacon into a heavy saucepan over medium heat, and when there is sufficient fat, add the onion and garlic and sauté gently for 5 minutes. Add the milk, water, herbs, salt, and pepper, and poach the fish in the stock for 3 to 5 minutes, keeping the temperature below the boiling point. When the fish is cooked, remove and fillet it, then set the flesh aside. Return the remains to the stock and poach for another 15 minutes to extract all the flavor, then strain. Bring the stock to a boil in a saucepan with a tightly fitting lid, add the wild rice, cover, and steam over low heat for about 45 minutes, or until the rice is cooked; add bite-sized pieces of fish to the soup and heat through for a minute. Pour into individual bowls and add a spoonful of cream or a knob of butter to each bowl just before serving.

Several historical accounts mention that the Indians made a wild rice and fish soup, so we thought we would experiment with one too. It was well worth the effort, we decided.

Wild Spinach and Smoked Trout with Spinach Sauce

SERVES 4

¾ CUP WILD RICE
1⅓ CUPS WATER
1–2 HEADS RED CHICORY (RADICCHIO)
2 TEASPOONS FINELY CHOPPED FENNEL LEAVES
1 MEDIUM-SIZED SMOKED TROUT
SALT AND PEPPER TO TASTE

SAUCE:
2 CUPS FRESH SPINACH LEAVES
½ CUP SOUR CREAM
SALT AND PEPPER TO TASTE

Wash the rice thoroughly and drain. Bring the water to a boil in a saucepan with a tightly fitting lid, add the rice, cover, and cook over low heat for 45 minutes, or until all the water is absorbed. Transfer the rice to a bowl and allow it to cool.

Wash the red chicory and dry with paper towels or in a salad spinner. Set aside 6 to 8 large, outer leaves. Finely slice the remaining leaves and add them, along with the fennel, to the cooled rice. Flake the trout, removing any bones and skin, and add it also. Mix and season to taste.

To make the sauce, first wash the spinach thoroughly, then cook it, covered, in the water remaining on the leaves, for 8 minutes, over low heat. Strain out as much liquid as possible. Put the spinach and sour cream in a blender and blend at high speed until the mixture is smooth and a vibrant green. Add salt and pepper to taste.

Pour the sauce into a small bowl and place it in the center of a large plate. Arrange the reserved chicory leaves decoratively around the bowl and spoon the wild rice salad into them.

This recipe comes from Jacqui Hurst.

Pinyon pine cone

PINE NUTS

Pinyon Pine, *Pinus edulis*, a bushy, cone-bearing tree, grows on plateaus and lower mountain slopes at elevations of 4,600 to 7,400 feet, often with juniper. The ripe, open cones should be gathered in August.

Found mainly in n.e. AZ, s.w. CO, NM, NV, TX, UT, WY.

Digger Pine or **Bull Pine**, *Pinus sabiniana*, a cone-bearing tree with a thick, scaly trunk, grows on foothills and lower mountain slopes at elevations below 5,000 feet, frequently with blue oak. The second-year cones should be gathered in August.

Found mainly in CA.

Other species bearing tasty pine nuts are the single-leaf pinyon (*Pinus monophylla*), the Parry pinyon (*P. quadrifolia*), and the sugar pine (*P. lambertiana*).

The nuts of all *Pinus* species are edible, although some are much more agreeable to eat than others, and consequently formed an important and nutritious article of food for the Indians who lived in the areas where they grow. According to Chesnut (1902), a nutritive-value analysis of *P. sabiniana* revealed that the kernels were principally composed of a rich, fatty oil (51 percent) and crude protein (28.5 percent).

Chesnut says that the pitchy exudation from all parts of the pine was used to fasten feathers to arrows and that "in former times, the Yukis [of northwestern California] used to smear their bodies with it and then cover themselves with feathers in order to present a more formidable appearance in times of battle." Also, after pricking a tattoo design into the skin with a sharpened bone of one of the awl-like leaves of a California nutmeg, they rubbed the pine-pitch soot into the design (the soot was esteemed as the best pigment for the purpose).

The Yukis also made the wood of the pine into poles, and with the more pliable wood next to the roots they constructed baskets for carrying acorns.

Medicinally, Chesnut says, the Yukis used the pitch extensively as a protective and healing covering for burns and sores. They drank an infusion of the bark, and also had a novel way of using the small twigs and leaves in the treatment of rheumatism and bodily bruises: "A fire is built over some rocks and allowed to burn down. The pine twigs are then thrown upon the warm ashes and the patient, wrapped well in blankets, lies down upon them. Water is occasionally sprinkled on the rocks beneath so that steam, together with the volatile oil from the leaves is constantly given off. After inhaling this and sweating most profusely for 8–10 hours, the patient is said to be invariably able to move without pain."

Although pine nuts can be eaten raw, many of them are more digestible roasted. Frederick Colville (1892) describes how they were collected and prepared for consumption: "In early autumn, after the seeds have matured, but before the cone scales have opened, the cones are beaten from the trees, gathered in baskets, and spread out on a smooth piece of ground exposed to the heat of the sun. The scales soon become dry and crack apart, and the seeds are shaken out by blows from a stick or the more persistent ones rattled out by hand. The empty cones are then removed from the ground and the seeds gathered in baskets. Large quantities of pine nuts are thus collected, and most of them are cached in dry places among the rocks for use during the year. They are said to remain fresh and edible for several years if properly stored."

Today, to prepare pine nuts for food, they are put into a basket with some live coals and shaken or stirred until they are roasted. In this state pine nuts are often sold in markets in California and other western states, being disposed of precisely as peanuts are in the East. Shelled, the roasted nuts may be munched whole or ground in a wooden mortar with a stone pestle and eaten dry or made into a soup.

The nuts of *Pinus edulis* are probably the tastiest. They can be eaten either raw or roasted, or they can be ground into flour and added to pancake, muffin, or cake recipes or to soups and stews, to give body and flavor. Ground pinyon nuts can be boiled with honey and water to make a nutritious baby gruel or cooked with vegetables to make a tasty vegetarian soup. Whole, roasted nuts make a crunchy addition to salads and risottos or sprinkled on quiches and pies.

Pasta and Pinyon Nut Salad

SERVES 4–6

½ RIPE AVOCADO

3 TABLESPOONS MAYONNAISE

5 CUPS COOKED GREEN PASTA SHELLS

1 GREEN BELL PEPPER, THINLY SLICED

1 BUNCH SCALLIONS, THINLY SLICED
   (WHITE PART ONLY)

SEVERAL SPRIGS OF FRESH CILANTRO,
   FINELY CHOPPED

SMALL BOX FRESH ALFALFA SPROUTS

½ CUP SHELLED PINYON NUTS

Put the avocado and mayonnaise through a sieve to make a smooth green paste, then coast the pasta shells thoroughly with this dressing. Stir the pepper, scallions, and cilantro into the salad, sprinkle the top with alfalfa sprouts, and lastly add the pinyon nuts.

The crunchiness of the nuts is a perfect counterbalance to the smooth texture of the pasta and avocado.

JUNIPER BERRIES

Rocky Mountain Juniper, *Juniperus scopulorum*, a large, evergreen shrub with reddish gray, scaly bark, grows on ridges, cliffs, and dry, rocky hillsides up to 9,800 feet. It flowers in April, but the fruit takes two years to ripen and is covered in a blue bloom.

Found mainly in AZ, ID, s.w. MT, s.w. ND, NM, w. SD, UT, e. WA, WY. In Canada: BC.

Checkered-Bark Juniper, *Juniperus deppeana*, a medium-sized tree, is remarkable for the way in which the bark breaks into neat, square plates, thereby giving it its common name. It grows on dry mountain slopes to an elevation of about 6,500 feet, and the fruit ripens in the fall of the second year.

Found mainly in AZ, NM, TX, and MEX.

According to Palmer (1878), the Indians of Southern California consumed intense quantities of the California juniper fruit, which is sweet and could be eaten as soon as it was ripe. When dried, it was either ground fine and made into bread, which he describes as having a "chaffy and saw-dust consistency," or boiled in water to make a mush. He concludes: "It must be nutritious, as the Indians got fat on it." Similarly, the Utes ate the fruit of the Utah juniper either raw or made into bread, and they used the fibrous bark to make saddles, breechclouts, skirts, and sleeping mats.

Colville (1892) explains how husting bows for killing small game were made from the desert juniper: "The Indian prefers a piece of wood from the trunk or a large limb of a tree that has died and seasoned while standing. One must remember that at low altitudes in these desert mountains moist rot of dead wood never occurs, but that a mature tree subjected to the intensely dry heat of the region is in perfect condition for this use. The bow rarely exceeds three feet in length, and is strengthened by glueing to its back a covering composed of strips of deer sinew laid lengthwise along it. The string is made of twisted sinew, or sometimes of cord prepared and twisted from

Checkered-bark juniper

from other trees, to name a specific juniper is much more difficult, and the berries of some varieties are much stronger in flavor than others. You will probably need to experiment before finding one you enjoy eating.

T-Bone Steaks with Juniper Berries

SERVES 4

4 T-BONE STEAKS
1 (8–10 OUNCE) JAR OF WHOLE-GRAIN
    DIJON MUSTARD
¼ CUP CRUSHED JUNIPER BERRIES

First of all, get the fire going really well so that you have a bed of glowing coals or wood. Throw a few handfuls of juniper needles on the fire to release the strong, aromatic smell, which will flavor the meat.

Spread the steaks generously on one side with mustard and crushed juniper berries, then barbecue them on the open grill, mustard-side-up first, for 3 to 4 minutes, then turn and repeat. The amount of time depends on how rare you like your meat. If you are in the middle of the desert, as I once was, and have no plates, serve the steaks on a bed of juniper branches.

Rocky mountain juniper berries

Indian hemp." Peter Kalm, in a diary entry of 1749, says that because of its pleasant smell, the shavings and chips of Virginia juniper were put among linen to secure it against worms.

Although the Indians were fond of eating juniper berries, many other people find their rather resinous taste unpleasant if they are eaten in any quantity. The berries are best picked as they ripen, usually after two seasons, and used as a seasoning. A few fresh, crushed berries sprinkled over veal or lamb, before roasting, impart an interesting but extremely pungent flavor to the meat. The roasted and dried berries can also be ground and used as a coffee substitute.

Although junipers are quite easy to distinguish

OAKS

White Oak, *Quercus alba*, a large tree with flaky, ash-gray bark, grows in moist or dry woods in sandy or gravelly soil. It fruits from August to September.

Found mainly in AL, AR, CT, DE, GA, IA, IL, IN, KY, n.w. LA, MA, MD, s. ME, MI, e. MN, MO, MS, NC, s. NH, NJ, NY, OH, PA, RI, SC, TN, n.e. TX, VA, VT, WV. In Canada: s. ONT, s. QUE.

Chestnut Oak, *Quercus prinus*, a medium-sized tree with dark, furrowed bark, grows in dry or moist rocky woods and on bluffs, ridges, and crests. It fruits from August to September.

Found mainly in n. AL, CT, DE, n. GA, s. IN, KY, MA, MD, w. NC, NJ, e. OH, PA, RI, n.w. SC, TN, VA, WV. In Canada: s. ONT.

California White Oak, or **Valley Oak**, *Quercus lobata*, a tall, deciduous tree, grows below 2,000 feet on slopes, in valleys, and on foothills. It flowers from March to April, and fruits in September and October.

Found mainly in CA.

California white oak acorns

The numerous species of oaks, both white and red, to be found throughout North America provided an important source of food for natives, explorers, and animals from the earliest times. Thomas Heriot, in his description of Virginia in 1585, wrote about "oak-acorns, which also by the experience and use of the inhabitants, we find to yield very good and sweet oil."

In a description in Alexander Young's *Chronicles of the Pilgrim Fathers, 1602-25*, an Indian dwelling includes two or three basketfuls of parched acorns "among sundry other things such as harts horns, eagles' claws, two or three deer's heads and a piece of broiled herring."

William Bartram (1791) tells us that turkeys became extremely fat and delicious from feeding on the sweet acorns of the live oak.

Chesnut (1902) gives an extremely detailed account of the way the Indians of Mendocino County, California, prepared and cooked acorns for consumption: "When the acorns are ripe in autumn the men go out and beat them off the tree or cut off the small branches and throw them to the ground. The squaws collect them in a large conical carrying basket. These are carried on the back, but are suspended by a broad band from the forehead. Both hands are therefore free for picking up the acorns, which are thrown backward with unerring aim into the basket. As much as seven or eight large basketfuls—some 400 or 500 pounds—may thus be gathered by one family for a year's supply. At home the nuts are first spread out in the sun until thoroughly dry, when they are sometimes cracked either with the teeth or by means of a small stone and still further dried for future use, or are stored away in the houses with the shells on.

"When ready for use for kernels are usually dry and rather brittle. They are first thoroughly pulverised in a curious mortar, which contains essentially of three parts—a large, flat stone; a shallow, basin-like, but bottomless basket, and a stone pestle. The basket is held in place on the stone by the legs of the operator—always an old squaw or a superannuated brave, who alone has the requisite patience and unlimited time—and the pounding is done upon the flat stone. The basket serves admirably to prevent the particles from flying away, and it fits so closely and is held so firmly to the stone that no meal is lost. This process requires a very considerable amount of time, and consequently the everlasting thump, thump, thump, of the pestle is a characteristic sound heard at many of the Indian settlements about midday . . . After the tannin has been removed, the acorn meal has the consistency of ordinary dough. It is sometimes converted into bread while still in the sand by building a fire around it; but this method is objectionable on account of the sand which adheres to the bread and the loss of the oil, which, when hot, passes into the sand. A considerable quantity is scooped out from the center of the depression, and this, which is entirely free from sand, is reserved and afterwards made into bread. The remainder of the dough, with, perhaps, a little of the adhering sand is converted into soup. The sand rapidly settles to the bottom and does not, therefore, contaminate the soup in any way. Water-tight baskets were the only cooking vessels which the natives originally possessed, and they are still very largely used in the process of soup making, the source of heat being hot rocks, which are placed in with the meal and water. Two pieces of green wood, used like a pair of tongs, serve to carry the rocks from the fire to the basket and again to the fire. Before being placed in the basket, however, each is sometimes washed free from ashes by plunging it once or twice into a basin of water. When cooked, the mush has very much the same appearance as corn-meal porridge, but is usually brownish red. It has a slightly sweetish taste, but it is, on the whole, rather insipid and unsavoury. Nevertheless, it is very much esteemed by nearly all of these Indians even at the present time, and many Americans who are more or less accustomed to it prefer it to other kinds of mush. According to its consistency, or to the whims of the eaters, it is eaten by dipping one, two, or three fingers into the basket, which serves as a common receptacle, and thus conveying the thick, gruel-like soup to the mouth, or it may be dipped out by a big mussel shell. This shell is known to the Yukis are *nok*, a name which they apply to spoons also. Spoon and separate dishes have been recently in-

troduced. No salt is used in the mush, although it is generally used with all kinds of pinole.

"The dough selected for acorn bread is mixed with red clay before it is baked, the proportion being about 1 pound of clay to 20 of dough. This clay, several Indians explained, makes the bread sweet. Others stated that it 'acted like yeast.' The mixture is placed on a bed of soaproot, oak, maple, or even poison-oak leaves, which in turn rests on a bed of rocks previously heated by a small fire. The dough is then covered with leaves and a layer of hot rocks and dirt and cooked gently in this primitive oven for about twelve hours, usually over night. When removed the next morning the bread, if previously mixed with clay, is as black as jet. It is remarkable for being sweet, for the original meal and even the soup are rather insipid. The sweet taste is very evident, and is due in great measure to the prolonged and gentle cooking, which, favored by the moisture of the dough, gradually converts some constituent of the meal into sugar, as in the case of camas bulbs.

"All kinds of acorns are appreciated by the Indians of Mendocino County for their fattening power, and it is remarkable, especially in early life, how fat they become on this diet. Those acorns which contain the most oil are most highly valued for food, and it was the meal from these that used to be employed by the squaws to groom their warriors after they had returned from battle. The annual harvest was in former days heralded by a kind of thanksgiving dance, and during this performance a special acorn song was sung. The Concow version of this is as follows:

> The acorns come down from heaven.
> I plant the short acorns in the valley
> I plant the long acorns in the valley.
> I sprout, I, the black acorn, sprout, I
>   sprout.

"Oak wood is used very little for fuel or timber, but some kinds are frequently used for making tool handles, mauls, and paddles. The bark taken from the fallen trees is especially useful in the process of baking and in parching pinole seeds in baskets, because it burns slowly without flame for a long time . . ."

Although the acorns of all oaks are edible, those that come from white oaks are generally much sweeter and more palatable than those from red or black oaks. The latter are usually bitter and astringent because of their high tannin content. Even so, once the tannin has been removed, these acorns can be dried, roasted, and ground into meal, and then used to make fat- and protein-rich bread, cakes, and muffins, or cooked with meat to make a hearty stew.

TO REMOVE THE TANNIN

If you are camping or living near a clear, running steam, simply place dry, whole, shelled acorns or ground acorn meal in a cloth or bag and leave it in the stream for several days to leach. When the water runs clear around and through the bag, the tannin has been removed. If you are not fortunate enough to have a stream flowing through your inner-city apartment, soak the bag of nuts or meal in boiling water until the water turns brown, then drain and repeat the process until the water remains clear. Spread the leached nutmeats or meal in a pan and dry in the sun or a warm oven, then grind. Even meal will need regrinding before use.

Acorn Coffee

I find that if you boil the acorns whole for 15 minutes you make it easier both to get the shell and peel off and to reduce their bitterness. Boil and peel the acorns, then split and dry them. After they have dried for a day or so, grind them in a coffee grinder and roast them in the oven or under a grill, watching all the time to see they do not burn; they should be a good, brown, coffee color. Infuse about 1½ teaspoons per cup of boiling water for a few minutes before serving. The taste does not resemble coffee, but it is quite pleasant with milk and sugar.

CHESTNUTS

Allegheny Chinquapin or **Eastern Chinquapin**, *Castanea pumila*, a spreading shrub or small tree, is found in dry woods, on mountain slopes, in thickets, and in dry, sandy soil along the Atlantic coast. It fruits from September to October.

Found mainly in AL, AR, DE, FL, GA, KY, LA, MD, MS, MO, NC, NJ, OH, OK, PA, SC, TX, VA, WV.

American Chestnut, *Castanea dentata*. A fatal fungus blight has almost totally wiped out this species, although stumps can be found regenerating even to the extent of bearing fruit.

The generic name for the chestnut, *Castanea*, is derived from the town of Castanis in Thessaly, where the tree grew in great abundance. The American variety also grew prodigiously. The early explorers and pioneers found it everywhere. The 16th-century traveler Thomas Heriot says of American chestnuts: "There are in divers places great store: some they use to eat raw; some they stamp and boil to make spoon-meat, and with some being sodden, they make such a manner of dough bread as they use of their beans before mentioned."

They were also a wholesome source of food for the Jesuit missionary explorers, as we learn from an account by Father Marquette (1678)–who, as far as I can see, must be referring to a chestnut: "There are also, in the prairies, fruit resembling our filberts, but more tender; the leaves are larger, and spring from a stalk crowned at the top with a head like a sunflower, in which all of these nuts are neatly arranged; they are very good cooked or raw."

Chestnuts are flatulent if eaten raw, so it is advisable to boil or roast them. The nuts are such a good source of food that in some Mediterranean countries they are a staple food, often dried and ground into flour. In the Apennine Mountains of Italy and the Peloponnesus of Greece, in Sicily, Madeira, and the south of France, the poorer people used to subsist largely on a diet of chestnuts. Nor were they valued only by the poor. The ancient Persian nobility, according to Xenophon,

Allegheny chinquapins

coming into use. But both are good, and deserving of more attention than they have hitherto received.

"Those who regard a dish of boiled chestnuts as forming a vulgar dinner, can easily form them into pies, puddings, bread, cakes, etc. They may be boiled and mashed; or, if it should be preferred, they can be ground into a sort of flour before they are cooked. The flour and meal may also be mixed with various other kinds of flour or meal, to form such compounds as the fancy or the judgment may direct."

One compound from chinquapin flour to which our fancy and judgment direct us is marrons glacés. Other favorites are using chinquapins to make a turkey stuffing or a hearty soup, although the roasting of chestnuts or chinquapins in front of an open fire on a frosty winter evening requires a lot of beating. Remember to prick the skins first, unless you want to entertain the company with a minor war!

Chestnut Stuffing for Roast Turkey
STUFFING FOR A 15- TO 20-POUND TURKEY

2 POUNDS FRESH CHESTNUTS OR CHINQUAPINS
1 MINCED TURKEY LIVER
2½ CUPS PORK SAUSAGE MEAT, UNCOOKED
PINCH OF ALLSPICE
SALT AND PEPPER TO TASTE
⅓ CUP BUTTER
1 ONION, CHOPPED
¾ CUP BRANDY

Split the chestnuts or chinquapins (to keep them from exploding) and heat them for a few minutes in a hot oven, then peel them, making sure to get rid of the bitter inner peel. Cover the nutmeats with water, bring to a boil, and simmer, covered, for 15 minutes or until tender. Then strain and mince them. Put them in a large bowl, stir in the liver and sausage meat, and flavor with the allspice, salt, and pepper.

Heat the butter in a small pan, sauté the onion until soft but not brown, and add it to the mixture in the large bowl. Then pour in the brandy and mix well again. Using your hands, fill the inside of the turkey.

were fattened on chestnuts, and two thousand years later coffeehouses in Lucca and Persia served delicious chestnut pâtés, muffins, and tarts.

Chestnuts may be boiled, roasted, or made into puddings, cakes, bread, and porridge. In Europe, even the flowers are not neglected. John Evelyn (1679) tells us, "They also made fritters of Chestnut-flower which they wet with Rosewater, and sprinkle with grated parmegiano, and so fry them in fresh Butter, a delicate."

William Alcott (1842) gives an (unintentionally) amusing account of his views on the chestnut: "The chestnut, in its raw state, is highly nutritious to swine and many other quadrupeds. To say that it would be equally so to man, even were he early trained to its use, would be to affirm what I believe we could not very well prove . . .

"In the south of Europe the chestnut is much used for bread, puddings, etc; and is regarded as pretty wholesome. Of late it has been exported, considerably, to this country, and is gradually

Marrons Glacés

Split fresh chestnuts or chinquapins and boil them vigorously in their skins for a few minutes to make it easy to skin them. Remove the skins and simmer the nutmeats, covered, for about 20 minutes to soften them. Drain off the water, cover the nutmeats with a sugar syrup made of 4 parts sugar dissolved in 1 part water, and simmer them slowly, uncovered, for 1 hour. Make sure they do not stick or boil over. Remove them from the syrup with a slotted spoon and coat them thickly with sugar. Then put them on an ungreased cookie sheet and bake them for 3 to 4 minutes in a preheated 350°F oven. After taking them from the oven, squeeze a drop of lemon juice on each and dust them with sugar.

BUTTERNUT & WALNUTS

Butternut, *Juglans cinerea*, a large tree with deeply ridged gray bark, grows in rich woods and deciduous forests, and on floodplains. It flowers from April to June, and fruits in October and November.

Found mainly in CT, e. IA, IL, IN, KY, MA, s. ME, MI, e. MN, MO, w. NC, NH, NJ, NY, OH, PA, RI, TN, w. VA, VT, WI, WV. In Canada: s. NB, s. QUE.

California Walnut, *Juglans california*, a large tree with thickly furrowed, dark brown bark, grows in gravelly soils along streams and rivers, and in bottomlands usually below 3,300 feet. It flowers in April, and fruits in October.

Found in CA.

Black Walnut, *Juglans nigra*, a large tree with dark, furrowed bark, grows in rich woods and bottomlands, and on floodplains, and is commonly planted. It flowers from April to June, and fruits in October and November.

Found mainly in AL, AR, CT, DE, n. FL, GA, IA, IL, IN, e. KS, KY, n. LA, w. MA, MD, s. ME, s, MI, s, MN, MO, MS, NC, NJ, NY, OH, OK, PA, RI, w. SC, s.e. SD, TN, e. TX, VA, s. WI, WV.

Many sources tell us that the Indians ate a great quantity of all kinds of nuts, including walnuts. As early as 1585, Thomas Heriot lists walnuts among the commodities of Virginia that could be merchantable: "There are two sorts of walnuts both holding oil: but the one far more plentiful than the other. When there are mills and other devices for the purpose, a commodity of them may be raised, because there are an infinite store."

Captain John Smith, writing in 1606, described how the Indians got around the difficulty of cracking walnuts in order to make nut milk: "When they need walnuts to break them between two stones, yet some part of the shels will cleave to the fruit. Then doe they dry them againe upon a mat over a hurdle. After they put it into a morter of wood, and beat it very small: that done they mix it with water, that the shells may sink to the bottome. This water will be coloured as milk, which they call Pawcohiccora, and keepe it for their use."

The nuts should be gathered in the fall when they drop from the trees, and although the shells are often difficult to crack (it is best to apply pressure at right angles to the seam), they are well worth the effort and very sweet to eat fresh. Alternatively, young nuts can be pickled whole.

A superb vegetable oil can be extracted by crushing, then boiling, the nuts and shells. The oil will give a distinctive flavor to a stir-fry or a salad. In early spring, the trees can be tapped for sap and the sap prepared in the same way as maple syrup (see page 173).

Pickled Walnuts

Gather immature nuts and scald them to remove the outer fuzz. Bring fresh water to a boil, add the nuts, and simmer them, uncovered, until the water discolors. Drain and repeat the process with fresh boiling water until the water remains clear.

Pack the nutmeats into a sterilized quart jar along with 1 dill flower, 3 walnut leaflets, 1 heaping teaspoon of pickling spices, 1 teaspoon of salt, and ¼ teaspoon of alum. Fill the jar with boiling cider vinegar. Seal and keep for at least 1 month.

Serve with cold meats.

Walnut Fudge

MAKES ABOUT 30 PIECES

2½ CUPS BROWN SUGAR
1½ CUPS LIGHT CREAM
1 TABLESPOON CORN SYRUP
½ TEASPOON VANILLA EXTRACT
1 CUP NUTMEATS

Put the sugar, cream, and syrup into a saucepan and bring to a boil over medium heat, stirring constantly. Continue to boil, stirring frequently, until the mixture starts to thicken (15 to 20 minutes). Remove the pan from the stove, add the vanilla, toss in the walnuts, and stir quickly until the fudge thickens. Pour into a buttered 6 x 6 x 1-inch pan, mark into squares with a knife, and leave to cool.

Walnut Ice Cream

"One pint of the meat of walnuts (the American are the best), pounded fine into a mortar; one pint of milk, one quart of cream, two small cupfuls of sugar, four eggs, one-fourth of a teaspoonful of salt. Beat the eggs with one cupful of sugar. Put them and the milk in the double boiler, and stir constantly until the mixture begins to thicken; then add the salt, and put away to cool. When cold, add the cream and nut meat, and freeze."

From *Miss Parloa's New Cook Book and Marketing Guide* (1880).

The nuts of the walnuts and hickories. Left to right: English walnuts, butternuts, bitternut hickories (below), black walnuts, shagbark hickories, shellbark hickories (above), pecans, mockernut hickories.

PECAN & HICKORIES

Pecan, *Carya illinoensis*, a tall tree with ridged bark, grows in bottomlands and woods in rich, moist soil. The thin-shelled nuts should be gathered in the fall when the leaves begin to turn.

> Found mainly in AL, AR, DE, n. FL, GA, IL, IN, KY, n. LA, MD, s. MO, MS, NC, e. OK, s. PA, SC, TN, e. TX, VA, WI, WV.

Shagbark Hickory, *Carya ovata*, a medium to tall tree with gray, shaggy bark, grows in rich woods and river bottoms and on dry upland slopes. The thin-shelled nuts should be gathered in early fall.

> Found mainly in n. AL, AR, FL, n. GA, ME, MI, MN, MS, NE, n.e. TX, WI. In Canada: s. ONT, s.w. QUE.

Big Shellbark Hickory, *Carya laciniosa*, a large tree with light gray, slightly shaggy bark, grows in rich woods and bottomlands and on floodplains. The thick-shelled nuts should be gathered in early fall.

> Found mainly in IL, IN, KY, MI, OH, TN, WV; locally in AL, AR, KS, MS, NJ, NY, OK, PA.

Mockernut Hickory, *Carya tomentosa* (synonym *C. alba*), is a large tree with dark gray, deeply furrowed bark. It grows in dry to moist soil on hills and slopes and in woods and river valleys. The thick-shelled nuts should be gathered in the fall as the leaves turn.

> Found mainly in AL, AR, CT, DE, n. FL, GA, s.e. IA, IL, IN, KY, n.w. LA, MA, MD, ME, MO, MS, NC, s. NE, s. NH, s. OH, PA, SC, TN, s.e. TX, VA, s. VT, WV. In Canada: s. ONT.

Hickory Nut Cake, Pecan Pie, and Pecan Penuche

Pecans and hickory nuts were an important article in the diet of the Indians whom the Spanish conquistador Cabeza de Vaca encountered in his march across the Southwest (1542): "Two days after Lope de Ovideo departed, the Indians reached the place we had been told of, to eat pecans. These are ground with a kind of small grain and furnish the sole subsistence of the people for two months of the year—and not every year, because the trees only bear every other year. The nut is the same size as [the walnut of] Galacia; the trees are massive and numberless." (Apparently, these groves where the Indians began nutcracking were 10 or 12 leagues above the Bay, on the lower Colorado, and tribes converged there from a distance of 20 and 30 leagues. In the course of the gathering season they worked a great distance upriver.)

Other early accounts explain how the Indians made a delicious juice from pecans. In 1749, Peter Kalm told the following story by a 92-year-old Swede, Nils Gustafsen: "They likewise prepared a kind of liquor like milk in the following manner: they gathered a great number of hiccory nuts and walnuts from the black walnut trees, dried and crushed them; then they took out the kernels, pounded them fine as flour, and mixed this flour with water, which took a milky hue from them, and was as sweet as milk."

There are many ways to use hickory nuts and hundreds of recipes into which they can be incorporated or substituted, so it is up to you to decide your personal favorite. They can be added to breads, cakes, cookies, or sweets. They can be mixed with honey to make nut butter, or the nutmeats can be ground and added to an oil-and-vinegar dressing to give a distinctive (and addictive!) flavor to salads. In early spring the trees can be tapped for sap and the sap made into syrup by following the method described for maple syrup (page 173). The hickory syrup can be used in any recipe calling for maple syrup or maple sugar.

Hickory Nut Cake

MAKES ONE 8-INCH CAKE

½ CUP (1 STICK) BUTTER
1½ CUPS SUGAR
¾ CUP WATER
2 CUPS FLOUR
WHITES OF 4 EGGS, BEATEN UNTIL FROTHY
1 CUP HICKORY NUTMEATS, FINELY CHOPPED
1 TEASPOON BAKING POWDER

Preheat the oven to 350°F. Beat the butter and sugar into a cream, then add the water and flour, and stir until smooth. Add half the egg whites, then the nuts, then the remainder of the whites, and the baking powder. Pour into an 8-inch-square flat pan lined with buttered paper to the depth of 3 inches and bake for 60 minutes.

This scrumptious cake recipe is taken from *Mrs. Rorer's Philadelphia Cook Book* (1886).

Pecan Pie

MAKES ONE 9-INCH PIE

PASTRY:
1½ CUPS ALL-PURPOSE FLOUR
¾ TEASPOON SALT
½ CUP (1 STICK) BUTTER OR BUTTER AND SHORTENING
2–3 TEASPOONS COLD WATER

FILLING:
2 EGGS
1 CUP LIGHT OR DARK CORN SYRUP
½–1 CUP BROWN SUGAR
1 TEASPOON VANILLA EXTRACT
    OR 2 TABLESPOONS RUM
¼ TEASPOON SALT
1 CUP PECAN HALVES
1 TABLESPOON BUTTER

First, make the pastry. Sift the flour and salt together. Add the butter and cut it into the flour with two knives, or rub it in with your fingers, until the mixture is in pieces the size of large bread crumbs. Add the water, a few drops at a time, and toss the mixture with a fork to combine the ingredients evenly. The dough should not be wet but just moist enough to hold together in a ball. Chill the dough in the refrigerator for 15 to 20 minutes before rolling out. Grease a deep 9-inch pie tin, line it with the pastry, and crimp the edges.

Then make the filling. Preheat the oven to 450°F. Beat the eggs in a mixing bowl and stir in the syrup, sugar, flavoring, and salt. Arrange half the pecans in a pattern on the pastry, pressing them into the dough slightly. Pour the filling mixture gently over the nuts, then arrange the rest of the pecans in patterns on the top. Dot with the butter and bake for 10 minutes, then lower the heat to 325°F and bake until the filling is almost firm to the center—about 30 minutes.

Allow the pie to cool in the pan for a couple of hours before serving so that the filling has time to harden and get deliciously chewy. If you are using a shallow, loose-bottomed tart pan, halve the filling quantities.

This is adapted from a recipe in James Beard's *American Cookery* (1972).

Pecan Penuche

MAKES 36 PIECES

2 CUPS DARK BROWN SUGAR
¾ CUP MILK
⅛ TEASPOON SALT
2½ TEASPOONS BUTTER, IN SMALL PIECES
1 TEASPOON VANILLA
¾ CUP CHOPPED PECANS

Oil an 8 x 8 x 2-inch pan. Mix the sugar, milk, and salt in a large, heavy saucepan, bring to a boil over medium heat, and cook, stirring constantly, until the sugar dissolves. Cover the pan and continue and cook, still over medium heat, for 3 minutes. Remove the lid and cook, without stirring unless the syrup starts to stick, for another 15 minutes, until the firm-ball stage is reached—244°F on a candy thermometer. (Alternatively, test by dropping a teaspoon of syrup in cold water; if the syrup remains almost intact, the right temperature has been reached.) Now remove the pan from the heat and reduce the temperature rapidly by putting the saucepan into a larger pan filled with cold water. Drop in the butter, and when it has melted, beat the mixture until it starts to thicken, then stir in the vanilla and pecans. You will need to work quite quickly as the candy thickens rapidly. Pour the mixture into the oiled pan and mark into squares. When firm (after half an hour in the refrigerator), cut it into pieces and put them into an airtight jar.

Once on the table, this candy disappears in minutes if your friends and family have a sweet tooth.

The recipe has been adapted from Fannie Farmer's *Boston Cooking-School Cook Book* (1896).

Hazelnuts

HAZELNUTS

American Hazelnut or **Filbert**, *Corylus americana*, a tall shrub with hard-shelled nuts, grows in thickets and woodlands, It fruits between July and September.

> Found mainly in n. AL, AR, CT, DE, n. GA, IA, IL, IN, e. KS, KY, MA, MD, s. ME, MI, MN, MO, NC, ND, e. NE, NH, NJ, NY, OH, n.e. OK, PA, RI, n. SC, e. SD, TN, VA, VT, WI, WV. In Canada: s. MAN, s. ONT.

Beaked Hazelnut, *Corylus cornuta*, a shrub with thin-shelled nuts, grows in rich thickets and clearings on the borders of dry or moist woodlands, and on mountain slopes. It fruits from August to September.

> Found mainly in n. CA, n. GA, IA, ID, IL, IN, e. KS, MA, ME, MI, MN, MO, MT, e. NC, ND, NH, NJ, NY, OH, OR, RI, SD, VT, WA, WI, WV, WY. In Canada: s. ALTA, s.e. BC, s. NB, NS, s. ONT.

Known as "ol mam" to the Yuki Indians, the rich, nutritious nuts of the hazelnut were gathered by the sackful in the fall, and supplies lasted until the following spring. Palmer (1870) says that the Indians east of the Missouri River and in Arkansas consumed enormous quantities at any one time— "an amount," he says, "which would be unsafe for more civilized stomachs."

Hazelnut Bread and Hazelnut Salad

Hazelnut Bread

MAKES 1 LOAF

1 CUP CHOPPED DATES
1 CUP HOT MILK
2 CUPS ALL-PURPOSE FLOUR
1 TEASPOON SALT
2 TEASPOONS BAKING POWDER
1 CUP CHOPPED HAZELNUTS
3 TABLESPOONS SHORTENING
¾ CUP BROWN SUGAR
2 EGGS, BEATEN

Grease a 9 x 5 x 4-inch bread tin thoroughly and preheat the oven to 350°F. Soak the dates in the milk and set aside. Combine the flour, salt, baking powder, and nuts in a bowl. Cream the shortening and sugar together in a second bowl and add the eggs. Mix well. Stir the flour mixture and the date mixture alternately into the creamed sugar and eggs, blending thoroughly after each addition, until all the ingredients are combined. Pour the dough into the bread tin, sprinkle the top with a little sugar and some chopped hazelnuts, and bake for about 50 minutes.

Hazelnut Salad

SERVES 2

4 RED LETTUCE LEAVES
1½ CUPS CUBED BLUE CHEESE
½ CUP SHELLED HAZELNUTS
½ ZUCCHINI, FINELY SLICED
½ APPLE, FINELY SLICED
2 STALKS CELERY, THINLY SLICED
2 TABLESPOONS HAZELNUT OIL
A FEW DROPS OF LEMON JUICE OR VINEGAR
SALT AND PEPPER TO TASTE

Line a large salad plate with lettuce and fill the center with the cheese, topped with the hazelnuts. Decorate around the cheese with the zucchini, apple, and celery slices. Just before serving sprinkle with the hazelnut oil, lemon, and seasonings.

Hazelnut Meringue and Hazelnut Nougat

Hazelnut Nougat

ENOUGH FOR ABOUT 20 NIBBLES

2 CUPS WHOLE HAZELNUTS, SHELLED
1 CUP SUGAR
1 CUP CORN SYRUP
½ CUP HONEY
1 EGG WHITE
3 TABLESPOONS WATER

Place the water, sugar, glucose, and honey in a saucepan and bring slowly to a boil over low heat, watching constantly at first—the mixture can quickly boil over. Meanwhile, in a large bowl, beat the egg white until stiff. Spread the hazelnuts on a marble or glass surface or on rice paper. Continue boiling the syrup until it almost reaches the soft-crack stage (270°F). Then remove the pan from the heat and gradually pour the hot mixture into the bowl with the egg white, whisking all the time. After 2 or 3 minutes it will turn pure white and start to stiffen. Keep on whisking until the whisk will hardly move, then spoon the mixture over the nuts. Leave for an hour to cool and set. The timing of the syrup and egg whisking is rather tricky, but the result always tastes delicious even if you take it a bit too far.

Hazelnut Meringue

SERVES 6

1 CUP HAZELNUTS, CHOPPED FINELY IN A BLENDER
1 CUP ALMONDS, GROUND FINELY IN A BLENDER
6 EGG WHITES
1½ CUPS SUGAR
1 CUP HEAVY CREAM
1–2 CUPS FRESH OR FROZEN FRUIT

Preheat the oven to 325°F. Mix the hazelnuts and almonds together. Whisk the egg whites to stiff peaks. Add half the sugar and whisk again until the mixture is stiff and shiny. Fold in the remaining sugar and the nuts. Brush three 9-inch layer-cake pans lightly with oil and line with circles of oiled baking parchment. Divide the mixture among the pans, spreading it evenly and lightly with a spatula to the edges of each pan. Bake for 45 minutes. Leave in the pans for 5 minutes and then turn onto cooling racks, carefully removing the paper from the bases. Leave until cold. Whip the cream until stiff, then assemble the layers of meringue with the whipped cream and fruit in between.

chapter nine
ROOTS & SAP

Wapato tubers, *Sagittaria latifolia,* page 170

COMMON BURDOCK

Common Burdock, *Arctium minus*, a biennial herb, grows commonly on wasteland, in vacant lots, and along roadsides. It flowers from July to October.

> Found in all states except those in the Deep South. In Canada: all provinces.

The ubiquitous burdock, which was introduced from Europe and Asia, requires considerable effort to harvest. The roots go down so deep that only a good spade can dislodge them. As early settlers found, the effort is well worthwhile. When Peter Kalm visited Fort Frederick in 1749, he found burdock growing profusely. The governor told him that the tender shoots were eaten in the spring like radishes, after the exterior peel had been removed.

Burdock has often been credited with a number of recuperative qualities. In early times it was used for the treatment of leprosy, and it has always been considered one of the finest blood purifiers. Mrs. Child (1836) says, "Housekeepers should always dry leaves of the burdock and horseradish. Burdock warmed in vinegar, with the hard stalky bits cut out, is very soothing, applied to the feet; they produce a sweet and gentle perspiration."

The roots, which should be collected from the first-year plants in June and July, can be boiled and served with butter as a vegetable, and the young leafstalks can be peeled and used in salads or casseroles. The Japanese cultivate burdock as a vegetable, and in England burdock beer is still popular.

Boiled Burdock Stems

Use the young shoots, leaf stems, and flower stalks. Peel to leave only the soft core, and slice into ¼-inch pieces. Simmer, covered, for 6 to 10 minutes in just enough water to cover the bottom of the pan. Drain well and serve with melted butter and freshly ground black pepper.

Burdock Boiled Dry

Cut young burdock roots into long, thin pieces the size of matchsticks. Place them in a heavy saucepan, cover them with water, and add a good dash of soy sauce and a small pinch of salt. Bring to a boil and simmer, covered, for 15 minutes, then remove the lid and continue cooking to allow the juices to evaporate and the soy sauce flavor to be absorbed by the cooked roots. Make sure that the burdock does not stick. The flavor of the burdock pieces will be strong and interesting—well worth the trouble of cooking them.

Roasted Burdock

Roll whole, cleaned burdock roots in fresh young burdock leaves, then wrap them in aluminum foil. Roast them in hot ashes for 45 to 60 minutes. Serve with soy sauce. In Japan, people who live in the mountains eat the roots prepared like this in fall and winter.

This and the previous recipe have been adapted from Cornellia Aihara's *Chico-San Cookbook* (1972).

GOAT'S BEARD

Goat's Beard, *Tragopogon pratensis*, a tall perennial or biennial herb with numerous yellow flowers, grows in fields and on rocky banks and roadsides. It flowers from May to July.

Found mainly in n.e. AZ, CO, CT, DE, IA, ID, IL, IN, KS, KY, ME, MA, MD, MI, MN, MO, s.w. MT, NC, NE, NH, NJ, n.w. NM, NV, NY, OH, PA, RI, SD, TN, UT, VT, VA, WA, WI, WV, WY. In Canada: s.w. BC, NB, NFLD, NS, s. ONT, PEI, s. QUE.

Introduced from Europe, goat's beard and the closely related purple-flowered salisfy *(Tragopogon porrifolius)* have grown wild over much of the United States. The very young leaves of either plant can be used in salad or as a potherb, but they are sometimes rather bitter and will need to be blanched. The ground, roasted roots have been used as a coffee substitute, but they are much more commonly eaten as a vegetable.

Salisfy

"Having scraped the salisfy roots, and washed them in cold water, parboil them. Then take them out, drain them, cut them into pieces, and fry them in butter.

"Salisfy is frequently stewed slowly till quite tender, and then served up with melted butter. Or it may be first boiled, then grated, and made into cakes to be fried in butter.

"Salisfy must not be left exposed to the air, or it will turn blackish."

This recipe is reprinted from Miss Leslie's *Directions for Cookery, in Its Various Branches* (1837).

Goat's beard

Groundnut tubers and the flowers that help you locate them.

GROUNDNUT

Groundnut, *Apios americana*, a perennial, twines around nearby plants in rich, moist soil in woodlands, on streambanks, and in thickets. It flowers from June to September.

> Found mainly in AL, AR, CT, DE, FL, GA, IA, IL, IN, e. KS, KY, LA, MA, MD, ME, MI, MN, MO, MS, s.e. NC, NE, NH, NJ, NY, OH, e. OK, PA, RI, SC, SD, TN, e. TX, VA, VT, WI, WY, e. WY. In Canada: s. ONT and s. QUE.

From the very earliest accounts we learn that the first explorers and settlers recognized the nutritive value of the groundnut, or hopniss, as the Indians called it.

Thomas Heriot, in his report on Virginia (1585), calls them Openauk and describes them as follows: "A kind of roots of round form, some of the bigness [of] walnuts, some far greater, which are found in moist and marsh grounds, growing many together one by another in ropes, as though they were fastened with a string. Being boiled or baked they are very good meat. Monardes call these roots beads, or Peter Nostri of Santa Helena."

In 1623, according to Alexander Young's account, the Pilgrim Fathers were trying to solve the problem of famine at the Weston Colony but were themselves victims of hunger: "For our own parts, our case was almost the same with theirs, having but a small quantity of corn left, and were enforced to live on *groundnuts*, clams, muscles, and such other things as naturally the country afforded, and which did and would maintain strength, and were easy to be gotten; all which things they had in great abundance."

The Swedish traveler Peter Kalm was extremely interested in the food of the Indians and gives this account of the groundnut in a diary entry of 1749: "Hopniss or Hapniss was the Indian name of a wild plant which they ate at that time. The Swedes still call it by that name, and it grows in the meadows in a good soil. The roots resemble potatoes, and were boiled by the Indians, who eat them instead of bread. Some of the Swedes at that time likewise ate this root for want of bread. Some of the English eat them instead of potatoes. Mr. Bartram told me that the Indians who live farther in the country do not only eat these roots, which are equal in goodness to potatoes, but likewise take the peas which lie in the pods of this plant, and prepare them like common pease. Dr Linnaeus calls the plant Glycine Apios." The Portuguese botanist Jose Correa de Serra thought so highly of the groundnut that he could not understand why neither the Indians nor the settlers attempted to cultivate it. In a letter of 1821 he wrote that groundnuts "deserve a place among our culinary vegetables."

Many people prefer this vegetable to the potato, and it can be eaten boiled, roasted, or fried. The seeds, if gathered while still bright green, can be boiled and eaten as peas.

Boiled Groundnuts

Collect as many tubers or "beads" as you can. This is hard work, following the twining vines to their source and digging to locate the roots. However, once you find one, you usually find several others joined to it by skinny roots resembling thin strings.

Scrub the tubers clean and simmer them, covered, in salted water for about 15 minutes. When they are tender, either serve them like boiled potatoes, with a generous knob of butter, or slice and toss them in bacon fat. Either way is tasty.

CHUFA OR YELLOW NUT GRASS

Chufa or **Yellow Nut Grass**, *Cyperus esculentus*, a perennial herb, grows in sandy fields, ditches, and waste places, and on the margins of ponds and streams. It flowers from June to October.

Found mainly in AL, AR, w. CA, e. CO, CT, DE, FL, GA, IA, IL, IN, KS, KY, LA, MA, MD, ME, MI, MN, MO, MS, MT, NC, ND, NE, NH, NJ, e. NM, NY, OH, OK, PA, RI, SC, SD, TN, TX, VA, VT, WI, WV, WY. In Canada: ALTA, s. MAN, NB, NFLD, NS, s. ONT, PEI, s. QUE, s. SASK.

Chufa or yellow nut grass

Chufa has been cultivated in many parts of the world because of its edible, nut-like tubers, and the existence of chufa tubers in ancient Egyptian tombs indicates that its history goes back thousands of years.

Havard (1895) says: "The chufa and the nut grass are extremely noxious weeds in the eastern and southern states and account for their rapid propagation by tuberiferous stolens and difficult extirpation. The Indians, however, looked on them with favor because of the small edible tubers, especially those of the chufa which are sweet and palatable and even now occasionally planted as food for swine."

According to Rafinesque (1823–30), mush, cakes, coffee, chocolate, and a fine, sweet, golden oil can be made from chufa. Furthermore, the roots are diuretic and useful after fevers.

The tubers contain a milky juice and have a sweetish, nutty taste. They can be eaten fresh or raw as a vegetable, or dried and ground into a delicious flour and used in cake, cookie, and candy recipes. Roasted until dark brown, then ground, chufa makes a coffee-like drink, and a cold drink called *horchata de chufa* in Spanish is very popular, particularly with children.

Horchata de Chufa

MAKES 3 CUPS

2 CUPS TUBERS, SCRUBBED CLEAN
¼ CUP SUGAR
2 CUPS WATER

Soak the tubers in water for 2 days to soften, then drain them. Puree them in a blender along with the sugar and the 2 cups of fresh water. Serve with crushed ice.

HORSERADISH

Horseradish, *Armoracia lapathifolia*, an introduced perennial, has escaped from cultivation and grows in moist soil. It flowers from May to July.

Found throughout North America.

Although horseradish was introduced into North America by the early European settlers and flourishes in the wild, it seems to be neglected by most of the modern books on edible wild plants, which pay little attention to it. Yet it appears to have been quite commonly used in the last century. Miss Leslie, in her *Directions for Cookery, in Its Various Branches* (1837), suggests using horseradish to make a horseradish vinegar.

Horseradish has been cultivated in its native area (Eastern Europe and Turkey) for over 2,000 years. The Germans and Slavs were probably the first people in Europe to use it, grated in sauces and pickles, and its use as a condiment reached England during the 17th century. Before this time, both the roots and leaves were used universally as a medicine, and it was one of the bitter herbs eaten by the Jews during Passover. John Pechy (1694) says of it: "It provokes the Appetite, but it hurts the Head."

A spade is essential when gathering horseradish, because the plant carries an extensive and complex root system. Pare away the brown layer with a sharp knife and grate the root for use. This

Horseradish

is best done out of doors. When you are preparing it, be careful: Horseradish makes the eyes run— it is almost worse than onions for making one cry.

Homemade Horseradish Sauce

½ CUP GRATED FRESH HORSERADISH ROOT
¾ CUP HEAVY CREAM
1 TEASPOON SUGAR
½ TEASPOON DRY MUSTARD
½ TEASPOON SALT
½ TEASPOON GROUND WHITE PEPPER
2 TEASPOONS WHITE WINE VINEGAR

Soak the horseradish root in cold water for an hour, then scrub it well and scrape clean. Grate the horseradish or cut it into very thin shreds with a sharp knife. Whip the cream to soft peaks and fold in the horseradish, sugar, mustard, salt, pepper, and vinegar. Serve cold with beef.

A fresh sauce made like this is infinitely better than the store-bought variety. It can also be made using the horseradish pickle (see the next recipe) in place of fresh horseradish. Rinse it thoroughly before use, squeeze out the excess liquid, and then fold it into the cream in the same way.

Horseradish Pickle

SERVES 4

4–6 LARGE POTATOES
2 TABLESPOONS GRATED HORSERADISH
2 TABLESPOONS FINELY CHOPPED PARSLEY
SALT AND PEPPER TO TASTE
1 CUP YOGURT

Boil the potatoes until tender, let them cool, then cube them. Mix the horseradish, parsley, and seasonings, and stir them into the yogurt. Add the potato cubes and mix gently.

INDIAN CUCUMBER

Indian Cucumber, *Medeola virginiana*, a perennial herb with a white underground tuber, grows in rich woods, along roadsides, and on the edges of bogs and swamps. It flowers from May to June.

Found mainly in AL, n.e. AR, CT, DE, GA, e. IA, IL, IN, KY, LA, MA, MD, ME, MI, s.e. MN, e. MO, NC, NH, NJ, NY, OH, PA, RI, SC, TN, VA, VT, WI, WV. In Canada: s. NB, NS, s. ONT, PEI, s. QUE.

Despite its name I have come across no reference to this plant in the accounts of early explorers or Indian traders. Doubtless some tribes ate the roots if they found them in sufficient quantity, and presumably this has gave rise to their name.

Once you find a patch of Indian cucumber, the roots are easy to dig up, but they are fairly small and you will need to find a great many to make a substantial dish. However, incorporated with other ingredients they make a tasty side salad; alternatively, you can pickle them with vinegar and spices.

Indian Cucumber Salad

SERVES 4

1 LARGE CUCUMBER
1 LARGE AVOCADO
12 INDIAN CUCUMBER ROOTS

DRESSING:
½ TEASPOON SALT
¼ TEASPOON PEPPER
1 CLOVE GARLIC, CRUSHED
2 TEASPOONS FRENCH MUSTARD
½ TABLESPOON CHOPPED FRESH DILL
    OR 1 TEASPOON DRIED DILL
½ CUP OLIVE OIL
1 TABLESPOON LEMON JUICE

Make the dressing first by putting all the ingredients into a bottle or jar with a screw top and shaking vigorously until they are well combined.

Line individual salad bowls with thin, transparent circles of finely sliced cucumber and pile tiny cubes of peeled avocado in the center. Carefully wash the Indian cucumber roots and slice them lengthwise. Be very gentle, as they are curiously brittle and snap easily. Decoratively arrange the strips of Indian cucumber between the cucumber circles, and just before serving, spoon 1 or 2 tablespoons of dressing into each bowl.

As well as looking pretty, this salad is an interesting combination of subtle flavors and contrasting textures.

ARROWHEAD OR WAPATO

Arrowhead or **Wapato**, *Sagittaria latifolia*, a perennial herb, has tubers that develop on its fibrous roots. It grows on the borders of swamps, bogs, ponds, streams, lakes, and ditches, flowers from July to September, and fruits from September to March.

Found throughout the United States and southern Canada.

The wapato or katnis has always been a major food source for Indian tribes throughout America and was frequently eaten by early explorers and settlers until they could successfully cultivate crops easier to harvest. Then they no longer needed to endure wading into cold, muddy water to collect the arrowhead roots.

Cabeza de Vaca (1542) relates a morbid tale of how he and his three companions named a certain island Mal Hado (island of doom). The water was so bad that five (unidentified) Christians were unable to pull up roots or catch any fish, and were consequently reduced to the extremity of eating each other! Although he does not give the roots a name, it is apparent from his description that they were in fact arrowhead roots, which normally provided the staple food of the Capaques and Han Indians of that area.

In a diary entry of 1749, Peter Kalm gives a long description of the arrowhead, saying that the Indians either boiled the roots or roasted them in hot ashes, and when the Indians had a plentiful supply "they desired no other food." In his opinion the roots "tasted well, though they were rather dry: the taste was nearly the same with that of the potato."

Lewis and Clark mention wapato roots on several occasions. On November 4, 1805, Clark records that they were invited to an Indian lodge and given "roundish roots about the size of a small Irish potato which they roasted in the embers until they became soft, this root they call *Wap-pat-to* the bulb of which the Chinese cultivate in great quantities called the Sa-gitti folia or

Wapato flowers

common arrow head . . . it has an agreeable taste and answers verry well in place of bread. We purchased about 4 bushels of this root and divided it to our party." A month later, Clark was unwell but found that wapato roots with elk's soup gave him great relief. "I found the roots both nourishing and as a check to my disorder."

Aquatic birds were reputed to be very fond of arrowheads, and they would feast on them in early spring, only to be feasted on themselves a little later in the year by the Indians.

The tubers grow in muddy water at the end of

long, thin, string-like roots sometimes as much as 12 inches away from the main stems. The Indians, usually women, would wade into the mud, loosen the roots with their toes, and wait for the tubers to float to the top of the water. Having been told that wapato root could be harvested all year round, we tried several times one September to follow the traditional method but without success. We came to the conclusion that we were a bit too early. Havard (1895) refers to Indian women harvesting roots in the depth of winter, and Palmer (1878) says the Mojave Indians of Arizona used to dig the bulbs as soon as the Colorado River subsided in the spring. So we decided to try gathering them toward the end of October, when the old roots had died, and we were more successful.

As it can be pretty cold wading barefoot in mud at the onset of winter, we suggest you do as we did and get an old garden rake or hoe with a long handle. Stir the mud vigorously for a few minutes to free the tubers from the old roots, then stop and *wait*. This is the essential point: The tubers are only just lighter than water, so it takes time for them to float to the surface.

They also vary considerably in size, sometimes being as small as peas and sometimes "as big as a man's fists," according to Peter Kalm. Generally they are about 1 inch in diameter and about 1½ inches long.

A good tip is to make a note of where the plants are growing in the summer so that you can dig in those areas during the fall.

Similar in taste to potatoes, though sweeter, they can be cooked in the same ways—boiled, roasted, fried, creamed. All are tasty. Alternatively, they can be dried, ground into flour, and used to thicken soups, stews, and casseroles. Boiled, peeled, and left to go cold, they are an excellent accompaniment to corned beef with a little oil and vinegar poured over them. Or try roasting them in the embers when you next have barbecued ribs or chicken.

JERUSALEM ARTICHOKE

Jerusalem Artichoke, *Helianthus tuberosus*, a tall, perennial herb, grows in rich or damp thickets, waste ground and fields, and on roadsides. It flowers from August to October.

Found in n. AL, CT, DE, n. GA, IA, IN, KY, MA, MD, MI, MN, e. MO, NC, ND, s. NH, NY, OH, PA, RI, n.w. SC, n.e. SD, TN, s. VT, WV. In Canada: s. MAN, s. ONT, s.e. SASK.

Harvard (1895) says that the Jerusalem artichoke was the most important native plant cultivated by the Indians. Apparently, it was taken to France by Lescarbot in 1612: "But although the Jerusalem artichoke is, so far, the only contribution [of] North America, exclusive of Mexico, to the vegetable garden of the world, and it can be said to be an aboriginal contribution, strange to note, it is now much more cultivated in the old world than in this continent."

An entry by Captain Meriwether Lewis is his journal on April 9, 1805, explains how an Indian squaw collected the wild tubers: "When we halted for dinner the squaw busied herself in searching for the wild artichokes which the mice [probably gophers] collect and deposit in large hoards. This operation she performed by penetrating the earth with a sharp stick about some small collections of drift wood, her labor soon proved successful, and she procured a good quantity of these roots."

Burr (1865) gives a concise account of the best ways of eating them: "The plant is cultivated for its tubers, which are pickled, like the cucumber, and sometimes eaten in their crude state, sliced, as a salad. When cooked they have somewhat the flavor of the true artichoke . . . that are suited to persons in delicate health when debarred from the use of most other vegetables."

Establish where the plants are during the summer, when they are in flower, then dig the tubers after the first frost, throughout the winter. Well scrubbed or peeled, they can be substituted for potatoes in many dishes. Because they contain inulin carbohydrates, they are particularly suitable for those on low-starch diets.

Jerusalem Artichoke Soup

SERVES 3–4

1 TABLESPOON BUTTER

1 MEDIUM-SIZED ONION, FINELY SLICED

1 CLOVE GARLIC, CRUSHED

2 MEDIUM-SIZED BAY LEAVES

SALT AND PEPPER TO TASTE

3 CUPS PEELED AND COARSELY CHOPPED
   JERUSALEM ARTICHOKES

2 CUPS WHOLE MILK OR HALF-AND-HALF

4 TEASPOONS SOUR CREAM

CHOPPED PARSLEY, FOR GARNISH

Melt the butter in a heavy saucepan and sauté the onion, garlic, and seasonings gently for 5 minutes, stirring occasionally. Do not allow them to burn. When the onion is soft but not brown, add the artichokes, mix well, and cook for 3 minutes. Then add the milk, bring to a boil, and simmer gently, covered, for another 30 to 40 minutes. Transfer the mixture to a blender and liquefy at high speed. Pour into individual bowls and add a teaspoonful of sour cream and a sprinkling of parsley as a garnish.

This soup has a very delicate but distinctive taste that our baby, Phoebe, loved—to our surprise.

DANDELION

The main entry for the dandelion is on page 21.

Dandelion roots should be dug in the winter. Choose year-old plants since the roots will have attained a decent size and should be slightly less bitter than younger specimens.

Dandelion Coffee

Dandelion coffee is really a misnomer. The drink made from the roots is not coffee and does not taste like it, though it is a palatable substitute for either coffee or tea.

Having collected a good supply of roots, clean them well and then dry them for about 2 days over a radiator or in an airing cupboard. Cut the dried roots into ½-inch lengths and roast them; I do it in the pan under the broiler. Make sure you turn them so you get an even roast. Just as with coffee beans, you can make the flavor stronger by roasting them to a darker color. Grind them in an ordinary coffee grinder and use the same quantity for each cup as you would use in making instant coffee. Strain as you pour into the cups.

The flavor is nutty and rather bitter. I need a little sugar, but then I have sugar in tea as well. If you roast the roots but don't grind them, they will keep very well in a sealed jar until ready for use.

Dandelion roots

MAPLE

Sugar Maple or **Hard Maple**, *Acer saccharum*, a medium-sized to tall tree with furrowed, dark gray bark, grows in rich, moist soil in hilly forests. Maples flower from late April to early June and fruit from June to September. In the fall the leaves turn red or scarlet or yellowish.

> Found mainly in CT, e. IA, IL, KY, MA, MD, ME, MI, e. MN, e. MO, w. NC, NH, NJ, NY, OH, PA, RI, TN, n.w. VA, VT, WI, WV. In Canada: NB, NS, s. ONT, s. QUE.

Red Maple or **Swamp Maple**, *Acer rubrum*, a medium-sized tree, occurs commonly in swamps and wet upland woods, flowering very early, in March and April, before the leaves form and fruiting from May to July, with red to yellow foliage in the fall.

> Found mainly in AL, AR, CT, DE, FL, GA, IA, IL, IN, KY, LA, MA, MD, ME, MI, MN, MS, MO, NC, NH, NJ, NY, OH, PA, RI, SC, TN, VA, VT, WI, WV. In Canada: NB, NFLD, NS, ONT, QUE.

Other maples that have commonly been used for syrup include the silver maple, *Acer saccharinum*, and the black maple, *A. nigrum*.

Early explorers and botanists soon discovered that wherever sugar maples were available they provided an important, much-prized article of food, as John Dunn Hunter (1823) confirms: "In districts of the country where the sugar maple abounds, the Indians prepare considerable quantities of sugar by simply concentrating the juices of the tree by boiling, till it acquires a sufficient consistency to crystallize on cooling. But, as they are extravagantly fond of it, very little is preserved beyond the sugar-making season. The men tap the trees, attach spigots to them, make the sap troughs; and sometimes, at this frolicking season, assist the squaws in collecting sap."

However, not all tribes were so greedy. Edward Palmer (1870) describes how the North American Indians turned sugar-making to financial advantage: "The sap collected from the trees is carried in bark buckets and boiled down in the usual way.

Sugar-making forms a sort of Indian carnival, and boiling candy and pouring it out on the snow to cool is the pastime of the children. The women make the sugar, which is put up for sale in boxes made of white birch bark and called mococks. The boxes designed for sale are of all sizes, weighing from twenty pounds to seventy and are generally exchanged for merchandise. Winnebagoes and Chippewas are the largest manufacturers, the former often selling to the North-west Fur Company fifteen thousand pounds a year."

COLLECTING SAP AND MAKING SYRUP

Maples can be tapped as early as January and as late as May, but the best time is on a warm, sunny day after a frosty night, when the sap will flow profusely. About 3 feet above the ground, on the south side of the tree, under a large limb, bore a hole at a slightly upward angle and about 3 inches into the trunk, then drive the tap (spile) in far enough to hold a bucket but not so hard that the wood splits.

Collect the sap and store it in a cold place. If you intend to make syrup, you will need about 3 gallons of sap to produce 1 pint of syrup.

We were unable to make our own maple syrup (for reasons that will become apparent in a moment!), but the syrup we used in our recipes was given to us by Mike Arney, who had made it from his own trees the previous year. He followed the method he had learned as a child.

When the temperature was up to 45°F in the daytime but still below freezing at night (on this occasion, March 20), he got up very early in the morning and chose his largest trees to tap. The bigger the trees the greater the yield, as long as the trees are healthy. He made wooden taps from hollowed-out elderberry wood, but in some areas of New England aluminum taps can be bought at the hardware store. He collected the sap as it gathered in his buckets and kept it in a cool place until he was ready to begin boiling it down.

As the whole process is very steamy and messy, Mike said it was best done outdoors, although if you are making only a small quantity of syrup you can work indoors, using all four burners on the stove. Mike said the first thing to do is build a long fire pit with stones and bricks along each side, on which you can securely balance the shallow evaporation pan and the cauldron in which is sap is preheated. Make sure to leave plenty of room to stoke and replenish the fire.

As the sap in the preheating cauldron got very hot, Mike would pour it into the shallow pan to finish off the boiling process. By continuously preheating the sap before pouring it into the shallow pan, Mike was able to keep it on the boil and, as it thickened and reduced, refill it from the cauldron.

The simplest way of finding out when the syrup is ready is by testing it with a candy thermometer. The best consistency for the maple syrup is when it reaches 7°F above the boiling point of water, at your altitude. As the syrup approaches this temperature, the addition of a few drops of cream will stop it from boiling over. If you need to filter out the niter, you can use two cone-shaped coffee filters for the job. Next, bottle the syrup in sterilized jars, and store them in a cool, dark place. Once you have opened one, keep it in the refrigerator; otherwise the syrup will go bad.

It took Mike a whole week to tap his trees and fuel his fire, but he considered that the 14 gallons of syrup he was able to store in his larder to eat with his breakfast pancakes were well worth every minute.

Maple Sugar

To make maple sugar, boil 1 pint of maple syrup in a saucepan, stirring continuously, until it reaches a temperature of 225°F on a candy thermometer. Remove the pan from the stove and stir the mixture until it loses its sheen, then pour it quickly onto waxed paper or into shallow, buttered tins about ¼ inch deep. When partially hardened, it can be scored with a knife.

Remember that boiling syrup is dangerous business. Keep children well out of the way.

Creamy Maple Pralines
MAKES ABOUT 24 PIECES

3 CUPS MAPLE SYRUP
1 CUP LIGHT CREAM
½ TEASPOON BAKING SODA
1½ TABLESPOONS BUTTER
3 CUPS SHELLED PECANS OR HICKORY NUTS

Put the syrup, cream, and soda into a deep saucepan. Cook the mixture over medium heat, stirring continuously, for about 35 minutes, until it thickens and form a soft ball when dropped into cold water, or until it reaches 235°F on the candy thermometer. Remove from the heat, stir in the butter immediately, and then add the shelled nuts. Beat the mixture for 2 or 3 minutes, until it starts to thicken. Then either pour it into a shallow, buttered tin (6 by 8 inches) and score it into squares when partially hardened, or drop small spoonfuls onto waxed paper.

Maple Cocktail

Put equal parts vodka and maple syrup into a glass, stir, and serve cold, either with or without crushed ice.

This mixture is my own favorite postprandial tipple.

Maple-Glazed Pear Pyramid

SERVES 8

16 FIRM PEARS
1 BOTTLE (1 LITER) RED WINE
2 TEASPOONS CINNAMON
2 TEASPOONS NUTMEG
WATER
1½ CUPS MAPLE SYRUP

Carefully peel the pears, leaving the stalks on, and place them bottoms down in two or three large saucepans. Combine the wine and spices, and pour them over the pears; add water until the pears are covered with liquid. Bring to a boil and gently simmer, covered, for half an hour, or until the pears are cooked. To ensure a good red color on the pears, let them cool in the cooking liquid for 3 or 4 hours, or overnight if possible.

To create a pyramid of pears, form a ring of seven pears on their sides with the stems pointing outward. Attach each pear to the next with a toothpick, horizontally, leaving an empty central space about 2½ inches across. Put in vertical toothpicks to hold the next ring of pears; then, again using horizontal toothpicks to balance them, make a ring of five pears on top of the bottom ring, this time leaving only a 1½-inch space in the middle. Repeat with the next ring of three pears, moving inward again to leave a ½-inch space in the middle. Finally, place one pear on top of the pyramid.

After the pyramid is assembled, prepare the glaze. Pour the maple syrup into a saucepan and bring to a boil. Control the heat so that the syrup bubbles continuously and gradually reduces. To test whether the syrup is reduced enough, dribble a little on one of the pears. If it sets, the syrup is ready; if not, continue to simmer and test again a few minutes later. When it is done, pour it over the pears, and the glaze will form within a couple of minutes. Serve immediately.

This dish an ideal dessert for a large dinner party because it makes such a beautiful centerpiece. **NOTE:** The glaze will go watery soon after contact with the juice from the pears, so it is important to do the glazing just before serving.

Bibliography

Aihara, Cornellia. *The Chico-San Cookbook*. Oroville, CA: Chico-San, Inc., and the George Ohsawa Macrobiotic Foundation, 1972. Reprinted as *Macrobiotic Kitchen*, San Francisco: Japan Publications, 1982.

Alcott, William A. *The Young Housekeeper*. Boston, 1842.

——. *Vegetable Diet*. New York, 1851.

Allouez, Claude. "Narrative of a Voyage Made to Illinois by Father Claude Allouez, 1676." In *Discovery and Exploration of the Mississippi River*, edited by John D. Shea, pp. 70–81. New York, 1852.

Ammons, Nelle. *Shrubs of West Virginia*. Grantsville, WV: Seneca Books, 1975.

Andrews, Julia C. *Breakfast, Dinner and Tea: Viewed Classically, Poetically and Practically*. New York, 1859.

Angier, Bradford. *Field Guide to Edible Wild Plants*. Harrisburg, PA: Stackpole Books, 1974.

Baegeart, Jacob. "An Account of the Aboriginal Inhabitants of the Californian Peninsula." In *Annual Report of the Board of Regents of the Smithsonian Institution*, pp. 352–369. Washington, DC, 1864.

Bartram, John. *An Account of East Florida with a Journal kept by John Bartram of Philadelphia*. London, 1767.

Bartram, William. *Travels through North and South Carolina*. Philadelphia, 1791.

Beard, James. *American Cookery*. Boston: Little, Brown, 1972.

Beverley, Robert. *The History and Present State of Virginia . . . by a Native*. London, 1705.

Blot, Pierre. *What to Eat, and How to Cook It*. New York, 1846.

Boston Mycological Club. *Mushroom Recipes*. Cambridge, MA: Boston Mycological Club, 1970, 1974, 1979, 1980.

Brackett, Babette, and Maryann Lash. *The Wild Gourmet: A Forager's Cookbook*. Boston, Godine, 1975.

Britton, Nathaniel, and Addison Brown. *An Illustrated Flora of the Northern United States and Canada*. 3 vols. New York: Dover, 1970.

Brown, Susan Anna. *The Book of Forty Puddings*. New York, 1882.

Bullock, Helen. *The Williamsburg Art of Cookery, or, Accomplish'd Gentleman's Companion: Being a Collection of Upwards of Five Hundred of the most Ancient and Approv'd Recipes in Virginia Cookery* [an early, undated manuscript]. Williamsburg, VA: Colonial Williamsburg, Inc., 1952.

Burr, Fearing. *The Field and Garden Vegetables of America*. Boston: J. E. Tilton and Company, 1865.

Cabeza de Vaca, Alvar Nunez. *Adventures in the Unknown Interior of America, 1527–37*. (Original title: *Los Naufragios y Comentarios, 1542*.) Translated and edited by Covey Cyclone. New York, 1972.

Campbell, Susan, and Caroline Conran. *Poor Cook*. London: Macmillan, 1981.

Carr, Lucien. "The Food of Certain American Indians and Their Methods of Preparing It." In *Proceedings of the American Antiquarian Society*, n.s., 10 (1895): pp. 155–190.

Carter, Charles. *The Compleat City and Country Cook: Or, Accomplish'd Housewife*. London, 1736.

——. *The Complete Practical Book: Or, A New System of the Whole Art and Mystery of Cookery*. London, 1730.

——. *The London and Country Cook: Or, Accomplish'd Housewife, containing Practical Directions and the best Receipts In all the Branches of Cookery and Housekeeping*. London, 1749.

Cartier, Jacques. "The First relation of Jacques Cartier of St. Malo of the New Land, Called New France, newly discovered in the year of our Lord, 1534." In *Voyages and Travels*, edited by John Pinkerton, vol. 12, pp. 629–640. London, 1812.

——. "The Third Voyage of Jacques Cartier, 1540." In *Voyages and Travels*, edited by John Pinkerton, vol. 12, pp. 665–674. London, 1812.

Carver, Jonathan. *Travels through the Interior Part of North America, 1766, 1767, 1768*. Bulletin of the Lloyd Library, vol. 2. Cincinnati, 1903–7.

Catlin, George. *Manners, Customs and Condition of the North American Indians*. 2 vols. New York, 1841.

Chadwick, Mrs. J. *Home Cookery*. Boston: Crosby, Nicholas, and Co., 1853.

Chesnut, V. K. "Plants used by the Indians of Mendocino County, California." *Contributions from the United States National Herbariam* (Washington, DC) 7 (1902): pp. 295–408.

Child, Mrs. [Lydia Maria]. *The American Frugal Housewife, Dedicated to Those Who Are Not Ashamed of Economy*. Boston, 1836.

Child, Theodore. *Delicate Dining*. London, 1891.

Coles, William. *Adam in Eden, or Nature's Paradise*. London, 1657.

Colville, Frederick Vernon. "The Panamint Indians of California." *American Anthropologist* 5 (1892): pp. 351–361.

——. "Some Additions to Our Vegetable Dietary." In *Yearbook of the Department of Agriculture*, pp. 205–214. Washington, DC, 1895.

Correa de Serra, M. Joseph [José F. Correa da Serra]. "Vegetables used as Esculents in North America. Letter to Richard Anthony Salisbury, July 17th, 1821." *Transactions of the Horticultural Society of London* 4 (1822): pp. 443–446.

Culpeper, Nicholas. *Culpeper's Complete Herbal*. 1649. Reprint (based on the original edition), New York: W. Foulsham & Co., n.d.

Cushing, Frank Hamilton. *Zuñi Breadstuff*. Indian Notes and Monographs, vol. 8. New York: Museum of the American Indian, Heye Foundation, 1974.

Cutler, Manasseh. *An Account of Some of the Vegetable Productions Naturally Growing in This Part of America.* 1785. Reprint, Bulletin of the Lloyd Library, no. 7, reproduction series no. 4. Cincinnati, 1903.

Digby, Sir Kenelm. *The Closet of the Eminently Learned Sir Kenelme Digby Kt. Opened: Whereby is Discovered Several Ways for Making of Metheglin Sider, Cherry- Wine etc. Together with Excellent Directions for Cookerys: As also for Preserving, Conserving, Candying etc.* London, 1669.

Dodge, Natt N., and Jeanne R. Janish. *Flowers of the Southwest Deserts.* 10th ed. Globe, AZ: Southwest Parks and Monuments Association, 1980.

Elias, Thomas S., and Peter A. Dykeman. *Field Guide to North American Edible Wild Plants.* New York: Outdoor Life Books, 1982.

Ellet, Elizabeth Fries. *Summer Rambles in the West.* New York, 1853.

Evelyn, John. Acetaria, a Discourse of Saliets. London, 1699.

——. *Sylvia: or a Discourse of Forest Trees.* London, 1679.

Farmer, Fannie. *The Boston Cooking-School Cook Book.* Boston, 1896. Reprint, London: Macmillan, 1982.

——. *The All-New Fannie Farmer Boston Cooking School Cookbook.* 10th ed. Boston: Little, Brown, 1959.

Foster, Charles. *Home Wine Making, Brewing and Other Drinks.* Charlotte, VT: Garden Way, 1983.

Frampton, John. *See* Monardes, Nicholas.

Gerard, John. *The Herball; or General History of Plants very much enlarged and amended by Thomas Johnson.* London, 1633.

Gibbons, Euell. *Stalking the Wild Asparagus.* 1962. Field guide ed. New York: McKay, 1970.

——. *Stalking the Wild Herbs.* 1966. Field guide ed. New York: McKay, 1970.

Gibson, Sheila, Louise Templeton, and Robin Gibson. *Cook Yourself a Favour.* Drogheda, Ireland: Johnston Green Publishing (Ireland), 1983.

Gilmore, Melvin Randolph. "A Study in the Ethnobotany of the Omaha Indians." *Collections of the Nebraska State Historical Society* (Lincoln, NE) 17 (1913): pp. 314–357.

——. "Uses of Plants by the Indians of the Missouri River Region." 1911-12. In 33rd *Annual Report of the Bureau of American Ethnology,* pp. 53–152. Washington, DC, 1919.

Glasse, Hannah. *The Servants Directory, or the House-Keeper's Companion.* London, 1760.

Gray, Asa. *Gray's Manual of Botany.* 8th Centennial ed. Edited by M. F. Fernald. 1950. Reprint, New York: Van Nostrand, 1970.

Grigson, Jane. *Jane Grigson's Vegetable Book.* London: Michael Joseph, 1978.

——. *The Mushroom Feast.* London: Michael Joseph, 1975.

Hakluyt, Richard. *The Principal Navigations, Voyages, Traifiques and Discoveries of the English Nation.* 12 vols. The Hakluyt Society, n.s. Glasgow: James MacLehose, 1903-5.

Hale, Mrs. S. J. *Receipts for the Millions.* Philadelphia, 1857.

Hall, Alan. *The Wild Foods Trailguide.* New York: Holt, Rinehart and Winston, 1976.

Hargreaves, Barbara, ed. *The Second Country Cookbook.* London: Hamlyn Publishing Group, 1974.

Haskin, Leslie L. *Wild Flowers of the Pacific Coast.* 1934. Reprint, New York: Dover, 1977.

Havard, Valery. "The Drink Plants of the North American Indians." *Bulletin of the Torrey Botanical Club* (Lancaster, PA) 23 (1896): pp. 33–46.

——. "The Food Plants of the North American Indians." *Bulletin of the Torrey Botanical Club 22* (1895): pp. 98–120.

Heriot, Thomas. "A Brief and True report of Virginia." 1585. In *Voyages and Travels,* edited by John Pinkerton, vol. 12, pp. 590–601. London, 1812.

Hertsberg, Ruth, Beatrice Vaughan, and Janet Greene. *Putting Food By.* 2d ed., revised and enlarged. Brattleboro, VT: Stephen Greene, 1975.

Hill, John. *The British Herbal.* London, 1756.

——. *The Useful Family Herbal.* London, 1755. Howarth, Sheila. *Herbs with Everything.* London: Pelham, 1976.

Humelbergius Secundus, Dick. *Apician Morsels; or tales of the table, kitchen, and larder.* London, 1829.

Hunter, John Dunn. *Memoirs of a Captivity among Indians.* London, 1823.

Jenks, Albert Ernest. "The Wild Rice Gatherers of the Upper Lakes." In *19th Annual Report of the Bureau of American Ethnology,* pt. 2, pp. 1013–1137. Washington, DC, 1897-98.

Kalm, Peter. *Travels into North America 1748-51.* Translated into English by John Reinhold Forster. 2 vols. London, 1772.

Leslie, Miss Eliza. *Directions for Cookery, in Its Various Branches.* Philadelphia, 1837.

——. *Miss Leslie's New Cookery Book.* Philadelphia, 1872.

——. *Miss Leslie's Seventy-Five Receipts for Pastry, Cakes and Sweetmeats.* Boston, 1828.

——. *New Receipts for Cooking.* Philadelphia, 1854.

Lewis, Meriwether, and William Clark. *Original Journals of the Lewis and Clark Expedition, 1804-6.* 8 vols. Edited by R. G. Thwaites. New York, 1904-5.

Lincoff, Gary H., and D. H. Mitchel. *Toxic and Hallucinogenic Mushroom Poisoning.* New York: Van Nostrand Reinhold, 1977.

Lincoln, Mrs. D. A. *Mrs. Lincoln's Boston Cook Book.* Boston, 1896.

Lincoln, Waldo. *American Cookery Books, 1742-1860.* Revised and enlarged by Eleanor Lowenstein. Worcester, MA: American Antiquarian Society, 1954.

Locquin, Marcel V. *Mycologie du Gout.* Paris: Guyot, 1977.

Lomask, Martha. *The All-American Cookbook.* London: Piatkus, 1981.

Long, John. *Voyages and Travels of an Indian Interpreter and Trader*. London, 1791. .

McIlvaine, Charles, and Robert K. Macadam. *One Thousand American Fungi*. Reprint of 2d rev. ed. (1902), New York: Dover, 1973.

Madlener, Judith Cooper. *The Sea Vegetable Book*. New York: Clarkson N. Potter, 1977.

Markham, Gervase. *Countrey Contentment or the English Huswife*. London, 1623.

Marquette, James. "Relation of Father James Marquette, 1678." In *Discovery and Exploration of the Mississippi River*, edited by John O. Shea, pp. 8-40. New York, 1852.

Marten, Peter, and Joan Marten. *Japanese Cooking*. London: Andre Deutsch Ltd., 1972.

Mason, Mrs. Charlotte. *The Lady's Assistant*. London, 1755.

Masterton, Elsie. *Blueberry Hill Cookbook*. Reprint, Camden, ME: Down East Books, 1982.

Medsger, Oliver Perry. *Edible Wild Plants*. New York: Collier Books, 1939.

Monardes, Nicholas. *Joyfull Newes out of the Newe Founde Worlde. Written in Spanish by Monardes and Englished by John Frampton*. 1577. Reprint, Tudor Translation Series, vol. 2, no. 9, New York: Knopf, 1925.

Morrell, Jennie M. "Some Maine Plants and their Uses 'Wise and Otherwise.'" In *Rhodora. Journal of the New England Botanical Club*, vol. 3, pp. 129-132. Boston, May 1901.

Moser, Meinhard. *Keys to Agarics and Boleti*. London: Phillips, 1983.

Mosser, Marjorie. *Good Maine Food*. New York: Doubleday, 1939.

Mueller, Jo. *Mushroom Cookery*. Charlotte, VT: Garden Way, 1980.

Munz, Philip A. *A California Flora*. Berkeley, CA: University of California Press, 1968.

"Mycophagist's Corner." Edited by Bob Peabody. *Newsletter*, New Jersey Mycological Association, various dates.

Niethammer, Carolyn. *American Indian Food and Lore*. New York: Collier Books, 1974.

Nutt, Frederic. *The Compleat Confectioner*. London, 1807.

Ohsawa, Lima. The Art of Just Cooking. Brookline, MA: Autumn Press, 1974. Republished as *Lima Ohsawa's Macrobiotic Cookbook: The Art of Just Cooking*, 1981.

Old-Fashioned Mushroom Recipes. Nashville, IN: Bear Wallow Books, 1981.

Old-Fashioned Persimmon Recipes. Nashville, IN: Bear Wallow Books, 1978.

Palmer, Edward. "Food Products of the North American Indians." In *Report of the Commissioner of Agriculture*, pp. 404-428. Washington, DC, 1870.

——. "Plants Used by the Indians of the United States." *The American Naturalist 12* (1878): pp. 593-606, 646-655.

Parloa, Maria. *Miss Parloa's New Cook Book and Marketing Guide*. Boston, 1880.

Pechy, John. *The Compleat Herbal of Physical Plants*. London, 1694.

Peck, C. H. *Annual Report of the New York State Botanist*. New York State Museum, 1895.

Peterson, Lee Allen. *A Field Guide to Edible Wild Plants*. Boston: Houghton Mifflin, 1977.

Radisson, Pierre Esprit. *Voyages among North American Indians, 1652-1684*. Translated and edited by Gideon D. Skull. Boston, 1885.

Rafinesque, C. S. *Medical Flora, or Manual of Medical Botany of the United States*. 2 vols. Philadelphia, 1828-30.

Recipes for the Million: A Handy Book for the Household. London: T. Fisher Unwin [c. 1897].

Rhoads, Sharon Ann. *Cooking with Sea Vegetables*. Brookline, MA: Autumn Press, 1978.

Robinson, Matthew. *The New Family Herbal and Botanic Physician*. London: Wm. Nicholson, n.d.

Roman, Liz. *A Fenland Village Cookery Book*. Cambridge, Eng.: Wicken Fete Committee and the Wicken Society, 1977.

Rorer, Mrs. S. T. *Mrs. Rorer's New Cook Book*. Philadelphia, 1902.

——. *Mrs. Rorer's Philadelphia Cook Book*. Philadelphia, 1886.

Sargent, Charles Sprague. *Manual of the Trees of North America*. 1905. 2 vols. Reprint: New York: Dover, 1965.

Shelton, Ferne, ed. *Mountain Cookbook*. High Point, NC: Hutcraft, 1964.

Simon, Andre L. *Mushroom Recipes*. 1951. Reprint, New York: Dover, 1975.

Smith, Alexander H. *The Mushroom Hunter's Field Guide Revised and Enlarged*. Ann Arbor: University of Michigan Press, 1974.

Smith, Helen V., and Alexander H. Smith. *How to Know the Non-Gilled Fleshy Fungi*. Dubuque, IA: Wm. C. Brown, 1973.

Smith, John. *The Generall Historie of Virginia, New England, and the Summer Isles*. 1624. Reprint, 2 vols., Glasgow: James MacLehose, 1907.

Snell, Walter H., and Esther A. Dick. *The Boleti of Northeastern North America*. Lehre, Germany: J. Cramer Verlagsbuchhandlung, 1970; distributed in North America by SH Service Agency, New York.

Stewart, Katie. *The Times Cookery Book*. London: Pan Books, 1974.

Sturtevant, Edward Lewis. *Sturtevant's Edible Plants of the World*. 1919. Edited by U. P. Hedrick. Reprint, New York: Dover, 1972.

Symonds, George W. D. *The Shrub Identification Book*. New York: Morrow, 1963.

Time-Life Books, *The Time-Life American Regional Cookbook*. Boston: Little, Brown, 1978.

Toklas, Alice B. *The Alice B. Toklas Cookbook.* London: Brilliance Books, 1983.

Tritton, S. M. *Guide to Better Wine and Beer Making for Beginners.* New York: Dover, 1969.

Venning, Frank D. *Wildflowers of North America.* New York: Golden Press, 1984.

Weeden, Norman F. *A Sierra Nevada Flora.* Berkeley, CA: Wilderness Press, 1981.

Winslow, Mrs. *Mrs. Winslow's Family Almanac and Domestic Receipt Book for 1866.* New York, 1866.

Young, Alexander. *Chronicles of the Pilgrim Fathers of the Colony of Plymouth from 1602–1625.* Boston, 1841.

WILDFLOWER AND TREE GUIDES

Brockman, Frank C. *Trees of North America,* Revised and Updated. New York: Golden Press, 2001.

Niehaus, Theodore F., and Charles L. Ripper. *A Field Guide to Pacific States Wildflowers.* Boston: Houghton Mifflin, 1976.

Niering, William, and Nancy Olmstead. *The National Audubon Society Field Guide to North American Wildflowers, Eastern Region.* Revised by John W. Thieret. New York: Knopf, 2001.

Peterson, Roger Tory, and Margaret McKenny. *A Field Guide to Wildflowers of Northeastern and North-central North America.* Revised edition. Boston: Houghton Mifflin, 1998.

Petrides, George A. *A Field Guide to Trees and Shrubs.* 2d ed. Boston: Houghton Mifflin, 1972.

National Audubon Society. *The National Audubon Society Field Guide to North American Wildflowers, Western Region.* Revised edition. New York: Knopf, 2001.

MUSHROOM GUIDES

Lincoff, Gary H. *The National Audubon Society Field Guide to North American Mushrooms.* New York: Knopf, 1981.

Miller, Orson K., Jr., and Hope Miller. *North American Mushrooms.* Guilford, CT: Globe Pequot Press, 2006.

SEAWEED GUIDES

Gosner, Kenneth L. *A Field Guide to the Atlantic Seashore.* Boston: Houghton Mifflin, 1999.

Waaland, J. Robert. *Common Seaweeds of the Pacific Coast.* Seattle, WA: Pacific Search Press, 1977.

Index